Welfare and the Welfare State

The welfare state plays a key role in people's everyday lives in developed societies. At the same time, the welfare state is contested and there are constant discussions on how and to what degree the state should intervene, influence and have an impact on the development of society. Recent years have seen an accelerated transformation of the welfare state in the light of the global financial crisis, demographic change and changes in the perception of the state's role in relation to social welfare. This raises fundamentally new issues related to social policy and welfare state analysis. This book provides:

- an introduction to the principles of welfare
- a conceptual framework necessary for understanding social policy at the macro-level
- a comparative approach to welfare states globally
- an overview of new ways to organise and steer welfare states
- an introduction to welfare state politics and underlying economic framework
- an account of equality and inequality in modern societies
- new directions for welfare states.

The book's focus on core concepts and the variety of international welfare state regimes and mechanisms for delivering social policy provides a much needed introduction to the rapidly changing concept of welfare for students on social policy, social studies, sociology and politics courses.

Bent Greve is Professor of Welfare State Analysis at Roskilde University, Denmark. He is regional and special issues editor of *Social Policy & Administration*, and has written over 20 books on welfare, including ten books in English, and many articles in international and national journals.

Welfare and the Welfare State

Present and future

Bent Greve

Routledge
Taylor & Francis Group

LONDON AND NEW YORK

First published 2015
by Routledge
2 Park Square, Milton Park, Abingdon, Oxon OX14 4RN

and by Routledge
711 Third Avenue, New York, NY 10017

Routledge is an imprint of the Taylor & Francis Group, an informa business

British Library Cataloguing-in-Publication Data
A catalogue record for this book is available from the British Library

Library of Congress Cataloging-in-Publication Data
  Greve, Bent.
  Welfare and the welfare state : present and future / Bent Greve. — 1 Edition.
    pages cm
  1. Welfare state.   2. State, The.   3. Social policy.   4. Globalization–Social
  aspects.   I. Title.
  JC479.G748 2014
  330.12'6—dc23

                                                              2014008099

ISBN: 978-1-138-79363-7 (hbk)
ISBN: 978-1-138-79364-4 (pbk)
ISBN: 978-1-315-76102-2 (ebk)

Typeset in Arial
by RefineCatch Limited, Bungay, Suffolk

Printed and bound in Great Britain by
TJ International Ltd, Padstow, Cornwall

Contents

Figures

Tables

Boxes

Foreword

The welfare state is central in people's everyday lives. At the same time, the welfare state is contested and debated, and is argued to be in a crisis. Welfare and welfare states used to be a national issue and prerogative. Today welfare and welfare states are not only influenced by national decisions, but also are influenced by regional and global aspects.

State, market and civil society all play a role in the development of society and their interaction can have profound impact on the way societies work and function, particularly with regard to who has access to income, goods and services.

However, there is a strong need to know basic concepts and how they can be understood and interpreted. This book provides an overview of the central concepts through a state, market and civil society lens. It also attempts to provide the reader with knowledge on distribution in societies and how this interacts and influences different groups and their position in society.

A comparative approach has been used as this better enables us to understand our own country's welfare. A comparative approach offers a mirror that helps us see differences and similarities between countries and their welfare states. It also helps to underline and see the linkages to the impact of global and regional issues on welfare states and their development.

Finally, the book attempts to present challenges and future perspectives for welfare states and their development.

Bent Greve
Roskilde and Bagsværd, January 2014

Part I

Central concepts

Chapter 1

Introduction

Contents

1.1 What are the central issues?

The welfare state, in all developed societies at least, plays a key role in people's everyday lives. At the same time, the welfare state is contested and there are constant discussions on how and to what degree the state should intervene, influence and have an impact on the development of society, including on the market and civil society. Many questions arise: should there be a stronger or a leaner welfare state, or a larger role for families, the voluntary sector or the market? Such issues have been discussed for many years, as have subjects concerning the welfare state in crisis. Different measures have been used, such as direct cutbacks in the form of retrenchment, more marginal changes or just gradual changes. At the same time, for centuries the sovereign and the state have played a role and the boundaries between state, market and civil society have been analysed, debated and discussed from many and varied perspectives.

Recent years have seen an ongoing transformation of the welfare state in the light of the global financial crisis, demographic change and changes in the perception of the state's role in relation to social welfare. The legitimacy and nature of the state's role is constantly changing, not only in relation to its overall size and role, but also within certain areas of welfare policies. For instance, the type and level of support for individuals might differ depending on whether we look at social assistance or old age pensions (Svallfors, 2012). Support for old age pensions and services has been and still is higher than for those receiving social assistance. Thus the old debate about the deserving poor and the undeserving is still very much alive. Recent years have also seen new risks emerging so that the 'old' risks (Taylor-Gooby, 2004) of reaching the age of retirement, becoming ill or unemployed, or having a work injury, have been supplemented by new types of risk related to changes in the family and family formations, including the breakup of families. New risks and new challenges for individuals in welfare states also mean that there might be a conflict between various kinds of needs in different sectors and parts of the economy, and that these are changing over time. Thus the balance between the state, the market and civil society, and also within and between different aspects of the welfare state's services and income transfers has been constantly reconstructed, including who has which responsibility and who is expected to finance and/or deliver different types of welfare transfers and services. The continuation and anticipation of more and better welfare services also implies a risk that voters' expectations will not be fulfilled and thereby possibly reduce the legitimacy of the welfare state.

Over the last 30–40 years, we have seen a shift in the focus of the welfare state, from concentrating on income transfers to offering more services beyond health care, in which childcare and care for the elderly have been the most prominent. The expansion of the welfare state in some countries, especially in the provision of services, raises new issues concerning the understanding and possible role of the welfare state, particularly during a period of increased financial pressures. Issues include the extent to which the welfare state should provide services and to whom, of what quality and under what conditions, and, in contrast, what should be delivered by the state, the market and civil society.

The welfare state, in its different national varieties, plays a profound role in most people's everyday lives. Thus the welfare state influences society's development, including the preconditions for helping to ensure social cohesion and the development of social capital. Furthermore, many welfare states have goals related to equality and employment.

This book will scrutinise the foundations of the welfare state and explain why we have a welfare state (Esping-Andersen, 2002). In addition it will examine why it is difficult to demarcate the roles of the state and the market with any precision, and why the welfare state's boundaries in relation to civil society, including families, the third sector and voluntary work, are difficult to define and are constantly changing. Furthermore, it will examine how the interaction between state, market and civil society is important in order to understand the welfare state and how the welfare state differs between countries. The book provides an overview of the different interpretations and explanations of what a welfare state is and how it works. The approach chosen is interdisciplinary, and draws on sociology, political science, economics and social policy. The book does not have a specific focus on one country's welfare system, but tries to balance between presenting principles in approach to welfare and examples from a variety of countries and systems, and thereby covering different welfare systems. This also helps clarify variations in approaches to and understanding of the welfare state. Looking at how the welfare state is structured and changing in different countries can provide a mirror that helps us understand the welfare state of our own country, while at the same time making it possible to understand the varieties of approaches that can be and are used to achieve a high level of welfare.

In recent years, the focus on economic growth as a way of promoting welfare has been questioned and there has been a growing interest in well-being and the broader aspects of what constitutes a good society. Furthermore, approaches have changed from mainly focusing on the short term to a longer-term perspective including intergenerational aspects. This therefore raises the fundamental question: What is welfare? In order to understand the welfare state one needs to understand its central concepts, and especially the understanding of welfare, and also how different principles of delivery and financing in the state, the market and civil society influence people's welfare. The ability to finance the welfare state, to ensure qualified labour and to establish trust in societal development are highly important issues for the development of welfare in many countries.

The book offers an international perspective on how the welfare state might be influenced by the European Union (EU), especially in the member states. It therefore also highlights how welfare, including its historical development within nation states, is now influenced by globalisation and European norms of welfare.

This book provides both insights and knowledge which will make it possible to analyse and interpret the ongoing societal changes in welfare states. Core concepts and arguments for and against the welfare state are presented so that the complexity of modern societies can be understood. The book should therefore be useful for all students of social policy, social care, sociology, welfare states, political science and welfare economics and other subjects where there is a need to be familiar with core concepts and issues related to a central theme in modern societies: welfare and welfare states.

1.2   Overview of the book

The book is divided into four parts. Part I presents the core concepts related to what welfare is and different ways to achieve goals in the welfare state, including central theoretical arguments for using the state, the market and civil society to deliver and/or finance welfare. This distinction of the three sectors as means to provide welfare, together with different welfare regimes, is the guiding principle in the book.

Part II focuses on the core providers of welfare: the state, the market and civil society. It addresses how best to achieve an aim in the welfare state by using the state, the market or civil society or a combination of these, and in what welfare regimes these goals seem to be best achieved. The central goals of the welfare state are inclusion (versus exclusion), equality (versus inequality) and a high level of employment.

Part III analyses central aspects and topics in welfare states by showing how the principles and elements from the first two parts can be used when analysing the welfare state. This includes, for example, how different approaches to welfare influence equality, inclusion and the welfare of different groups based upon gender, age, race and disability. Therefore the third part presents how to understand what has been seen as essential to the development of welfare states: the degree of equality and inequality and the impact of the state and the market especially in different welfare regimes.

The final part then takes a more international perspective, examining whether welfare state policies are still mainly a national prerogative or whether they are influenced by globalisation, and especially the impact of the EU on the options and possibilities of national combinations of the state, the market and civil society. It also presents trends in the development of the welfare state, including new ways of steering and organising the welfare state, in the light of ongoing transformations and challenges, and finally points towards the future of the welfare state.

The first part of the book presents the framework. Chapter 2 asks us to step back and ask: What is welfare? Answering this question is essential if we are to understand the development of the welfare state, what it is, and what it can be. An important issue here concerns the need to know why it is so difficult theoretically to find the boundaries and limits between the state, the market and civil society in welfare. The issues involved here are both empirical and normative, such as deciding the correct balance between individual freedom and societal intervention. The ability to prioritise between ends and means and between limited available resources is also becoming increasingly important.

Therefore both objective quantitative indicators of well-being and subjective aspects of citizens' understanding of the good society are important. Subjective well-being can be important in a modern welfare state. A happy nation might also be one that has a good welfare state. Social indicators and ways of measuring the impacts and outcomes of welfare state interventions in societal development might thereby be important. Institutions, structures and the way they influence equality and justice in modern societies are important as well.

Concepts central to understanding the welfare state in its different guises, such as the universal or targeted welfare state, including elements such as selectivity and take-up rate, are considered. The relative generosity of the welfare state is often discussed by looking into income replacement rate, which is therefore also presented. Furthermore, a variety of criteria – such as age, income and different social contingencies – may be applied for entitlement to benefits in different welfare state regimes. Benefits can also be divided into whether they are means tested or not. Even when the right to a benefit is established, there are several types of delivery, such as in kind and/or in cash. Income transfers and social services as elements are discussed.

How these different approaches can be used in different welfare policies is indicated in order to gain an understanding of how they are implemented in diverse welfare states, for example in areas such as pensions, unemployment benefits, social assistance, disability benefit, health care, old-age care, child-care, education and the labour market. The level and composition of public welfare in different types of welfare regimes is further presented.

Chapter 2 then presents a distinction between state, market and civil society that will be used as a way of understanding the welfare state and its role. This is used in combination with how this is dealt with in different welfare state regimes. Finally, it touches upon the aspects central to many welfare regimes: how to balance efficiency and equity.

Understanding what a welfare state is and what different welfare state regimes are, is the focus of Chapter 3. This chapter starts by presenting an overview of the debate about what a welfare state is; having defined what welfare is, one needs to find out what can be understood by a welfare state, since providing social welfare is not exclusive to the state, but is shared with the market and civil society. Types of welfare regimes are thereafter presented, how they differ and how the understanding of welfare regimes informs us about what to expect in different countries with regard to welfare. This includes how typologies can be used as part of the analysis of what a welfare state is and different understandings of the welfare state. The chapter argues for the choice of countries used in the book as a way of presenting varied approaches and types of welfare states in Europe. A new perspective on the welfare state – the social investment perspective – is finally shown as this is a way of presenting competing views on the welfare state: as a burden or an investment in the future. The social investment perspective is seen as a contrast to the Keynesian and neoliberal approach (Morel et al., 2012).

This also emphasises that politics matters, and that one needs to be aware of logics and ideologies behind changes in the welfare states, including types of drivers for changes. Types of changes and possible reasons for choosing between these are presented in the chapter.

Part II then looks in more detail into the role and rationality of the state, the market and civil society in relation to the delivery and financing of welfare and societal functioning. It thereby follows a tradition of looking into the mixed way of providing and financing welfare (Johnson, 1999). Chapter 4 is on the state and Chapter 5 on finance, which is seen as so important that it needs to be presented in a separate chapter. The next two chapters (6 and 7) are on the market, with a separate chapter on the labour market given its profound role and impact on people's everyday lives, and also its impact on public sector income and expenditures. The second part ends with Chapter 8 on civil society, especially the role of the family and the voluntary sector. They can be seen as different providers of welfare given that families have stronger social bonds and commitments than the voluntary sector and the rest of society. This distinction is not central here.

The different ways states seek to achieve the aims and purposes of the welfare state are the topic of Chapter 4. This is based upon a classical and historical approach originally presented by one of the most influential figures in the development of social policy in the United Kingdom, Richard Titmuss (Alcock et al., 2001; and see Box 1.1). Starting with Titmuss's understanding of social policy the chapter explores three different but interlinked approaches to the delivery of welfare – public, fiscal and occupational welfare – and examines how they are defined and measured and how they are linked together, including the possible impact of access to and distribution of resources. The chapter includes a short empirical overview including a discussion of measurement issues. This further relates to the fact that most of the present economic constraints on the welfare state mainly focus on the public side, and less on the more hidden elements and aspects of the welfare state, such as tax expenditures and occupational welfare.

Box 1.1 Who was Richard Titmuss?

Richard M. Titmuss (1907–73) was one of the most influential writers, alongside Beveridge, in the UK on Social Policy and its development, and how to structure and analyse core issues related to the welfare state. He was professor in Social Administration at the London School of Economics from 1950 until his death.

The following extract reflects the perspective here in this book:

> Considered as a whole, all collective interventions to meet certain needs of the individual and/or to service the wider interests of society may now be broadly grouped into three major categories of welfare: social welfare, fiscal welfare and occupational welfare. When we examine them in turn, it emerges that this division is not based on any fundamental difference in the functions of the three systems (if they may be so described) or their declared aims. It arises from an organizational division of method, which, in the main, is related to the division of labour in complex, individuated societies.
>
> (Titmuss, Lecture at the University of Birmingham, 1955; in Alcock et al., 2001, p. 63)

How to finance the welfare state has, in the wake of the ongoing financial crisis, become even more important. Chapter 5 presents the central principles of financing the public sector, and probes into the possible short- and long-term

central concepts

consequences of the financial crisis for welfare, as well as how international developments influence national options for financing the welfare state. Demography as a specific challenge for the financing of welfare states and debates revolving around ageing societies are examined. The use of welfare technology and social innovation in changing the welfare state offer new approaches to solving the economic and demographic pressures on the welfare state. This also raises the question of whether new ways of financing the welfare state are necessary for ensuring its long-term sustainability. Sustainability concerns both financial issues and the legitimacy of the welfare state.

Chapter 6 then switches the focus to the role of markets in the welfare state. First the chapter presents how and when a market will work, and also how market failure and government failure, as opposing arguments, are different reasons why diverse pathways to welfare have been chosen in different countries. Market failure is seen as a major reason why there is a need for state intervention. The marketisation of welfare services as a way to cope with an increase in demand and a wish to be more efficient will be discussed, together with the impact of choice. Finally, the possible outcome in relation to social cohesion, and equality and inequality in relation to both outcomes and access to welfare services, will be presented. The market has a role as a provider, but it also has an economic interest in providing these services. That the market in itself has an interest in public demand for services does not explain where the borders between the market and civil society should be, or that in some areas there might not even be a market if families take care of their own members or close networks exist. Further, this might influence who will finance and provide welfare.

The labour market as a specific but very important market is the focus of Chapter 7. Its importance goes beyond being a market for the demand and supply of labour as it also relates to individuals' options, their possibility of getting an income, social relations and the feeling of being included in society. An analysis of employment and unemployment as key elements of how the society functions is part of the chapter. The role of trade unions and employers' organisations in the welfare state is explored in relation to the changes in the composition of the labour market. Impacts due to the internal market in the EU and global movement of workers will also be touched upon, including reasons for cross-border migration and mobility. Given the central role of having a job and its impact on life conditions during a working life it is necessary to assess the workings of the labour market. Core issues such as 'flexicurity' and active labour market policy are also discussed.

Chapter 8 examines the role of civil society and families. It concentrates on the debate concerning 'the Big Society' and the intention of the partnership between the state and civil society, including expectation of a larger role for the voluntary sector in the delivery of welfare. That discussion has also awakened the debate of the expected role of the state and civil society in ensuring welfare, including care. This chapter will present concepts and ideas related to the role of civil society as it is today, including families. This is also a way to discuss the borderlines and possible changes to them, including whether welfare should be understood as a cost for society or, as suggested in recent debates, as a social investment, for example, by providing care for children enabling both mothers and fathers to enter the labour market. The intergenerational perspective related to the role of the family will also be explored. Social capital as a concept and the role and influence of the civil sector from an international perspective will be presented. Finally, civil society and the role of families with regard to social cohesion is discussed.

Having set the scene with state, market and civil society and welfare regimes, Part III examines the central aspects of the welfare state and central issues in everyday life for citizens in welfare states. It concentrates on two important aspects related to the development of welfare society:

1   Understanding and measuring inequality (a topic which has had a central place for many years).
2   How to see and understand social inclusion and exclusion.

These are linked to four specific groups/segments often perceived in different ways as not being treated fairly or at higher risk of being socially excluded:

1   gender: mostly women
2   disability: people with disabilities
3   age: mostly young people and older people
4   race and ethnicity: ethnic and racial minority groups, immigrants, refugees, asylum seekers.

Chapter 9 takes up the normative issues of justice and measures of inequality looking at both classical (income) and more modern (capabilities) measures. In addition the chapter takes up the subject of how equality/inequality has an impact on how society works and, in turn, how this might influence well-being, health and so on in modern welfare states. The chapter will introduce concepts and methodologies appropriate for understanding inequality and the implications of different types of inequality, ways to measure and discuss it and ways to change this in different welfare state regimes. The monetary as well as non-monetary factors linked to inequality, poverty and deprivation are presented. This is finally connected to new types of risk, including the consequences for family structure and the breakup of families.

Inequalities have also often been perceived as being related to differences resulting from social inclusion or exclusion. Chapter 10 investigates different groups' position in the welfare state focusing on gender, disability, age and ethnicity. This includes issues such as whether societies are making new divisions between those included and excluded and whether the welfare state can reduce, reinforce or change the roles of, for example, gender and ethnicity. What is the mainstream explanation of, for example, ethnic segregation, and how can we see its impact on welfare states and their way of functioning?

Migration and its impact on welfare states is also included, given that both within the EU and globally there are issues that might have an impact on the development of the welfare state. These types of questions thus reinforce a new approach to inequality and equal opportunities in modern societies. Another question is whether this is different in various welfare regimes.

Having presented these central aspects of modern welfare societies in the third part, the fourth and final part moves on to discuss possible impacts on welfare states from globalisation and Europeanisation, and their consequences. This part also includes new approaches in the ways the welfare state may be organised and steered.

The governance of the welfare state is changing. There appears no longer to be just one type of management and one way of structuring the welfare state. Chapter 11 turns to this development. However, given the fiscal constraints on welfare states, there has increasingly been a focus on more effective, leaner and more strongly managed welfare states, while at the same time a stronger focus on users' perspectives, and involvement of the market and civil society. Furthermore increasing attention is given to being informed about decision making on what works and what does not work. Evidence-based policy is thus increasingly important. Therefore the chapter also discusses how to measure policies and social intervention in social policy, including the impact of context and how one is able to ensure consistency about knowledge of what works best. The tradition of health care also enters the heart of social policy studies and is used in policy making and administration. Furthermore, there has been increased attention to trying to influence behaviour not only in the traditional way by using economic incentives (taxes and duties, economic support), public information campaigns and legal intervention (for example, bans on smoking) but also by nudging people to change their behaviour.

Chapter 12 examines the EU's role in relation to the welfare state, and whether it differs depending on welfare state regimes, and how this might change the role of the state, the market and civil society. The reason for this is the presumed increasing role played by the EU in the options and possibility of pursuing national welfare state policies. The chapter presents the EU's historical role and principles on welfare state policy, including those related to gender and migration. Introducing the Open Method of Coordination and the role of the European Court of Justice, the chapter then goes on to discusses whether welfare state policies are still national. It questions whether we are witnessing a convergence of welfare states, not just in terms of public welfare, but also occupational and fiscal welfare, and the respective roles of the state, the market and civil society. Another issue is whether recent changes in nation states' options will imply a movement towards much more similar welfare states in the developed world, which is what Esping-Andersen (1990) proposed, with three worlds of welfare capitalism reduced to one. This includes also the debate on whether welfare states are national or by now so aligned as part of global and European development that diverse welfare regimes are withering away in favour of one way of combining state, market and civil society.

Finally, Chapter 13 sums up the discussions and presents some ideas about the future of the welfare state. This includes returning to the debate on demographic and financial pressures on welfare states in the light of recent developments, and also whether the legitimacy of the welfare state is challenged by the changed role and interaction between state, market and civil society in the light of the globalisation and Europeanisation of the welfare state.

References

Alcock, P., Glennerster, H. and Oakley, A. (2001), *Welfare and Wellbeing. Richard Titmuss's Contribution to Social Policy*. Bristol, Policy Press.

Esping-Andersen, G. (1990), *The Three Worlds of Welfare Capitalism*. London, Polity.

Esping-Andersen, G. (ed.) (2002), *Why We Need a New Welfare State*. Oxford, Oxford University Press.

Johnson, N. (1999), *Mixed Economies of Welfare. A Comparative Perspective*. London, Prentice Hall.

Morel, N., Palier, B. and Palme, J. (2012), *Towards a Social Investment Welfare State? Ideas, Policies and Challenges*. Bristol, Policy Press.

Svallfors, S. (ed.) (2012), *Contested Welfare States. Welfare Attitudes in Europe and Beyond*. Stanford CA, Stanford University Press.

Taylor-Gooby, P. F. (2004) New Social Risks and Welfare States: New Paradigm and New Politics? In Taylor-Gooby, P. F. (ed.), *New Risks, New Welfare*. Oxford, Oxford University Press, pp. 209–48.

What is welfare?

Some basic concepts

Contents

2.1   Introduction

This chapter examines the concept of welfare from the perspectives of social policy, economics, sociology and philosophy. This will consequently enable us to define 'welfare'. Both macro and micro perspectives will be used, and both subjective and objective approaches will be taken into consideration. Social indicators and new measurements of well-being, including happiness, will also be discussed as they reflect different understandings of the topic, and have entered the debate on the welfare state since the more traditional use of money (and gross domestic product – GDP) as the measure of welfare has been increasingly questioned. These discussions form the basis for understanding the notion of the welfare state. Social policy is thus a broader set of policies such as social security, education, health care and housing (as in kind as well as in cash) and is thus part of the welfare state's activities.

Having discussed and defined welfare, this chapter will present key principles, concepts and policies in relation to welfare and the welfare state as this will show the variety of principles that can be used, and to varying degrees are used, in the welfare state. This also forms a background for the presentation of the welfare state in Chapter 3, and the different ways to finance and deliver welfare as shown in Part II.

The welfare state has been defined in different ways despite it having had a central role in many societies for many years. This diversity might be a result of the disagreement over why we should have a welfare state. This chapter gives a short outline of the possible boundaries of the welfare mix and how this might change and has changed over time.

Understanding welfare in societies, and not only with objective quantitative data, has in recent years implied a new focus on social indicators, including the happiness and well-being of people in different societies. How this is and can be done in order to supplement classical ways of depicting welfare states is the focus of Section 2.5. Another possible aim of the welfare state, such as equality and efficiency and how they interact, will also be touched upon in Section 2.6. Finally, Section 2.7 will sum up the chapter.

2.2   What is welfare?

This topic will be presented by employing four overall perspectives based upon whether we look at macro-level (state, market) or micro-level (civil society) aspects in combination with the possible use of subjective or objective indicators. These perspectives are captured in Figure 2.1, and will run through several themes discussed in the book such as well-being, poverty, inequality, etc.

Figure 2.1 indicates that there are at least four different approaches to welfare. One can approach it from a societal perspective in an objective way, for example, by looking at the overall level of production (often measured objectively by GDP per capita) or more subjectively, by examining trust in government. Welfare can also be seen from an individual point of view (for example, subjectively, as the perception of being poor, or as an objective measure of the number living at risk of poverty). The number of people at risk of living in poverty is an objective measure, based upon an understanding of the level of income needed to avoid living in poverty (see also Chapter 9), it might also have in-built subjective understandings. A reason for including the objective/subjective distinction is that persons often compare their life-situation to that of others. For example, even if one has a high income, if the neighbours have a higher income this can

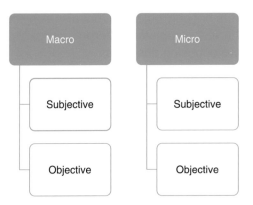

Figure 2.1 Perspectives on welfare.

influence the individual's well-being, and welfare is therefore also influenced by subjective issues, and measuring this is not simple. There is further, in relation to social services, the possibility that even when a service is good, the individual's perception is not the same. For example, it might be that objectively it is safe to walk the streets at night, but elderly people are subjectively afraid of doing so.

Approaches to welfare can include concepts such as happiness, security, preferences, needs, deserts and relative comparison (Fitzpatrick, 2001). A way of describing well-being could be that a person is happy if

> she spent most of her time engaged in activities that she would rather continue than stop, little time in situations she wished to escape, and – very important because life is short – not too much time in a neutral state in which she would not care either way.
>
> (Kahneman, 2011, p. 391)

In Box 2.1 is another understanding of well-being.

Box 2.1 A common understanding of well-being

In the UK the Department for Environment, Food and Rural Affairs has together with other departments developed the following common understanding of well-being:

> Well-being is a positive physical, social and mental state; it is not just the absence of pain, discomfort and incapacity, it requires that basic needs are met, that individuals have a sense of purpose, that they feel able to achieve important personal goals and participate in society.
>
> (in Allin, 2007, p. 46)

Well-being thus renders not only objective, but also subjective elements. This is one approach to welfare. A completely different approach to the understanding of welfare refers to two opposing positions:

> Perfectionism: welfare refers to a life that is, morally speaking, 'lived well'.
> Non-perfectionism: welfare refers to all-purpose means to attain one's aims and/or the satisfaction of one's desires and preferences.
>
> (Fives, 2008, p. 3)

These different approaches show that there is not just one understanding of what the concept of welfare includes. Besides the aspects mentioned above, the approaches should also include the understanding of well-being.

The first important question is how to define welfare; in this book it is defined as:

> the highest possible access to economic resources, a high level of well-being, including the happiness of the citizens, a guaranteed minimum income to avoid living in poverty, and, finally, having the capabilities to ensure the individual a good life.
>
> (Greve, 2008, p. 50)

These aspects are discussed next. Crucial to the definition is the idea that welfare is related to aspects of the greatest importance for individuals' lives. Additionally it involves an understanding, albeit implicitly, of how a good society, which has many individuals who have a variety of preferences, can be developed in such a way that citizens find it a good society to live in. This involves the question of what role the welfare state should play, and who should provide welfare. This will be explored further in Chapter 4.

Welfare has been discussed in many and very varied disciplines. The notion of utility has been the basis of the economists' debate, sociologists have concentrated on the concept of well-being, and philosophers have focused on trying to understand what the good life is. These differences also have implications for the way welfare and the corresponding use of social indicators are understood.

Social policy and welfare state policies can be seen as instruments that can be used in order to try to achieve the highest possible level of welfare for the citizens in a country. Social policy can be interpreted in a very narrow or a very broad sense, although when trying to depict what welfare is, as in the above definition, this is less important.

In economic theory, the interest in relation to welfare has primarily been on individuals' choices as they are expected to relate to what is best for the individual. Furthermore, the utility derived from the amount of goods and services an individual can buy is regarded as reflecting the best position for a person. Individuals' decisions on how to use their money and time are thus seen as the best way to maximise societal welfare. The market has an essential role in

central concepts

welfare economics. Recent developments within behavioural economics have shown an increased interest in other approaches, including non-monetary aspects, and how they influence our welfare and the decisions we take.

In sociology, topics related to social cohesion and well-being in a broader sense have been important issues in relation to welfare. A higher level of welfare would then be possible to reach in various ways including, for example, having many friends and relatives. Thereby income is not the only important aspect in welfare. There is a need for diverse data to describe and measure welfare, including the use of social indicators. One of the most important contemporary sociologists, Anthony Giddens, has focused on what he has labelled positive welfare. Giddens proposes that the welfare state be regarded as a social investment state, and thus his focus is on features such as active health, autonomy, education and well-being (Giddens, 1998, 2007). This is in line with much research today, which shows the possible positive impact of the welfare state, for example, by providing affordable and high-quality day care for children. This is not only for the children's benefit, but it also allows more equal access to the labour market for men and women.

Welfare can also be based upon need. For example, Allardt states, 'the amount of welfare is defined by the degree of need-satisfaction' (1976, p. 228). Allardt also points out that, by focusing on needs, welfare can be seen as having two levels, one dealing with standard of living and the other with quality of life. The implication is that one has to take into consideration material and immaterial resources as well as human relations when evaluating and describing the level of welfare in a society. This suggests a set of social indicators that would give a major role to issues such as having, loving and being, and also ways to measure these. It also reflects that for a good life basic needs must be met (shelter, food) before looking into other amenities.

Whether the welfare state can help in increasing welfare or whether the welfare state increases dependency is often disputed (George and Wilding, 1994). However, the welfare state can at least establish the framework for a higher level of welfare and enhance the ability to achieve it, and there are different principles in order to do so, which is the focus of the next section.

2.3 Some basic principles, concepts and policies

There are at least three different approaches possible when the welfare state wants to deliver welfare to its citizens: need, merit and equality (see Table 2.1). How these approaches are combined depends on national traditions and history, and on the ideological foundations of different welfare states, and therefore they are different in various welfare regimes.

Benefits based upon need and means testing might, but would not necessarily, be at a low level. Low level and means-tested benefits were the understanding of the 1942 Beveridge Report. It can be argued that the principles in the Beveridge Report formed the background for the welfare state, especially in

Table 2.1 Types of benefit and principles of justice

Principles of justice	Benefit types – policy orientation
Need	Means-tested income maintenance and services (health, education, and housing); special needs provision; and universal human needs.
Merit	Social insurance schemes; conditionality of welfare receipt; equal opportunity (meritocracy); and counseling and training.
Equality	Guaranteed unconditional basic income; universal public services; equalisation of income; fair equal opportunity; and affirmative action.

Source: Fives (2008, p. 7).

the UK. For a summary of the contents of the report and also a short presentation and a modern interpretation, see: http://www.sochealth.co.uk/public-health-and-wellbeing/beveridge-report/. The Beveridge Report focused on 'want, disease, ignorance, squalor and idleness' (Timmins, 1996). Today, attention is directed to employment, housing, health, education and income level in order to achieve a high level of both societal and individual welfare.

Means testing is advocated to ensure that the welfare support goes to those most in need, whereas benefits that are not means tested might also be given to people with higher incomes. Examples of non-means-tested benefits in welfare states can be different kinds of support for people with disabilities to pay for equipment aids. The basic state pension, although often low, is often non-means tested, as are family allowances, as these are argued to be a transfer from taxpayers without children to families with children.

Benefits based upon merit imply that a person has done something and then has the right to a benefit. This is typically the case in social insurance systems. While working, the individual earns the right to certain benefits, for example, unemployment insurance or pension savings.

When benefits are based upon equality and with an equal amount for all who qualify, this is for some seen as a basic income. This can only be argued to a limited extent to exist in welfare states, as there often is a number of criteria in order to be eligible for the benefit. Equality in access to service is within this approach, and in many welfare states there is equal access, for example, to health care. Fair and equal opportunities in society overall are also emphasised by this understanding of principles of justice. The book will return to different understandings of justice in Chapter 9 on equality. Another central topic refers to the difference between a universal or selective approach to welfare.

Universalism refers to 'the aim of making services available and accessible to the whole population in such ways as would not involve users in any humiliating loss of status, dignity or self-respect' (Titmuss, 1968, p. 129). The implication of a principle of universalism is not that everyone should have a right to all kinds of benefits. There may still be specific criteria for eligibility for certain

central concepts

benefits based on two of the three principles depicted in Table 2.1. This can also include access to welfare being based upon reaching a certain age (old age pension), or having children of a certain age (child benefits, family allowances) or a specific social contingency (work accident, sickness).

Universalism is the idea that access to benefits and services is based upon citizenship or having permanent residence in a country. This is in contrast to selectivism in which access to benefits is dependent on being a member of a specific social insurance, or having paid membership fees. In most welfare state regimes, access to hospitals is based upon universalism, whereas many pension systems are to a large degree a combination of (often a relatively low) universal state benefit and supplements based upon previous savings to either a pension fund or savings account. The universal approach might be subject to change due to the impact of the EU (cf. also Chapter 12).

In contrast to universality is selectivity, whereby only groups or persons selected beforehand can have access to benefits. Selectivity can be combined with means testing so that groups with a specific need (lack of income, for example) can have a benefit or access to services on different conditions than other citizens.

Having decided who will have access to benefits and on what criteria, the next step is to decide the level of the benefits. This is often measured by the replacement rate, which is the level of welfare benefits compared with the income before being eligible for the benefit. It is often measured so that it is the replacement rate after tax income that is compared, that is the impact of the tax system is included. The level of the replacement rate can be a guide to the generosity of a welfare state, and this can be a dividing line between different types of welfare regimes (see also Chapter 3).

The level of the replacement rate need not be the same across different income transfers. It is often highest for short-term benefits, such as unemployment benefits, where the benefit can help a person or family to continue their lifestyle even for a short time on becoming unemployed, whereas the expectation is that the living standard might have to be reduced if benefits are received for a longer time span. Therefore the replacement rate of the state pension is often at a lower level, especially given that this is, in principle, a foreseen contingency, whereas unemployment and disability are generally unanticipated.

However, even when there are rules for benefits and how to calculate them this might not imply that all who are eligible for a benefit actually receive it. Not all citizens ask for the benefit or are aware that they have the right to claim it, or the right to receive any economic support from the welfare state. The percentage of those who are eligible and who receive the benefit is termed the take-up rate. A low take-up rate can also be due to the fact that for some people receiving welfare benefits is a stigma.

Another distinction is whether the benefit should be given in cash or in kind. The argument for in-cash benefit is that this gives the recipient the best option for the possible combination of goods and services he/she prefers. In some cases, the argument for benefits in kind is that this ensures that, for example, the person in need of food gets food and does not perhaps buy alcohol or drugs instead. The support for benefits in kind might therefore in certain cases be higher, with this paternalistic approach (Barr, 2004). In certain policy areas benefits in kind is the main principle, such as, for example, the case of education. Here the welfare state often provides education free of charge in order to ensure that children receive education, instead of paying an amount of money to the parents to pay for their children's education and risking that they will use it for other purposes. Education is often also an example of what is labelled a merit good, that is a good that left to the provision of the market will not, based on an overall societal interest, be used in a sufficiently high level (see further in Chapter 4 on the state).

Welfare policies can aim to support people in case they are in need, but can also try to prevent certain social issues arising (Berghman et al., 2013). This includes information on how to live a healthy lifestyle, using fiscal instruments to reduce consumption of alcohol, but also the new idea of nudging people (see also Section 11.5) to live a healthier life. Education is also seen as a way to prevent people being socially excluded, and make them better able to get and keep a job. Prevention in order that individuals are better able to take care of themselves, by rehabilitative efforts, especially in care for the elderly, has been another approach used in welfare states in recent years.

Many of the principles described above have been developed in relation to income transfers from the welfare state to the individual. They can also to a certain extent be used in the area of welfare services, which, despite discussion on the future of the welfare state, have been developing in many countries over the last 20–30 years.

Policies on welfare services in the classical welfare state areas such as care, labour, housing and health can thus be built upon different types of criteria, different replacement rates and rules for access, and thereby use of a variety of instruments. Criteria range from universality in access to selectivity, and can vary from being free at the point of use to a variety of user charges. User charges can also vary, for example, depending on an individual's income and wealth. Even when the need for services is decided, there is still a debate on who will have to provide them – the state or the market.

2.4   State, market and civil society

Welfare services and income transfers can be delivered in many and varied ways, and these were explained in the previous section with many and various criteria regarding level, payment and reasons for eligibility. Still, this does not tell us who has the responsibility to finance and provide these benefits, although many of the principles are developed with an eye to what the state has been doing. A classical way of depicting this is by looking into the role of the state, the market and civil society. This can have different names such as welfare mix and the mixed economies of welfare. The focus here is on the various combinations of the actors.

These sectors (e.g. state, market and civil society) have different ways of being able to provide welfare and also have different rationalities in order to deliver it, ranging from payment at the market rate to public provision without paying, to care within the family. In Chapters 4–8 the logic and ability of these sectors to provide welfare for individuals is shown, including how this can differ among different kinds of welfare state regime, as presented in Chapter 3. The combination, labelled the welfare mix, is presented in Chapter 8, where the reasons for and abilities to provide welfare by the state as well as the market and civil society are shown.

In relation to the state this presentation is split into two chapters, with financing by the state as a separate chapter, given that financing the welfare state has been central in the arguments on the size of the welfare state and what it is able to provide for its citizens.

A core reason for state welfare is that the market left to itself will in many areas not provide either services or economic security for citizens. Market failure has thus been a core reason for the welfare state's development (see, for details, Section 6.2, which also discusses government failure). Still, there is also a normative issue at stake given that different ideological underpinnings can be used as arguments for a stronger or weaker state, market and/or civil society. They have, further, had different roles historically over time and these are ever changing – and the balance will presumably continuously change. Hence it is necessary to understand why and how the different sectors provide and support welfare.

The role of the market in most economies is to distribute goods and services in accordance with the preferences of buyers and sellers. Therefore in principle welfare benefits and services in several areas could also be provided by the market. The discussion revolves around the consequences of using the market as provider, related to issues of both equality and efficiency. The labour market has a very specific place and importance in the welfare state, as for many people it is where the possibility of consumption through income is guaranteed.

Civil society has historically been important in providing care and also some security for food and shelter. Whether and how to balance the state and civil society is an ongoing debate as the welfare state has taken over part of the care for children and frail elderly people. This balance is therefore central also for individuals' welfare and well-being.

2.5 Social indicators – new ways of measuring well-being

Research has shown that it is possible to collect meaningful and reliable data on subjective as well as objective well-being. Subjective well-being encompasses different aspects – cognitive evaluations of one's life, happiness, satisfaction, positive emotions such as joy and pride, and negative emotions such as pain and worry; each of them should be measured separately to derive a more comprehensive appreciation of people's lives.

(Stiglitz et al., 2009, p. 16)

As this quote indicates, it is possible to measure well-being. Social indicators are seen as a new way of measuring well-being which can provide a broader picture of societal development and include monetary as well as non-monetary factors, and thereby give a better description of the overall level of societal welfare. Therefore, there have been attempts to be more precise in describing well-being. Examples of social indicators include being alone, or having a decent living standard. A distinction between objective and subjective well-being indicators is also made, as this makes it possible to combine objective information with how the individual values his/her life in different welfare areas. Recent years have further seen an upsurge in published data intended to reflect more than the classical measure of GDP per capita. This also includes data on happiness and other indicators relevant to the quality of life. Table 2.2 shows the possible combination of monetary/non-monetary issues and objective/subjective indicators, and provides an example of each of the four possible combinations.

The implication of these different types of measurement is that there is a need for quantitative data based upon registers or other objective collected data, and qualitative data based upon individual interview surveys. Register data comes from information in registers (which are not available in all countries, given the different traditions concerning registration), or at least in such a way that it is possible to combine different data for persons who have been receiving, for example, different welfare benefits. Box 2.2 illustrates the variety of indicators provided by the Organisation for Economic Cooperation and Development (OECD). This information can be used for an analysis of welfare, and also shows that welfare is and will be different for diverse persons.

Table 2.2 Combination and types of monetary/non-monetary elements in a objective/subjective framework

	Monetary	Non-monetary
Objective	Income per inhabitant	Average life expectancy
Subjective	Feeling that there is not enough money	Personal evaluation of quality of life

Note: In each cell only one example of an indicator is given; in social policy analysis they can be different and along many lines, see, for example, also Box 2.2 with OECD indicators.

central concepts

Box 2.2 OECD's social indicators

Median equalized household income in US dollar purchasing power parities (USD PPPs)

Employment to population ratio for population aged 15–64

Unemployment rate for the population aged 15–64

PISA mean scores on the reading literacy scales

Gini coefficient of income inequality

Poverty rate

Percentage finding it difficult or very difficult to manage on current income

Percentage of average gross wage to reach a poverty threshold of 60% of median income for lone parents with two children

Life expectancy at birth/Infant mortality rate

Rate of positive experience

Percentage of persons satisfied with water quality

Percentage of people expressing high level of trust in others

Corruption index

Pro-social behavior

Voting rates

Tolerance of diversity

Source: OECD (2014), Society at a Glance 2014 OECD Social Indicators. Paris, OECD.

It is obvious that establishing measurements for some of these indicators is more difficult than for others. The OECD's social indicators point to certain areas of greatest prominence for the individual's life and society's functioning. Therefore these are important areas for most people when trying to describe their level of welfare. Issues such as employment and unemployment will be returned to several times in this book, as well as issues related to equality such as poverty rates and the Gini coefficient. Several of the other indicators are also important to describe and analyse welfare. This includes life expectancy, but also whether people can trust each other and the degree of tolerance in society.

The list is not exhaustive of indicators, but it presents the elements of importance in order to understand welfare. Furthermore, a risk of using too many indicators is that this would reduce the ability to grasp how a country is ranked compared to other countries in relation to the level of welfare.

The OECD also has another list of indicators, where it is possible to look into and also compare one's own country with other countries' performance and stance within 11 areas related to well-being, including three subjective

Table 2.3 OECD's 11 topics and indicators to measure 'How's Life?'

Topics	Indicators
Housing	Rooms per person Housing expenditure Dwelling with basic facilities
Income	Household disposable income Household financial wealth
Jobs	Employment rate Long-term unemployment rate Personal earnings Job security
Community	Quality of support network
Education	Educational attainment Years in education Students skills in maths, reading and science
Environment	Air pollution Water quality
Civic engagement	Voter turnout Consultation on rule-making
Health	Life expectancy Self-reported health
Life satisfaction	How people evaluate their life as a whole
Safety	Assault rate Homicide rate
Work–life balance	Employees working long hours Time devoted to leisure and personal care

Source: http://www.oecdbetterlifeindex.org/ (accessed 10 June 2014)

indicators: subjective well-being, personal security and work–life balance (cf. OECD's work on well-being at: http://www.oecdbetterlifeindex.org/). Table 2.3 provides an overview of the 11 indicators and sub-elements.

One measurement of well-being is the individual's subjective evaluation of his/her level of happiness, and the measurement and understanding of this has received growing interest in recent years. Happiness of the citizen has been a goal for individuals and for a long time in many societies has been part of an understanding of what constitutes a good society. It does seem that the most developed welfare states are often the happiest (cf. Table 2.4).

A central issue concerns the way research on 'happiness' can inform us on core aspects related to when people are happy and the reasons why, and thereby which policy recommendations should be given in a specific policy area. Box 2.3 summarises the findings of a recent report (cf. also Greve, 2012).

Table 2.4 The 20 happiest countries in the world

1. Denmark 2. Finland 3. Norway 4. Netherlands 5. Canada

6. Switzerland 7. Sweden 8. New Zealand 9. Australia 10. Ireland

11. United States 12. Costa Rica 13. Austria 14. Israel 15. Belgium

16. Luxembourg 17. United Arab Emirates 18. United Kingdom 19. Venezuela 20. Iceland

Source: Helliwell et al. (2012).

Box 2.3 Information on happiness

- Happier countries tend to be richer countries. But more important for happiness than income are social factors like the strength of social support, the absence of corruption and the degree of personal freedom.
- Over time as living standards have risen, happiness has increased in some countries, but not in others (such as, for example, the United States). On average, the world has become a little happier in the last 30 years (by 0.14 times the standard deviation of happiness around the world).
- Unemployment causes as much unhappiness as bereavement or separation. At work, job security and good relationships do more for job satisfaction than high pay and convenient hours.
- Behaving well makes people happier.
- Mental health is the biggest single factor affecting happiness in any country. Yet only a quarter of mentally ill people get treatment for their condition in advanced countries and fewer in poorer countries.
- A stable family life and enduring marriages are important for the happiness of parents and children.
- In advanced countries, women are happier than men, while the position in poorer countries is mixed.
- Happiness is lowest in middle age.

Source: http://www.earth.columbia.edu/articles/view/2960
(accessed 17 October 2012)

Without going into detail about the reasons for people's happiness, the summary in Box 2.3 shows that the support provided by welfare states has an impact on people being happy, and consequently the welfare state may play a role in providing the conditions for happiness even though it is unable to provide happiness as such. Health is, for example, a good predictor of the individual's well-being and happiness. Welfare states that provide a good and sufficient level of health care thus, all other things being equal, should expect a higher level of happiness among their citizens. Providing jobs and economic growth can also help in increasing happiness and well-being in a country. A higher level of security can help in increasing well-being and a family policy that supports families will in principle also be able to contribute to a society's well-being. It is also the case that being socially excluded might reduce the level of happiness and well-being (Eurofound, 2012; see also Chapter 10).

Subjective well-being is, according to the OECD, related to individuals' life evaluation, affect (personal feeling or emotional states) and eudaimonia (sense of meaning and purpose of life) (OECD, 2013). This is then used as a starting point for guidelines for measuring subjective well-being, and thus to supplement the objective data of a society's welfare. Referring back to Table 2.2, we can conclude that in order to understand welfare one needs to look into subjective as well as objective measures.

2.6   Balancing perspectives of equity and efficiency

Even when we know what increases welfare, including the factors of well-being and happiness in a society, this still has to be balanced with other goals. Societies need to be efficient given that there are only limited resources available. The size of a year's production (e.g. gross national product – GNP) can only be used once, so there will be competition among many goals in the welfare state for scarce resources. Therefore, as will be discussed further in Chapter 11, there has been a constant quest for reliable evidence of what works and pressure to use best practices as a way of optimising the use of scarce resources, thus ensuring that there is maximum output for the available resources; and that the goals set can be achieved with as few resources as possible given that there are also other goals to be achieved. Thus spending on one activity reduces the option of spending on another, which is often called the opportunity cost.

Another issue relates to the fact that the most simple and administrative solutions might be less equitable, and the balance between equity and effi-ciency is often thus a central feature of welfare states. The ambition to have less bureaucracy therefore often conflicts with principles of equality. This is, for example, the case with a fixed amount of money per child in a family, as used in many family allowances systems, which is a simple measure, but not neces-sarily equitable. This is because in such a system those with a high level of income will receive the same amount of money as those with a low income, although from a relative perspective the same amount of money is more impor-tant for the low income than high income earners. On the other hand, making such a system even more equitable implies a need to find a mechanism to reduce the allowance for high income earners, which can also be administra-tive, and hence more expensive. At the same time it is fair in the sense that it redistributes money from families without children to families with children and using a concept of justice between families with and without children instead of income as a parameter changes the understanding of the balance.

central concepts

This raises at least two issues concerning a just system. One is normative, related to how to define when one person is rich. Another is at what rate the allowances should be reduced. A high rate of reduction in benefit with higher income can then imply a negative incentive to work more, or if the level is relatively low there is a risk of poverty traps, that is even when working more hours or changing to a job with higher income, the family will still have a disposable income below the poverty line.

The balance between easy and simple administration may thus be in conflict with equity, but also in conflict with the overall possible level of spending, as the absence of means testing or a reduction for higher income earners will make income transfers more expensive for the public sector.

There is also a continuing debate about the possible disincentives arising from the financing and delivery of welfare. The welfare state should try to minimise the negative impact and avoid as many distortions as possible. This is often applied, for example, in the ongoing discussion concerning the possible impact on individuals' job search behaviour when they are receiving unemployment benefits (cf. also Chapter 7).

2.7   Summing-up

This chapter has set the scene for the presentation of various core issues concerning the welfare state in the following chapters. Welfare is not an unambiguous concept; however, it is still possible to get at least some idea of the central issues related to what welfare is.

Welfare can be understood at both a macro- and a micro-level, and both objective and subjective approaches are possible. Therefore it is important when describing welfare to know how the data have been gathered and what they cover. Welfare is also central when connected to the state, that is the welfare state. In all developed countries, the welfare state plays an essential role in relation to different kinds of risk and different degrees of need, a point which will further be pursued in the coming chapters.

Recent years have seen an upswing in trying to capture more subjective aspects of welfare by looking into happiness, well-being and other social indicators. This points to how broad and diverse the concept of welfare can be.

Welfare states are not all alike due to historical and national traditions. They therefore use different approaches and ways to distribute services and income transfers. Using different approaches has different impacts, and thus also a possible difference related to equity and efficiency.

References

Allardt, E. (1976), Dimensions of Welfare in a Comparative Scandinavian Study. *Acta Sociologica*, vol. 19, no. 3, pp. 227–39.

Allin, P. (2007), Measuring Societal Wellbeing. *Economic and Labour Market Review*, vol. 1, no. 10, pp. 46–52.

Barr, N. (2004), *The Economics of the Welfare State*, 4th edition. Oxford, Oxford University Press.

Berghman, J., Debels, A. and Van Hoyweghen, I. (2013), Prevention: The Cases of Social Security and Health Care. In Greve, B. (ed.), *Routledge International Handbook of the Welfare State*. Abingdon, Routledge, pp. 47–58.

Beveridge, W. (1942), *Social Insurance and Alliel Services*. Presented to Parliament by command of His Majesty, HMSO CMND 6404.

Eurofound (2012), *Third European Quality of Life Survey – Quality of Life in Europe: Impacts of the Crisis*. Luxembourg, Publications Office of the European Union.

Fitzpatrick, T. (2001), *Welfare Theory: An Introduction*. Houndsmills, UK: Palgrave.

Fives, Allyn (2008), *Political and Philosophical Debates in Welfare*. Houndsmills, Palgrave.

George, V. and Wilding, P. (1994), *Welfare and Ideology*. Hemel Hempstead, Harvester Wheatsheaf.

Giddens, A. (1998), *The Third Way: The Renewal of Social Democracy*. Cambridge, Polity Press.

Giddens, A. (2007), *Over to You, Mr Brown*. Cambridge, Polity Press.

Greve, B. (2008), What Is Welfare? *Central European Journal of Public Policy*, vol. 2, no. 1, pp. 50–73.

Greve, B. (2012), *Happiness*. Abingdon, Routledge.

Helliwell, J., Layard, R. and Sachs, J. (eds) (2012), *World Happiness Report*. New York, The Earth Institute, Columbia University.

Kahneman, D. (2011), *Thinking Fast and Slow*. London, Penguin Books.

OECD (2013), *OECD Guidelines on Measuring Subjective Well-being*. Paris, OECD.

Stiglitz, J., Sen, A. and Fitoussi, J.-P. (2009), *Report by the Commission of the Measurement of Economic Performance and Social Progress*. Paris, Commission of the Measurement of Economic Performance and Social Progress.

Timmins, N. (1996), *The Five Giants: A Biography of the Welfare State*. London, Fontana Press.

Titmuss, R. (1968), *Commitment to Welfare*. London, Allen & Unwin.

Chapter 3

Welfare states and welfare regimes

Contents

3.1   Introduction

Chapter 2 described what welfare is and key concepts related to well-being and the main social principles related to access and delivery of welfare. This chapter continues by looking into the question of what welfare states are, and how we can understand these, including different perspectives of why there is a welfare state in most developed countries around the world.

Countries around the world belong, according to many articles and analyses, to different welfare regimes. This chapter will therefore also focus on some issues of methodology related to analysing welfare states and welfare regimes, welfare typologies and the ability to use them as devices to describe societies and societal development. This includes arguments for the choice of countries used in the book as examples of countries belonging to different regimes and thereby different understandings and representation of kinds of welfare state; there is often a different mix between state, market and civil society, which as is argued in Section 2.4 will have an impact on who receives, pays for and delivers welfare.

The chapter is structured so that first there is a discussion on how to understand welfare states, then how to measure and describe welfare regimes, followed by a discussion of whether they have changed. Then different perspectives of the role of the welfare state are considered, especially from a social investment perspective, but also contrasting this to neoliberalism, Keynesian and the Third Way approaches. Section 3.8 sums up the chapter.

3.2   What is the welfare state?

A definition of welfare, as outlined in Chapter 2, does not by itself define what a welfare state is, neither does it inform us what kind and type of welfare state different countries might have. Who delivers and who finances welfare can be a question of diverse structures and approaches in various countries (cf. Chapter 4 for the principles). This section will show what a welfare state is, including how the concept of a welfare state has been interpreted differently by different approaches. The development of different types of welfare regimes will be outlined, and in more detail, in Section 3.3. The classification of welfare state regimes will be used as a structuring device here and later in the book by using countries from different regimes to indicate how different welfare states solve the tasks and use various approaches in order to achieve the goals of the varied welfare states.

The term 'welfare state' itself is contested within social and political analysis. On a narrow understanding, it refers to the role of the state, since the Second World War, in education, health, housing, poverty relief, social insurance and other social services (Timmins, 1996). A broader approach would focus on the welfare state as a particular form of state, a distinctive form of polity or a specific type of society, and also a specific form of capitalism that can help to aid capital accumulation, regulate and discipline labour and be the result of working class power (Korpi and Palme, 1998). After the Second World War the focus was on how to cope with 'want, disease, ignorance, squalor and idleness', as presented in the Beveridge Report on social insurance.

· The welfare state can be seen as having at least three different tasks: redistribution, social investment and intergenerational transmissions. Furthermore, the welfare state often has a role in coping with market failure (see Section 6.2 for a more detailed presentation of this concept), and also varied ways to help individuals in cases of social risks and different groups (see especially Chapter 10).

There is no common agreement about what a welfare state is (see Box 3.1). However, it is often related to state intervention aimed at reducing the risk of market failure, ensuring a decent living standard and a certain degree of equality and intergenerational distribution. The welfare state thus often plays a central role in relation to essential issues of people's daily lives such as housing, employment, income security, health and education. Reducing market failure and ensuring at least options for many are arguments for public sector intervention without this exactly addressing the level and type of intervention to be used in order to redress the impact of market failure.

Box 3.1 Examples of definitions of welfare state

- 'A polity so organized that every member of the community is assured of his due maintenance with most advantageous conditions possible' (*Oxford Dictionary*, 1955).
- 'A welfare state is a state in which organized power is deliberately used in an effort to modify the play of market forces' (Briggs, 1961, p. 226).
- 'By a welfare state is understood an institutionalized system where the actors, the state, market and civil society interact in various relations with the purpose of maximizing society's welfare function and where the degree of public involvement is sufficiently high to be able to counteract the consequences of market failure, including ensuring a guaranteed minimum income' (Greve, 2002, p. 94).
- 'The coordination of mutually dependent political or economic systems that are structurally differentiated' (Kaufmann, 2012).

Here the welfare state will be understood as an entity which provides welfare for its citizens and helps in alleviating the negative impact on the welfare of society and individuals of the impact of different kinds of market failure. A welfare state can have different kinds of organisation and structures; thus the focus is on its impact on and interventions for people in a given society.

The definition of a welfare state does not show in detail the varying approaches and goals of welfare states among countries, and how they are organised and structured. Esping-Andersen's (1990) path-breaking work on three worlds of welfare capitalism has laid the foundation for an immense amount of research into the similarities and differences between countries in the way they organise, structure, deliver and finance welfare, and to systematise welfare states into different groups of welfare regimes. Important aspects distinguishing the three regimes from each other are (Esping-Andersen, 1990):

a) decommodification (the extent to which an individual's welfare is reliant upon the market);
b) social stratification (the role of the welfare state in maintaining or breaking down social stratification); and
c) the private–public mix (the relative roles of the state, the family and the market in welfare provision).

Decommodification is still important, and the level of replacement rate for benefits in cash is an indicator of it. Social stratification is also relevant to examining social inclusion/exclusion, (cf. Chapter 10). The public–private mix will be used here as central in the presentation as this shows how different actors and institutions in welfare states can and will provide welfare in different welfare state regimes. Other elements that have been included in the analysis include issues such as: defamilialism, universalism and marketisation. Based on this analysis one can also look into indicators in different regimes (such as the degree of equality, goals of full employment). For an overview of the debate see Powell and Barrientos (2011). Table 3.1 sets out five types of welfare regimes and their specific characteristics.

Table 3.1 shows the aspects used to categorise welfare states, including the elements historically derived from Esping-Andersen; decommodification, stratification and the different role of the state, market and civil society in different welfare regimes. It also includes the different dominant welfare ideologies and their principles (cf. also Section 3.7) on social investment and other approaches.

It is a clear indication of the variation in the use of state, market and civil society (here mentioned as family and individual). In three of the five models the family plays a central role in the provision of welfare; thus having a family is central in order to be provided for in case of need, albeit most regimes have some support for those with no family. The state on the other hand, for example, has a strong role in the Social and Christian-democratic type of welfare states, but a weak role in the liberal type, whereas the opposite is the case with regard to the role of the market in relation to provision of welfare.

Table 3.1 shows five different types of welfare regimes, including regime types in emergent welfare states (cf. also Section 3.6), such as China, South Korea and Brazil. The first three regimes types – the Social and Christian-democratic and liberal types – is the classical three, whereas the pro-welfare in South East Asia and the anti-welfare conservative in Latin America show welfare regime types with deviation from the classical ones. This deviation is influenced by the Bismarckian approach.

There has been considerable academic discussion about whether or not there are more than three worlds or whether all countries fit exactly into the model (cf. also Section 3.3). This also implies that the Christian-democratic

Table 3.1 Regime-specific characteristics in five types of welfare regimes

	The Social Democratic Welfare Regime in Scandinavia	The Christian Democratic Welfare Regime in Continental Europe	The Liberal Welfare Regime in Anglo-Saxon countries	The Pro-Welfare Conservative Welfare Regime in East Asia	The Anti-Welfare Conservative Welfare Regime in Latin America
Dominant welfare ideology	Social Democratic	Christian Democratic	Liberal/Neoliberal	Pro-Welfare Conservative	Anti-Welfare Conservative
Dominant mix of welfare institutions	Universal social security and welfare services	Bismarckian social insurance, NGO-based welfare services	Asset and means testing, limited social insurance, company-based welfare services	Universal social investment in education, health care, housing; Bismarckian social insurance and/or provident funds	Bismarckian social insurance and/or provident funds; universal and means-tested social assistance, health care services
Emphasis on:					
State	Strong	Strong	Weak	Increasing	Decreasing
Market	Weak	Weak	Strong	Decreasing	Increasing
Family	Weak	Strong	Weak	Strong	Strong
Individual	Strong	Weak	Strong	Weak	Weak
Degree of decommodification	High	Medium	Low	Medium-low	Medium-low
Degree of stratification	Low	Medium	High	Medium	Extremely high
Degree of individualisation	High	Low	High	Medium	Medium

(Continued)

Table 3.1 Continued

	The Social Democratic Welfare Regime in Scandinavia	The Christian Democratic Welfare Regime in Continental Europe	The Liberal Welfare Regime in Anglo-Saxon countries	The Pro-Welfare Conservative Welfare Regime in East Asia	The Anti-Welfare Conservative Welfare Regime in Latin America
Countries/regions that belong to this general overall group	Sweden, Norway, Finland, Denmark, Iceland	Germany, Austria, Netherlands, Belgium, France, Switzerland, Portugal, Spain, Italy, Poland, Czech Republic, Hungary, Slovenia, among others	United States, Australia, New Zealand, Canada, United Kingdom	Mainland China, Hong Kong, South Korea, Japan, Taiwan, Thailand, Malaysia, Singapore, Indonesia, among others	Chile, Argentina, Brazil, Uruguay, among others

Source: Adapted from Aspalter (2013).

welfare regime could be split into specific regimes for southern and eastern Europe. The debate on the number and types of welfare regimes is the reason for integrated presentation of a greater variety of welfare models and also to show how different countries might fit into different types of welfare state. Despite this, as a heuristic device the original three worlds from Esping-Andersen (1990), which have often been given different names (Social Democratic, Liberal and Conservative) can be used to structure an analysis and also to have an initial idea of what a country's welfare state model can be expected to look like. No country will normally fit perfectly into any one type in all aspects, but certain common characteristics will be present, and this therefore makes it possible to use countries as representatives to show how they deliver and finance welfare, and what their welfare mix is.

Based upon these regimes, this book will mainly use data for the following countries: Social Democratic (Denmark and Sweden), Liberal (UK), Conservative (Germany, France), southern Europe (Italy, Spain), eastern Europe (Czech Republic, Hungary). This will therefore include all the classic welfare regimes and the new EU member states from eastern and southern European countries where classification has often been debated (Ferrera, 1996). There are five countries from northern and western Europe, and four from southern and eastern Europe. This division is chosen as it is sometimes argued that convergence has taken place making the countries in Europe more alike with a north/west group and a south/east group. All the countries are members of the European Union and given the increased influence of the EU on welfare state development and common data available this makes the use of these nine countries convenient to indicate differences and similarities among welfare states. Due to data limitations no countries from Latin America or South East Asia are included here. Some references will also be made to the USA, Australia and Canada.

An argument in favour of the existence of a north/west and south/east divide in Europe regarding welfare state approaches also relates to the fact that:

Accounting for both the tax-system and the role of private social benefits reveals that the proportion of an economy's domestic production to which recipients of social benefits lay claim is similar in countries often thought to have very different gross public expenditure levels. For example, total net social spending in Austria, Canada, Denmark, Finland, Italy, the Netherlands, Portugal and the United States are within a few percentage points of each other.

(Adema and Ladaique, 2009, p. 50)

3.3   What are welfare regimes?

The development of welfare regime typologies has been criticised for the choice of countries, that the regime typology is gender blind, for not including an analysis of the role of the family, and for an imprecise choice of data which focuses on public welfare but not on other types of provision. Finally, it has been argued that the choice of parameters and understanding of types of changes, such as direct retrenchment by cuts in spending or incremental adjustment in the size and use of the state, make it difficult to have specific models. Nevertheless as argued previously it is a good starting point and also it is a way of holding a mirror up to one's own country's welfare state. Comparing one country with another, differences and similarities can highlight central issues related to welfare provision and financing.

Box 3.2 Three ideal worlds of welfare capitalism

Social-Democratic World of Welfare Capitalism: the social-democratic welfare state is characterised by a comprehensive system of social protection. The high level of social service is revealed by, among others, the high wage replacement rate of the state retirement pension schemes. These generous social security benefits result in high average and marginal tax rates. The social-democratic state pursues active labour market policies. The labour force participation of women is high, which is facilitated by generous parental leave schemes.

Conservative World of Welfare Capitalism: the conservative welfare state is characterised by the generous occupational benefits; unemployment and disability insurance schemes for (former) employees. As such, conservative welfare states are sometimes referred to as corporatist welfare states. The position of the traditional male breadwinner is also safeguarded by the protective services for children and parenthood, relatively high child benefits and long-term pregnancy, childbirth and parental leave. In the field of labour relations, collective agreement often plays a central role. Both the labour participation of women and of older men is much lower than in the social-democratic state.

Liberal World of Welfare Capitalism: the social security system in the liberal world can be characterised as 'residual'. The replacement rate of most benefits (e.g. unemployment benefit) is relatively low and they have a limited dura-tion. Much emphasis is placed upon means-testing social assistance schemes. A distinguishing feature of collectively financed social security in later life is the relatively low flat-rate state pension benefit. Compared to the social-democratic welfare state, there are few public facilities for children and parents and the labour market is less regulated compared to the corporatist state, but the participation rate of women tends to be higher than in the corporatist world.

(Deeming and Hayes, 2012, p. 813)

central concepts

In Section 3.2 the main elements included when trying to depict and describe different welfare regimes were presented, for example, the use of concepts such as decommodification, social stratification and the private–public mix. Other elements, since the first works of Esping-Andersen, that have been included by various authors in the analysis contain issues such as: defamilialism, degree of universalism and degree of marketisation. In the following section, first a more detailed description of the original three worlds of welfare capitalism is presented, followed by different approaches and ways to understand welfare states and welfare regimes.

In Box 3.2 the three ideal worlds of welfare capitalism are presented. Countries in the Social-Democratic model are often described as the Nordic countries in Europe, and sometimes Belgium and the Netherlands are also included in this group. The Liberal model is countries like Australia, New Zealand, Canada, the UK and the USA, whereas the Conservative model is countries in central Europe like Germany and France and, outside Europe, Japan.

There has been considerable academic discussion about whether or not there are more than three worlds or whether all countries fit exactly into the model. This debate is the reason why above there is an integrated presentation of a greater variety of welfare models and how different countries might fit into different types. Despite this, as a heuristic device the original three worlds, which have often been given different names (Social Democratic, Liberal and Conservative), can be used to structure an analysis and also to give an initial idea about what a country's welfare model can be expected to look like. No country will normally fit perfectly into any one type in all aspects, but certain common characteristics will be present.

Even before Esping-Andersen published his book, *The Three Worlds of Welfare Capitalism* (1990), there were various attempts to systematise and describe welfare states in different countries, and to try to compare them with other countries. The reason for this is that comparison acts as a mirror and offers a reflection of what one country is doing compared with other countries. It also opens up the possibility of learning policy lessons from other countries. The historical approach was especially to look into income transfers as this was the main measure welfare states implemented. However, it has been argued in particular that there are problems with measuring welfare regimes in relation to welfare services as:

1   it ignores the different countries' specific welfare mix, e.g. the way welfare is delivered by different providers
2   there are often sector-specific ways and overlapping approaches, e.g. overlap between old-age care and health services.

However, looking at what has been labelled the 'worlds of welfare services', a relatively similar approach emerges when analysing what the welfare states are doing (Stoy, 2012 p. 353):

Liberal: Australia, Canada, Finland, France, Iceland, Ireland, New Zealand, UK

Conservative: Austria, Belgium, Germany, Netherlands, Switzerland, USA

Social Democratic: Denmark, Norway, Sweden

Rudimentary: Czech Republic, Greece, Hungary, Italy, Poland, Portugal, Slovak Republic, Spain.

The countries used for comparison here are again represented in all four types with eastern and southern European countries in the more rudimentary approach to welfare services, UK and France in the Liberal, Germany in the Conservative, and Denmark and Sweden in the Social Democratic. This classification is an example of how a country can shift according to the classification, as France here belongs to the liberal and not the conservative central European model.

Other criticisms of the model have revolved around the fact that the main focus as already mentioned has been on income transfers, but also that it has been blind to gender differences in what the welfare state is financing and delivering. This has especially been in relation to family policy and the possible role of the welfare state as a social investment state (see also Section 8.3 on the work–family balance).

From a more methodological point of view, the discussion and criticisms have been related to what is called the dependent variable problem, that is how to conceptualise, operationalise and measure a concept (Vis, 2013). For example, we need to understand and interpret the level of generosity of a welfare state and how it can be analysed: Is the support to be offered over a short or long time? Is it for people of working age or the elderly? Is it related to the level of poverty? How to ensure that data are of the same quality and validity in all the countries analysed? Another criticism also relates to the fact that the data used in most analyses are of a quantitative nature, and only more limited qualitative data, including well-being and quality of life, which, as shown in Chapter 2, can be highly important in order to achieve individual welfare. Furthermore, the time horizon used when analysing welfare state development is important because of changes over time, so sometimes data are not precise enough to show what welfare states look like currently. Finally, the fact that the institutional structure and the implementation of welfare policies can have an impact is not included in the analysis.

The quality and effectiveness of welfare delivery are often not included, because how to measure and compare the quality of services delivered is not always very clear.

Box 3.3 contains a recent summary of research related to welfare regimes and the knowledge gained in these areas.

central concepts

In a nutshell, an academic consensus has been reached in the past two decades that:

1 the welfare regime typology is here to stay as an analytical tool because there is clearly 'something in it,' although the empirical applicability of the concept remains problematic;
2 a minimum of three but possibly more welfare regime prototypes can be identified;
3 the historical origins of welfare regimes lie in the religious and state building history of Western Europe; and
4 welfare regimes differ not only in the structures of inequality and social stratification they (re-) produce, but also in the way in which they seek to achieve this goal as well as in their normative justifications thereof.

(Rice, 2013 p. 94)

(Note: In Rice's article there are many references to all the four points, which have been omitted here.)

3.4   Welfare regimes and welfare typologies

Is there a relation between welfare typologies and welfare state regimes? The first question is: What is a welfare typology? This is used to describe whether a country belongs to, for example, the regimes described in the previous section. An ideal type, on the other hand, is a construct where one can argue whether or not a country belongs to it; in an ideal type of analysis the question is to what extent a country belongs to an ideal type (Vis, 2013). A further distinction relates to the real-typical and ideal-typical approach. The real-typical approach focuses on the details and the way welfare state institutions work, whereas the ideal-typical method focuses on average ways of working in different regimes or clusters (Aspalter, 2013). Here the main focus is on the ideal-typical method as a way of and ability to present the broader viewpoints on welfare states and their development, although the risk is that differences within national systems are not really explored. This will have to be done in more specific national studies.

The first issue relates to whether there has been change in the structure, financing and ideas and thereby movement away from one type to another type. Recent years have seen many and varied changes in welfare states. Some countries have been responding to new social risks. Some countries have had the ability to deliver more welfare when becoming richer. The fact that most countries have become richer since the beginning of this century despite the fiscal crisis of recent years is shown in Table 3.2.

Table 3.2 Development in GDP per capita since 2000 (index 100) in selected EU countries and the USA

	2000	2005	2009	2010	2011	2012	2013	2014	2015
EU27	100.0	109.3	111.8	113.9	:	:	:	:	:
Czech Republic	100.0	122.2	136.1	139.5	142.0	140.6	139.1	141.6	144.7
Denmark	100.0	106.4	104.6	106.1	107.2	106.8	107.1	108.9	110.9
Germany	100.0	103.0	105.8	110.0	113.7	114.5	115.0	117.0	119.2
Spain	100.0	117.4	122.7	122.4	122.5	120.5	118.9	119.5	121.5
France	100.0	108.3	109.8	111.7	114.0	114.0	114.3	115.3	117.3
Italy	100.0	105.0	101.9	103.7	104.2	101.6	99.7	100.4	101.6
Hungary	100.0	122.6	120.0	121.2	123.2	121.1	122.0	124.2	126.8
Sweden	100.0	114.2	116.1	123.8	127.4	128.6	130.0	133.7	138.4
United Kingdom	100.0	115.7	115.7	117.7	119.0	119.3	120.9	123.6	126.5
United States	100.0	113.3	114.7	117.6	119.8	123.1	125.0	128.3	132.3

Source: Eurostat (nama_gdp_k) (accessed 4 January 2014).

Notes: The year 2000 has the index value of 100. This implies that, for example, the Czech Republic in 2013 had a GDP per capita 39.1% higher than in 2000. A decline in value from one year to another thus also implies a decline in the level of GDP. Data for 2013 to 2015 are estimates.

Despite the decline in the level of GDP in 2009 in all the countries included in the analysis, whereby countries have a lower overall level of production and thereby goods and services to use, Table 3.2. shows that all countries have been witnessing an increase in their overall level of wealth as measured by GDP since the year 2000, although in Italy it is expected to be almost the same in 2015 as in the year 2000.

Although GDP per capita does not necessarily fully reflect a society's wealth, well-being and happiness, it is an indicator of what economic options a country has available for both private and public consumption. We would expect that when a society becomes richer it will also want to have more welfare delivered – although whether this should be by the public sector or the market is open for interpretation. Growth in welfare state spending on social issues was therefore possible in most countries, until the last financial crisis started in late 2008. With real increase in GDP it has been possible to increase both public and private consumption, so not only welfare provided by the state has been increasing, but also it has been possible to buy more private goods. Using the same percentages of GDP on social policy issues will thus in times of economic growth make it possible in real terms to spend more, and without necessarily having to raise taxes. This also increases the likelihood that policy makers are more willing to expand social welfare in good economic times.

A contradiction here is that social welfare is more likely to be needed in times of slow economic development.

Historically, there has been a relation between economic development and the welfare state; sometimes in economic jargon it has been argued that welfare is a 'luxury' good and when an economy becomes richer the demand elasticity is greater than one, implying that we demand more. Therefore, future development of the welfare states will also be highly influenced by the overall economic growth in the individual countries and around the world. In times of economic prosperity it is more likely that countries will spend more on welfare than in tough economic times. This also depends on the view of the role of the welfare state.

However, economic issues, such as economic growth, are only one part of what can be understood as well-being and welfare. This possible contradiction may imply that the welfare state will be difficult to develop further given the risk and lack of resources if the overall economic growth no longer has a positive development, making it possible to finance the welfare state. Furthermore, a conflict between issues of well-being and happiness that might be difficult to measure compared with hard economic facts may also imply a contradiction given that GDP, as argued in Chapter 2, does not include well-being as a parameter for societal development.

3.5   Change and drivers for change

Welfare states have changed as we have seen in the previous section, and will be discussing throughout the book. However, even if there has been change, it is not necessarily clear what types of change have taken place, and what have been the drivers behind those changes. Furthermore, change in paradigms and understanding of the role of the welfare state can influence the way welfare states develop. This section will discuss these topics and the principles related to the politics of the welfare state.

Table 3.3 provides an overview of different types of change in welfare states that may be the result of change in the economic and political options open to welfare states.

Table 3.3 Type of change

	Within path (incremental)	Radical/transformation
Gradual	Classical incrementalism TORTOISE	Gradual eventually fundamental STALACTITE
Abrupt	Radical conservatism BOOMERANG	Sudden radical EARTHQUAKE

Source: Farnsworth and Irving (2011, p. 33).

Table 3.3 shows that change can and will have different dimensions and directions. Here the distinctions are between gradual or abrupt change and within path (incremental) or more radical transformation. These types of changes also relate to the debate on path-dependency, path-breaking or incremental change (Thelen, 2004). Again one needs to be cautious about whether or not change is along one of the four dimensions depicted in Table 3.3. The table emphasises the varieties and possibilities of change in welfare states, and when undertaking empirical analysis is a good way to try to show how dramatic a change has been.

Path-dependency implies that policy makers continue along the same path, that is the way the welfare state has already been gradually developed. This is often seen as a central explanation of the changes in welfare states, as the cost for policy makers (risk of losing votes in an election and thereby power) is less if they only make small and incremental changes in the level and composition of welfare benefits and services. Still, many such changes can, but might not, gradually transform a welfare state from one type to another. This can be done by using instruments such as higher or lower benefits and/or more or fewer social policy areas covered. The gradual approach can also be more dramatic, with more fundamental changes in the long run, given that continuous changes might move a country away from its original path. This can be altered in one specific social policy area, such as has been the case with changes in pension systems. These have taken place in many countries with a move away from state universal pension systems towards greater dependence on savings and number of years on the labour market.

Changes can be abrupt, despite moving back to and being within the path; such a change is called a 'boomerang'. There could, for example, be a dramatic change in the unemployment compensation system, which after a short while more or less reverts to what it was originally. The last quarter in Table 3.3 combines abrupt changes with radical transformation, such as those which several countries witnessed in the wake of the financial crisis. These involved dramatic cuts in the overall level of spending on social policy and reduction in the areas in which the welfare state is involved.

An abrupt change could occur when the historical path of a country's welfare system is dramatically changed in another direction, that is a break in the path. Whether this occurs due to a window of opportunity – i.e. some would have liked to make the changes a long time ago, but the fiscal crisis first made it possible – or it is a dramatic change due to fiscal crisis, can be difficult to establish. Furthermore, the reason or reasons for a change might have implications for policy reaction when again there are economic possibilities to adjust the development, for example, when the economy starts to grow again. Changes might also be influenced by ideological preferences for state, market or civil society solutions, including different understandings of what gives the best results for society. Different understandings of the cost of a welfare state (cf. also Section 3.7), might be part of the rationalities for different decisions on how and to what extent to change a welfare state.

central concepts

A country's response to a political or economic crisis might therefore also be influenced by its historical traditions and development, and the present political ideology. It is therefore also difficult to predict a specific development, although many analyses of welfare regimes, despite using different measures and historical data and examining different aspects of welfare systems, confirm that clustering within certain regime typologies is possible. A concrete empirical analysis of changes is therefore necessary in order to understand how and in what way a country has changed its welfare system. Notwithstanding that the historical paths are different in those welfare states inspired by Bismarck (Germany being a prime example) or Beveridge (UK as a prime example) there might be convergence (cf. Section 12.3).

Regardless of such historical differences, similarities may exist across countries. In most countries there is, for example, universal access to hospitals and treatment in cases of acute sickness. There is also, however, a difference with regard to user charges for medicine, access to general practitioners, different specialists and private hospitals and so on. However, analysis using a health perspective also shows that despite universal access to hospitals, there are differences among welfare regime types. Thus it seems that infant mortality rates, low birth weight and life expectancy in general are also related to regime types. Results in these areas are, in general, better in the Social-democratic welfare regimes than in the Liberal model or in the southern European countries. Health, therefore, is better in the relatively generous and universal welfare countries than in countries within the Liberal model (Bambra, 2013). So, welfare regime typologies can also be used as a starting point for analysing specific social policy areas and trying to find patterns within these areas even if the institutional set-up in a social policy area appears similar.

As indicated previously, drivers for change could be the financial crisis as this puts pressure on the ability to finance the welfare state and has been used as an argument especially for retrenchment in several welfare states. The change in the demographic composition of society has also been used as argument for change. This, as shown in Section 5.4, has been due to possible impacts on public sector income and, as shown in Chapter 13, on public sector spending and change in the area of spending, for example, the need to spend more on elderly care and benefits and on health care, than childcare. A change from one area to another, such as from care of children to care of elderly, can be difficult as there are both fixed and variable costs involved. Fixed costs are related to buildings and staff who are needed even when there are few users, whereas the variable costs relate to those directly dependent on the number of users of a welfare service, such as the number of children, patients, etc. Therefore demographic changes can be difficult to cope with economically if the related change in delivery from one group to another has to be kept within the same amount of spending. The overall political economy of the welfare state in this understanding relates to how changed macro-economic conditions and changes in the demographic composition of the society influence the ability of the welfare state to fulfil the electorates' presumably constant expectation of more and better welfare delivery.

However, financial crises and demographic changes are not the only reasons for change. New social risks, such as family breakups, have also been a driver for changes in welfare state spending as has been the greater participation of women in the labour market which has required a greater need for more spending on day care for children. This is, given that it is a welfare service, in contrast to the historical intentions focusing on income transfers especially to cope with the risk of loss of income (in case of disease, work injury, disability, old age or family responsibility). Thereby the welfare states also moved towards provision of service and not only being income transfer welfare states.

The different preferences, which might be ideological, of welfare state actors may also have an influence on and can be drivers of the development of welfare states (Guiraudon and Martin, 2013). These include political decision makers, the administration, and different pressure and lobby groups.

Generally speaking, in welfare states it is the democratically elected parliament and government that decide, by a simple majority, what to do, although it is often within the given path dependent on previous decisions. There might be issues and areas where there is a need for a qualified majority. In the case of a simple majority, the vote by the median voter is of interest to policy makers. The (or those) party(ies) that get the median voters' support will be able to form a majority, as the median voter is the voter exactly in the middle. Therefore, the legitimacy of different kinds of benefits and services can influence what the political system decides in relation to welfare as this might help in gaining or maintaining a majority. It can, furthermore, be the case that voters simultaneously want to increase spending and decrease taxation. Therefore the politics of the welfare state can be a mix of representation of different voters' interests, but also be influenced by different ideologies and perceptions about the best way to pursue a societal development. The different paradigmatic understandings as depicted in Section 3.6 illustrate this.

Voters' support for and perception about who is and who is not deserving can thus also have an impact on policy makers' willingness to expand or contract specific welfare spending. The same applies to different understandings of justice and equality (cf. Chapter 9). 'Deserving' as a criterion for decisions on welfare spending is not new (see the quote in Box 3.4, written in the eighteenth century).

Box 3.4 Montesquieu's view on who to provide for

Montesquieu adopts this distinction between religious charity and political-social obligations by stating that the state's duties are not fulfilled by 'a few alms to the naked man'. The state must provide employment for those who are capable of working. Therefore, Montesquieu's definition of poverty is a very secular one. The poor are not those who are in need, the necessitous, that is; rather the poor are those who do not work. Montesquieu is very careful to specify that only the needs of those who cannot work – 'the old, the sick, and the orphaned' – must be provided for. All the others are no longer poor, as soon as they can work, and there are available jobs.

(Larrère, 2001)

Voters' understanding of 'deserving' might change, but historically the elderly in particular have been seen as deserving, whereas those who can work, but do not, have been seen as less deserving.

Pressure and lobby groups have an interest in a certain area in the welfare state gaining more support from the state. Their arguments may, for example, be related to justice and/or to a more efficient type of intervention. Theoretically, policy makers are expected to be open to demands in order to cope with pressure groups as they would like to gain votes. This was one of the public choice theorists' arguments (such as Niskanen, 1971). It was held that the government and public sector spending would constantly increase and take up an ever growing proportion of societal production. However, in most countries there is also a Ministry of Finance which keeps an eye on the overall level of spending and how this relates to the ability to finance expenditures. Therefore, after what was labelled the Golden Growth of the Welfare States from 1960 and until the first oil price crisis started in 1973, there has never been a strong and continuous growth in welfare spending as a percentage of GDP. So pressure groups might have had and still have in certain areas an impact on spending, but their efforts might be counteracted by those not wanting to increase the level of spending and taxation, or even in the more neoliberal approach to a reduction in the level of taxation. The same argument applies with regard to the possible impact of the bureaucracy and professionals.

Still, the counteraction is also due to the fact that there are limitations and that spending money on one area implies that the same amount of money will not be available to another area. Opportunity costs, as they are called, imply that there will be a constant battle between different goals and therefore also a political struggle between competing ends and programmes. The use of documentation and evidence to show that an intervention works (cf. also Section 11.4), is therefore also a way to try to document the need for involvement in one area and to make the decision makers willing to spend more.

Even if policy makers intend change in an area, difficulties might arise in the form of pressure from voters, interest groups, professionals and the administration. In such situations it may be necessary to wait for a window of opportunity where it is possible to make changes in the welfare state without risking being blamed for the change. If policy makers can argue it is necessary to reduce spending, as was the case during the financial crisis, in order to cope with and be able to reduce the budget deficit and be able to finance the welfare state into the future, then changes might be possible without politicians running the risk of losing too much voter support. Credit claiming and avoidance of blame for change can thus be important concerning whether there is change and how big those changes are in welfare states.

The ideology of the political decision makers is also an important issue. Historically, it has been argued that left-wing governments have expanded welfare states more than right-wing governments. Ideology (cf. also Section 3.7), can thus have an impact on the way welfare states are changed. One possibility is that overall changes in the perception of the state's role in how to ensure a good society may take place among voters and policy makers.

Drivers for change might thus come from a variety of sources and for a variety of reasons, and often they might even be intermingled making the reason behind change less clear-cut than one might expect. The combination of political preferences, possibilities of making decisions and the interaction between different interest groups can help in explaining that the development of welfare states does not necessarily follow logical paths and/or a specific rationality or ideology. Differences can also be due to the fact that in some countries one party usually has a majority in parliament (e.g. the UK) or there is a strong veto-player or decision maker as president (e.g. France), or that coalition decision making is the rule (e.g. Denmark). Parliamentary traditions, in addition to the other drivers mentioned, can also influence the way welfare states are changed.

Thus politics matters, and sometimes it seems as though, to use the title of Esping-Andersen's book, that it is 'Politics against Markets' (1985). This reflects the dichotomy between state and market, the struggle between different ideological approaches, but also change over time. At the same time, this struggle sometimes has overlooked the influence of civil society, including the role of the family. These contradictions and varieties are something we will return to several times throughout the book. Still, the principles and approaches to welfare state policy have been and still are influenced by a combination of available economic resources, ideology (including viewpoints on justice and equality), voters' perceptions, impact of pressure groups, and changes in legitimacy and support for deserving and non-deserving people.

Even though this is the case, knowledge about how the different actors (state, market and civil society) can finance, deliver and influence welfare is important. It is equally important to be aware of how different parts of the welfare state function and how this can sometimes impact disadvantaged groups.

3.6   Emergent welfare regimes

The analysis of welfare states and welfare regimes has often been strongly influenced by a European and North American perspective, though this has sometimes included Australia and New Zealand. However, in the rest of the world there are also different types of welfare states and welfare regimes, and some of these states could be labelled emergent or new types of welfare states. Thus there are different approaches in China, Japan, South Korea and India, to those developing in Latin America or in the Sub-Saharan countries.[1] There is much diversity in this development, which also in part is due to different economic options and possibilities.

In Sub-Sahara the approach is often characterised by:

- A residual, confessional and clientelistic approach to social protection
- A permanent emergency orientation of measures (Cerami and Wagué, 2013).

The Sub-Saharan countries also often have low state involvement due to lack of economic resources, and instead a high reliance on family, local and religious communities; however, this often provides poor social protection. They might further be highly dependent on money from donor countries or migrant workers. Their development of welfare support has come later than other countries, and therefore has had less time to develop especially in comparison to the more mature welfare states in Europe.

In other parts of the world welfare is still highly fragmentary, due to a lack of sufficient resources which are necessary to finance and develop comprehensive welfare programmes compared with Europe. They can also vary regarding size and areas of coverage. However, in most countries around the world there are programmes dealing with the classical risks such as disability, work injury, old age, sickness and unemployment. Family benefits can be found in many countries. Family benefits or social assistance can be dependent on many factors, but in some developing countries they have been made dependent on children's school attendance.

Emergent welfare states often have a higher reliance on civil society, especially the family, given the limited economic resources available. At the same time, some of the emergent welfare states, such as China, already face problems relating to demographic composition causing pressure on health care and pensions in particular. Still the size and structure of welfare in emergent welfare states has to be seen in the light of the time they started to develop their welfare states, and also their economic options available.

3.7 Social investment and other perspectives

Welfare states have historically coped with the risk for individuals or families of lack of sufficient income in the case of unemployment, old age, sickness and work injury. In more recent years welfare states have looked into how this could be understood as a social investment in the future by providing welfare services and income transfers in order to support societal development. Social investment might also be seen as a further development of Giddens's 'Third Way' (1998). The Third Way was built upon a set of values including equality and a programmatic approach (see Box 3.5). This approach is therefore arguably in contrast with two other ideological underpinnings of the role of the welfare state – the Keynesian and neoliberal perspectives.

Box 3.5 The Third Way Programme

The radical centre, The new democratic state (the state without enemies), Active civil society, The democratic family, The new mixed economy, Equality as inclusion, Positive welfare, The social investment state, The cosmopolitan nation, Cosmopolitan democracy.

(Giddens, 1998, p. 70)

A neoliberal approach would have a focus on how the market can solve societal issues and with as few as possible interventions in the economy. It can be said to a certain degree to have developed in the aftermath of the difficulty for Keynesian demand management in the 1970s to ensure full employment and stable economic development. A neoliberal approach would focus on how the market could best ensure economic growth and full employment. It therefore also sees the welfare state as a burden for societal development.

The Keynesian approach to a large degree argues that societal intervention is necessary to ensure smoother economic development and a high level of employment by supporting demand when necessary and by using the state, especially the financial instruments, to make growth and stability possible. It therefore prefers to have some kind of welfare state and welfare state intervention.

A focus of the social investment approach is that at least part of the welfare state's activities provides increased options for societal development. This includes, for example, how to combine work and family life by supporting day care (see also Section 8.3). Investment in education can help to ensure higher competitiveness, implying that social policy is supporting economic growth and job creation.

The mixed economy of welfare was also part of this understanding that welfare could be pursued in a mix of using a market, a state and a family approach.

Table 3.4 sums up the understanding of the three very different paradigms and approaches to welfare state development with regard to key principles, norms and instruments. Such differences are natural. The description is a schematic depiction of the possible varieties (see also Crouch, 2013). However, comparing these approaches indicates different understandings of the balance between state and market and, relatedly, different ideological underpinnings of welfare states. Here the focus is on three central approaches to welfare. Other

central concepts

Table 3.4 Three different paradigms and their values, norms and instruments

	Keynesian	Neoliberal	Social investment
Key values and principles	Social equality Jobs for all (men) Decommodification	Individual responsibility Any jobs Activation	Social inclusion Quality jobs Capabilities approach Equality of opportunity: prepare rather than repair
Key norms for public action	Big state Central economic planning Welfare state development	Lean state Deregulation Dismantling of the welfare state	Empowering the state Investment Recasting of the welfare state
Key instruments	Policies to support demand Development of social insurance schemes for income maintenance Development of the public sector Unemployment compensation	Monetarist economic policies to fight inflation Deregulation of the labour market Privatisation of social and health services, development of capitalisation to finance pension schemes Activation and workfare	Human capital investment policies to increase competitiveness and job creation Development of social services and policies to support the labour market: early childhood education and care; higher education and lifelong training; active labour market policies; policies to support women's employment Flexi-security

Source: Adapted from Morel et al., 2012, pp. 12–13, Table 1.1.

approaches include the New Right, the Middle Way, Democratic Socialism, Marxism, Feminism and Greenism (see George and Wilding, 1994).

Different ideological understandings might also have influenced the development of a particular welfare state. This is, however, not the focus here, although the possible impact of path-dependency on the development of a welfare state will be included in the presentation of the three paradigms in Table 3.4. It is further important to be aware that these paradigms present ideal cases, and that the more precise content varies over time and across countries.

The Keynesian paradigm, often seen as one of the central arguments for the development of welfare states, besides covering the historical social risk, focuses on the importance of full employment, a high degree of social equality and at least to a certain degree the abilities to have decommodification. Having these values and principles also implies a strong focus on and use of the state to intervene in the economy and society so as to achieve the welfare state goals. Representatives of the approach have argued that the welfare state is part of the solution to problems, such as a high level of unemployment, by using state intervention to create demand for goods and services, and by, for example, infrastructure investment and buildings. Unemployment compensation in the Keynesian view, for example, thus was built upon two types of argument: that this would help in increasing social equality, and that if the unemployed received a benefit they would still be able to buy goods and services helping to reduce the decline in economic activity. The public sector was also seen as the one which should cope with market failure and, overall, achieve a higher level of welfare by reducing the negative impact of market failure on societies' functioning. In the Keynesian understanding, the welfare state was thus a prerequisite for developing a high level of welfare and stable economic development.

After the economic crisis in the 1970s following higher oil prices it was argued that Keynesian demand management was no longer possible, as the ability to ensure public sector income was not present, and/or that this would imply a too high level of taxes and duties making the incentives too weak for both work and savings in the economies. The stagflation in the 1970s (a stagnant economy with high level of inflation) was by some seen as a consequence of the big state, and led in many welfare states and public discourses towards a more neoliberal stance.

The neoliberal approach focused on key values related to a higher level of individual responsibility, that any job would do and activation should focus on work-first. Specifically with regard to the welfare state, the approach's focus was on how to reduce the size of the welfare state by, if possible, dismantling it, and a greater use of the market as the main provider of welfare. In a neoliberal perspective, privatisation is central combined with as much deregulation as possible leaving overall economic development to the forces of the market. In this perspective, welfare states are seen as very costly and a burden to society, and taxes and duties as detrimental for societal development. A small welfare state with only very limited levels and comprehensiveness of benefits was argued to be the best cure and the way to ensure a positive economic development. Monetary policies (e.g. amount of money and interest rate policies) were seen as the main instruments for influencing economic activity. In the wake of the latest financial crisis, the neoliberal argument was that the impact would have been less strong if there had been fewer regulations. So, in contrast to a Keynesian perspective where the state has a role, this is not the case in the neoliberal perspective, where as much as possible should be left to the market and the markets' abilities to reach an equilibrium.

For some commentators both the Keynesian and Neoliberal approaches are too unrealistic in relation to actual societal trends, and they hold a more balanced perspective that in principle both market and state might fail in achieving their goals. The Social Investment perspective starts from a set of values and principles that focus on ensuring social inclusion, that there should be equality of opportunity (not necessarily outcomes) and that jobs should be of a high quality. In this perspective the state has a role, as state investment might help in ensuring society's way of functioning by creating jobs and social inclusion. Public sector activities thus are seen as an investment in the good society aimed at achieving a high level of activities. State spending is thereby not just a cost for society, but an investment in order to help the market work, but also that people in general are included in societal development. Private companies' development is, it is argued, thus supported by the state's activities. This is achieved by providing a good infrastructure, and supporting the educational and research system to enable societies to maintain their wealth and develop. A high quality education system is thus important and not just a burden for tax payers. The same is the case with regard to affordable and high quality day care as this makes it possible for both men and women to be on the labour market, thus ensuring the availability of a labour force. Welfare states thus support the private sector and are not seen as being in conflict with the market as the neoliberal approach would have it. Therefore a social investment approach also highlights the state's role in several areas besides those already mentioned – lifelong learning and a flexicurity labour market policy (cf. also Chapter 7). The implication is not that this perspective, nor the Keynesian perspective, is just in favour of spending more money and increasing taxes, it is more a perspective trying to reflect upon and discuss the pros and cons in different areas whether a state intervention will improve the overall level of welfare in society. Still, in contrast to the neoliberal approach, the social investment approach emphasises the possible positive effects of state intervention in order to achieve an overall higher level of welfare. Box 3.6 provides an example of a case for social investment. Another example relates to the fact that much private sector investment in new technology, including the Internet, might not have been possible without state intervention (Mazzucato, 2013).

Box 3.6 Example of a case of social investment

The agenda of the social investment state includes active labour market policy, not in the sense of 'workfare', i.e., bullying unemployed people to take any job available, but in providing training and help with job search, perhaps with removal costs.

(Crouch, 2013, p. 89)

The Third Way (see Section 8.2), also embraces issues of inclusion, a role for public as well as private initiatives and an investor approach (cf. Powell, 2013). However, the Third Way is less explicit about the possible positive role of the state than the social investment approach.

Different welfare state and welfare regimes might have used all these different approaches, for example, by first focusing on the Keynesian, then neoliberal and now perhaps a more social investment perspective. Thus, it is therefore possible that in different welfare states there can be traces of various ways of seeing the role of the state, and this might have changed over time. It can even be the case that the degree of marketisation differs in various areas of the welfare state. For example, the state plays a stronger role in hospitals than it does in pensions.

Throughout the book many of these elements and understandings of different approaches to welfare are part of the presentation. This is so in relation to the role of the state, the market and civil society as presented in Part II, but also how these approaches deal with the issues of equality/inequality and social inclusion and use different instruments. The perspectives have diverse impacts and influence on how welfare states have been and still are developed in different countries. However, the focus here is, in general, not on the ideological perspectives and reasons for welfare states, but more the functioning and argument for diverse types of interaction between state and market. It is important to be aware of why there are and might be different ways of financing and delivering welfare. Ideological preferences thus have a role, albeit they are not always clearly presented as such.

3.8   Summing-up

The aim of this chapter has been to focus on what a welfare state is, and how welfare states may be compared with each other. Welfare states will be understood as an entity providing welfare for its citizens and with the aim of reducing the negative impact of the market forces.

Welfare regimes can be used as a way of comparing countries, and this can then be used as a way to understand why welfare states look the way they do and to inform us on future possible development. Welfare regimes have been used in particular to describe the welfare states of European countries, however, they can also be used as a structural device for placing other welfare states around the globe in a way that makes comparisons possible. Section 3.6 also presented possible emergent welfare regimes.

Typologies thus help to show how different countries organise their welfare states in different ways regarding actors, financing and delivery of welfare, and indirectly also the interplay between state, market and civil society. Therefore they can be used in order to learn about many countries' welfare systems. Still, there might be differences in areas related to income transfer and delivery of services, and even within these areas some might be more universal and comprehensive than others. Three welfare models are often used, but several welfare state typologies also exist. Based upon this, the countries used for comparison throughout the book have been selected.

This chapter has also looked into different paradigms' understanding of what the role of the welfare state is. Different paradigms have different positions of what the role of the welfare state is and should be.

Changes of welfare states do not necessarily just take place. Therefore the chapter has also highlighted possible drivers for change and possible reasons and rationalities behind this kind of change. Three specific paradigms (Keynesian, Neoliberal and Social Investment) have been explained in more detail to illustrate how different perspectives might have an impact on welfare and welfare states' development.

Note

1 See Chapters 21–25 in Greve (ed.) (2013) and there is also an annual regional issue in *Social Policy & Administration* dealing with welfare states outside Europe, often with emergent welfare states.

References

Adema, W. and Ladaique, M. (2009), OECD Social, Employment and Migration Working Papers No. 92: How Expensive is the Welfare State? Gross and Net Indicators in the OECD Social Expenditure Database (SOCX), 13 November. Paris, OECD.

Aspalter, C. (2013), Real-typical and Ideal-typical Methods. In Greve, B. (ed.), *The Routledge Handbook of the Welfare State*. Abingdon, Routledge, pp. 393-406.

Bambra, C. (2013), Welfare Regimes, Health and Health Care. In Greve, B. (ed.), *The Routledge Handbook of the Welfare State*. Abingdon, Routledge, pp. 260-273.

Briggs, A. (1961), The Welfare State in a Historical Perspective. *Archives européennes de sociologie*, 2, pp. 221–59.

Cerami, A. and Wagué, A. (2013), Africa. In Greve, B. (ed.), *The Routledge Handbook of the Welfare State*. Abingdon, Routledge, pp. 252–259.

Crouch, C. (2013), *Making Capitalism Fit for Society*. Cambridge, Polity Press.

Deeming, C. and Hayes, D. (2012), Worlds of Welfare Capitalism and Wellbeing: A Multilevel Analysis. *Journal of Social Policy*, vol. 41, no. 1, pp. 811–29.

Esping-Andersen, G. (1985), *Politics against Markets. The Social Democratic Road to Power*. Princeton, NJ, Princeton University Press.

Esping-Andersen, G. (1990), *The Three Worlds of Welfare Capitalism*. London, Polity.

Farnsworth, K. and Irving, Z. (2011), *Social Policy in Challenging Times: Economic Crisis and Welfare Systems*. Bristol, Policy Press.

Ferrera, M. (1996), The 'Southern' Model of Welfare in Social Europe. *Journal of European Social Policy*, vol. 6, no. 1, pp. 17–37.

George, V. and Wilding, P. (1994), *Welfare and Ideology*. New York, Harvester Wheatsheaf.

Giddens, A. (1998), *The Third Way: The Renewal of Social Democracy*. Cambridge, Polity Press.

Greve, B. (2002), *Vouchers – nye styrings- og leveringsmåder i velfærdsstaten*. Copenhagen, DJØF's forlag.

Greve, B. (ed.) (2013), *Routledge International Handbook of the Welfare State*. Abingdon, Routledge.

Guiraudon, V. and Martin, C. (2013), Drivers for Change. In Greve, B. (ed.), *The Routledge Handbook of the Welfare State*. Abingdon, Routledge, pp. 283–292.

Kaufmann, F-X. (2012), *European Foundations of the Welfare State*. Oxford, Berghahn Books.

Korpi, W. and Palme, J. (1998), The Paradox of Redistribution and Strategies of Equality: Welfare State Institutions, Inequality, and Poverty in the Western Countries, *American Sociological Review*, vol. 63, no. 5, pp. 661–87.

Larrère, C. (2001), Montesquieu on Economics and Commerce. In Carrithers, D., Mosher, M. and Rahe, P. (eds), *Montesquieu's Science of Politics: Essays on the Spirit of Laws*. Lanham, MD, Rowman & Littlefield.

Mazzucato, M. (2013), *The Entrepreneurial State, Debunking Public vs. Private Sector Myths*. New York, Anthem Press.

Morel, N., Palier, B. and Palme, J. (eds) (2012), *Towards a Social Investment Welfare State? Ideas, Policies and Challenges*. Bristol, Policy Press.

Niskanen, W. (1971), *Bureaucracy and Representative Government*. New York, Aldine-Athartan.

Powell, M. (2013), Third Way. In Greve, B. (ed.), *The Routledge Handbook of the Welfare State*. Abingdon, Routledge, pp. 202–212.

Powell, M. and Barrientos, A. (2011), An Audit of the Welfare Modelling Business. *Social Policy & Administration*, vol. 45, pp. 69–84.

Rice, D. (2013), Beyond Welfare Regimes: From Empirical Typology to Conceptual Ideal Types. *Social Policy & Administration*, vol. 47, no. 1, pp. 93–110.

Stoy, V. (2012), Worlds of Welfare Services: From Discovery to Exploration. *Social Policy & Administration*, doi: 10.1111/spol.12006, vol. 48, no. 3, pp. 343–360.

Thelen, K. (2004), *How Institutions Evolve: The Political Economy of Skills in Germany, Britain, the United States and Japan*. New York, Cambridge University Press.

Timmins, N. (1996), *The Five Giants: A Biography of the Welfare State*. London, Fontana Press.

Vis, B. (2013), How To Analyse Welfare States and Their Development. In Greve, B. (ed.), *The Routledge Handbook of the Welfare State*. Abingdon, Routledge, pp. 274–282.

Part II

State, market and civil society

The state

Contents

4.1   Introduction

The state has a central role in welfare states due to market failure, to ensure financing and/or delivery of welfare goods including what is labelled merit-goods, which can also support a social investment perspective. Historically, the welfare state helped in ensuring social security in case of sickness, unemployment, old age and work accidents. However, even when we know the reasons and arguments for having a welfare state there still remains the question of who should deliver the services. This chapter uses Titmuss's (1958) understanding of social policy as the starting point and will explore the three different but often interlinked approaches to the delivery and financing of welfare, namely public, fiscal and occupational welfare. The chapter examines how the three approaches are defined and linked (including the possible impact of access to and distribution of resources) and how and if the different types of welfare can be measured. A short empirical overview concerning the level and structure of public welfare will be provided. This will include a discussion of the related measurement issues. The possible impact of fiscal welfare, including how it makes comparative analysis difficult, is shown.

The impact of using choice within the welfare state is further explored as it reflects different ways to welfare. Different ways to welfare also include who can choose and what the impact of using choice in the welfare states is. Finally, possible outcomes in relation to equality and inequality will be presented.

In principle, welfare can be provided by the following sectors, as shown in detail in Section 2.4:

The state: for example, hospitals and education
Civil society: including the family, for example, care of children and elderly people
The market: with the aim of profit, for example, health care, medicine and other types of care.

The focus of this chapter is mainly on delivery. The impact of being on the labour market will also receive attention (see further, Chapter 7).

The reason for having a welfare state also revolves around the efficiency of the state versus the market. Whether it is cheaper from an economic perspective to use a private rather than a public provider cannot be solved purely from a theoretical approach. This is because in order to make this calculation it is important to be able to define precisely what the private provider should supply, including a measurement of the quality of the production. The quality of production may be difficult to define and measure in the field of social policy, especially when interaction among people is included. Nevertheless, competition either with the private sector and/or within the public sector is often used as an instrument to help in ensuring that the public sector works effectively. This is based on the idea that a private provider who is not effective runs the risk of bankruptcy, whereas a public provider does not run the same risk, although management might be sacked and an inefficient institution risks being closed down.

Whether a private provider can deliver a cheaper and/or higher quality product depends on:

1   whether wages are lower in the private than in the public sector
2   whether the work organisation and management is more effective
3   whether the price alone reflects the possibility of delivering a lower quality
4   whether or not the workforce is worn out more quickly or the working environment is worse.

The last point might imply that there is a certain cost at a later stage which will have to be paid by the public sector (hospitals, disability pension, etc.). This also indicates that what at first sight looks like a cheap provision of welfare might not in the longer term be the same for the welfare state.

4.2 Public, fiscal and occupational welfare

This section will present and define public, fiscal and occupational welfare and provide the main reasons for having them and the principles guiding them, followed in Section 4.4 by more detailed information on fiscal and occupational welfare. It also elucidates the various modes of delivery.

Richard Titmuss was the first to point to the division between public, fiscal and occupational welfare in the UK in 1958. Since then the division has been used as a way of understanding different routes to welfare, including that some part of the financing might be hidden from the public. Despite this, analyses of welfare states often overlook the implications and possible distributional consequences of using different routes to the delivery and financing of welfare.

Public welfare is defined as those welfare services and income transfers paid for by the public sector. Public sector welfare is, according to definitions in the national accounts system, when more than 50 per cent of the cost of welfare comes from public sector finance. Hence a service can from a statistical point of view be included in the size of the public sector in the national accounts even if it is delivered by a private actor. It is thus the financing of the welfare service that is important, or the fact that the state has made the provision of it obligatory by law. This is, for example, the case with many of the social insurance systems in Europe. In most welfare states, public welfare is the dominant element in the provision of welfare, although fiscal and occupational welfare also play a strong role in many countries.

There is a link between fiscal welfare and public welfare as fiscal welfare can also support the financing of welfare for the individual, and therefore also support occupational welfare by giving tax incentives for companies to provide this (Sinfield, 2013). As Titmuss has pointed out:

> Allowances and relief from income tax, though providing similar benefits and expressing a similar social purpose in the recognition of dependencies, are not, however, treated as social service expenditure. The first is a cash transaction; the second an accounting convenience. Despite this difference in administrative method, the tax saving that accrues to the individual is, in effect, a transfer payment.
>
> (Titmuss, 1958, pp. 44–5)

Fiscal welfare is thereby welfare supported through the tax system (cf. also Section 4.4).

Occupational welfare relates to welfare delivered as a result of being on the labour market. The point here is whether and how this can supplement or substitute public welfare. Occupational welfare thus also has a central role in many welfare states as those people on the labour market might have better access to and more welfare than those outside the labour market (Farnsworth, 2013). For example, redundancy pay from an employer can be a substitute for unemployment benefit from the public system. Thus countries where employers are obliged to pay workers some compensation in the event of redundancy might have lower or reduced unemployment benefit expenditures in the statistics of public spending given that it is paid by the employer as a direct wage cost.

How these three approaches to welfare can be measured and how they are linked together, including the possible impact of access to and distribution of resources, will be discussed in the following section. Furthermore, it is important to recognise that it may be necessary to meet certain criteria to be eligible to receive income transfers or social services.

Income transfers might be organised so that the recipient is free to choose how to spend the money, or the transfers can, in the form of a voucher, be spent at certain places or give the right to receive certain types of goods and services, such as care. In some areas the right to a benefit is a benefit in kind rather than a cash benefit. This is shown in Figure 4.1.

Figure 4.1 illustrates, although in a simplified version, the variety of ways of providing welfare. Cash can be either free to spend (this includes, for example, pensions and unemployment benefits), as a service or a voucher for a certain purpose (this includes, for example, food stamps, housing support, some support for people with disabilities). Benefits in kind can be delivered by a specific institution (for example, day care, old-age care or hospital) to deliver

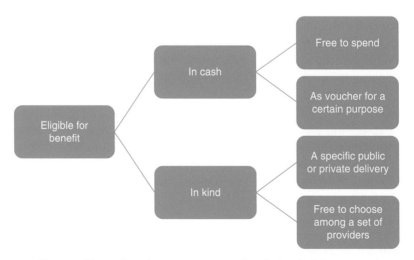

Figure 4.1 Types of benefits when a person or family is eligible to receive.

state, market and civil society

specific services, or it can be as a right to choose a provider (this can be public and/or private) to deliver a specific service (for instance, a general practitioner).

However, the right of access to certain social services does not in itself infer that it is free of charge. Many welfare states have user charges, for example, in relation to health care and care for children. Other restrictions or claims when receiving a benefit can be attached. This can, for example, include actively searching for a job or participating in education.

Given that cash benefits can be spent freely as the individual prefers, economists consider it to be the best form of welfare because it is assumed that people themselves know best how to spend their money. An argument for using restrictions is that a paternalistic approach might make more people willing to pay for the benefit, for example, to ensure that children of people with alcohol problems get food, or that the benefit ensures that children receive an education. Sometimes, the benefit is also directly related to buying help remedies, for example, to people with disabilities or the elderly, and therefore the use of the transfer is restricted. This indicates a choice among the overall highest level of welfare through individual freedom to ensure that the money is spent in accordance with the reason for giving the benefit.

Public financing for services can be done in order to ensure that all have access to services. In relation to education, society's support has been given in order to ensure the development of a high level of human capital. Therefore primary education is free in most countries, and in certain countries in South America and Africa there has been a demand from the state that in order to receive a benefit the children attend school, and if they don't the social benefit will be withdrawn. This is part of a social investment approach to ensure a high level of knowledge in a society.

In-kind services can be financed and delivered by the public sector, but need not necessarily be delivered by public sector institutions. Thus the relations between the public and private sector are often more mixed than appears at first sight.

4.3 The level and composition of state welfare in different types of welfare regimes

State welfare, here understood as all welfare provided by the public sector in a country, is a central element in the provision of welfare services in most European countries. Table 4.1 shows the overall level of spending on social protection in the EU and the nine selected countries.

Table 4.1 shows that Denmark and Sweden have the highest expenditure on welfare, closely followed by France and Germany, with the Czech Republic and Hungary being the lowest spenders. The same picture emerges whether we look at the percentage of GDP, although France here is the highest spender, or in absolute terms measured by euros per capita. The table also shows,

Table 4.1 Spending on welfare as percentages of GDP, euro per inhabitant and euro per inhabitant in purchasing power standard in 2011

	Euro per inhabitant	Euro per inhabitant in purchasing power standard	% of GDP
EU27	7.303	7.292	29.0
Czech Republic	3.025	4.231	20.4
Denmark	14.785	10.054	34.3
Germany	9.389	9.147	29.4
Spain	5.842	6.063	26.1
France	10.327	9.257	33.6
Italy	7.725	7.328	29.7
Hungary	2.281	3.891	23.0
Sweden	12.070	9.141	29.6
United Kingdom	7.641	7.403	27.3

Source: Eurostat (spr_exp_sum) (accessed 4 January 2014).

Note: In the dataset it is also possible to get information on the development over time and in fixed prices.

although implicitly, the differences in wealth among the countries. Denmark spends 6.3 times more per capita than Hungary when measured in euros, whereas as percentages of GDP it is not even double. As a contrasting example, the Czech Republic uses a lower percentage of GDP than Hungary, but has a higher absolute level of expenditure per inhabitant. The difference is less pronounced when taking the purchasing power in the different countries into consideration, for example, that in some countries you can get more for the same amount of euro than in others. Table 4.1 points to a north/west and east/south division in Europe in spending on welfare, albeit the UK and Italy spend around the same amount of money as a percentage of GDP.

However, even if we know the overall level of welfare spending this does not tell us how it is distributed among different areas and activities within the area of social protection. Table 4.2 shows, in percentage, the relative size of the different areas.

Table 4.2 clearly shows that expenditure on old age, such as pensions and care for the elderly, is the most important area in most welfare states. In Italy it is more than half of the public spending, in the UK and Czech Republic it accounts for above 40 per cent of expenditure. The other core area is spending on sickness (including sickness benefits and health care). There are some differences in the approach which also indicate the diversity of countries. The UK, for example, has a higher relative level of spending on housing, and a relatively low level of unemployment benefits. Another example is Denmark, which has the highest spending on disability and family but spends the least relatively on health care. The data only reflect public welfare spending, and thus not the part financed and delivered through occupational and fiscal welfare. Therefore,

state, market and civil society

Table 4.2 Central social expenditure areas in 2011 as percentages of GDP

	Total	Sickness/ health care and disability	Old age and survivors	Housing and social exclusion	Family	Unemployment	Other
EU27	29.0	10.3	12.7	1.0	2.2	1.6	1.2
Czech Republic	20.4	7.8	9.6	0.4	1.2	0.7	0.7
Denmark	34.3	11.0	14.2	1.7	4.1	1.8	1.5
Germany	29.4	11.6	11.4	0.7	3.1	1.3	1.3
Spain	26.1	8.8	11.2	0.4	1.4	3.7	0.6
France	33.6	11.1	14.5	1.6	2.6	2.1	1.7
Italy	29.7	8.7	17.4	0.1	1.4	0.8	1.3
Hungary	23.0	8.0	10.6	0.5	2.9	0.8	0.2
Sweden	29.6	11.3	12.5	1.1	3.1	1.2	0.4
United Kingdom	27.3	10.7	11.4	1.7	1.7	0.7	1.1

Source: Eurostat (spr_exp_sum) (accessed 4 January 2014).

Note: In the dataset more years and data for all EU member states are available.

for example, support to old age is higher in countries like the UK and Denmark through tax expenditures.

Thus there are different institutional approaches and emphases on different areas among welfare states. This reflects historical differences and a certain path-dependent approach to spending in different countries. Path-dependency refers to the situation where having first made a decision to provide a social transfer or social service, or a specific institutional structure, there will be a tendency to follow this already-decided path. This is also the case because it can be difficult to reduce spending in particular areas when people have got used to receiving a specific benefit or service.

Another difference relates to the fact that in some countries income transfers are taxable income, whereas in other countries they are not. Therefore a higher level of expenditure in absolute terms might not be the case when taking the impact of taxing income transfers into consideration. This is shown in Figure 4.2.

Figure 4.2 shows the countries with the highest net expenditure in declining order, that is when having taking the impact of the tax system into consideration. The square number is the ranking for gross public sector spending and the distance to the net level an indication of the changes due to including taxation in the calculation. The figure is a clear indication that the relation between gross public social expenditure and net social spending, that is taking into consideration the taxes clawed back from income transfers, is not always clear-cut. Countries with large deviations from and changes in positions include the USA,

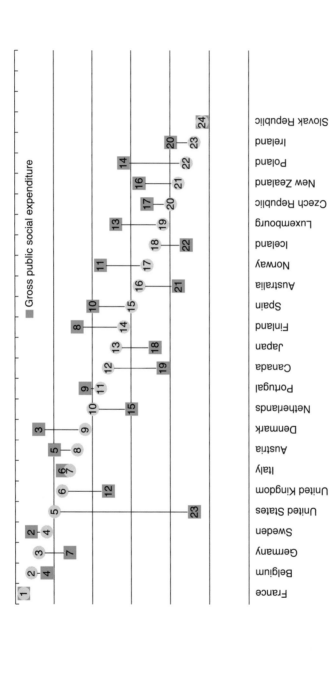

Figure 4.2 Social expenditure, country ranking, from highest spender to lowest in OECD countries, 2007.

Source: OECD. http://www.oecd.org/els/socialpoliciesanddata/socialexpendituredatabasesocx.htm

the UK, Denmark, Spain and Norway, moving them in different directions, for example, their position in ranking order goes either up or down. Thus spending on social policy is, using these data, higher in the UK, a liberal welfare regime where one might expect a lower level of spending, than in Denmark, which belongs to the Nordic welfare model where the expectation would be a high level of spending.

Figure 4.2 is not only an indication that at societal level there is an impact of the overall spending on welfare if the society is clawing back money through the tax system. This is also the case for individuals so that an income transfer which is non-taxable income will have a higher value for an individual than a transfer from which income tax will have to be paid. The same applies if social services are available free of user charges.

4.4   Fiscal and occupational welfare and their impact

This section will discuss how fiscal and occupational welfare play roles in the financing and provision of welfare. This takes place in different ways in various welfare regimes in core welfare areas, including health, social policy, education, housing, social security and pension. In health, for example, this can be by providing health care insurance, making easier and/or cheaper access to treatment more possible for those on the labour market.

A central question is: What are fiscal and occupational welfare?

Fiscal welfare refers to welfare financed and/or delivered through the tax system. This can be administered by the use of allowances, relief and exemptions from tax. Fiscal welfare is also referred to as tax expenditures as it is placed within the tax system, and consequently it is often termed hidden welfare, as it is not part of the classical way of calculating the cost of the welfare state, and is not included in information on public sector expenditures. The definition of tax expenditures is linked to departures from the normal accepted or benchmark tax structure.

It is not always clear what is understood by the normal tax benchmark structure, and consequently what the fiscal welfare is. Without this information this reduces the possibilities of getting information on different types of spending through the tax system. Another issue relates to the fact that in some instances there are temporary reductions in tax payment, for example, when using the money for investment there are tax deductions and then later for private purposes, taxes will have to be paid. Thus there is a question of whether or not a tax is postponed or is a full or permanent reduction of the tax to be paid. This is, for example, often the question related to savings for pension purposes.

This also raises the issue of how we should calculate the size of fiscal welfare. Nevertheless, in order to know the full impact and cost of the welfare state it is important to try to integrate knowledge on the size of fiscal welfare. This is also due to the fact that spending money in this way is another way of achieving electoral support in the welfare state and is an indication of how different routes to welfare can be used.

A specific problem relates to the fact that fiscal welfare often has a negative distributional impact, for example, the largest proportion of the fiscal welfare will be received by those having the highest level of income.

Occupational welfare can be understood in both broad and narrow senses. The broad perspective includes all types of employee fringe benefits, whereas the narrower perspective focuses on issues directly related to other types and provisions of welfare. How broad an approach one should use is a matter for debate. However, even if this is open to discussion, a good starting point is to analyse whether it supplements or substitutes elements of public welfare. A higher level of sickness benefit, as either agreed by the labour market partners or part of a salary packet, is an example of a benefit that supplements the public approach to sickness benefits. Occupational welfare also tends to have an upside-down effect, that is those with the highest income receive the highest proportion of occupational welfare.

Pensions are often said to be the main occupational welfare benefit as many people working on the labour market receive a portion of their earnings when they retire through a pension savings account. There are many types of labour market pension, but most importantly they are related to labour market participation, and therefore the size of the pension is often related to income when being on the labour market. The implication is that inequalities in working life are continued into the age of retirement.

Solid data about fiscal welfare (or tax expenditures) and occupational welfare are limited, especially if we are interested in international comparisons. They are therefore often overlooked in the presentation and discussion of welfare states and welfare regimes, and spending and approaches related especially to fiscal welfare are also often labelled the hidden welfare state. It is expected to be lower in universal types of welfare states like the Nordic and higher in liberal and central European welfare states. Data on occupational welfare can sometimes be studied by looking into the size of fringe benefits paid out by companies, and by surveys asking what welfare employers are providing besides the direct wage.

Fiscal welfare can be rather important (Greve, 2008), and can change the ranking of welfare spending among countries. In the same way, the impact of the tax system when taxing or not taxing social security changes the overall evaluation of the cost of a welfare state and thereby also the perception of high and low spenders in the area (cf. Figure 4.2). Table 4.3 provides estimates of tax expenditures in selected countries.

Table 4.3 is a clear reminder of the importance of fiscal welfare in many countries, with Italy having the highest proportion in relation to GDP. The implication is that looking at public sector spending data alone would be misleading when trying to describe welfare states. The welfare states thus have different routes to financing and delivering welfare. The specific mix between public, fiscal and occupational welfare varies across countries, and also changes over time. However, when trying to understand the relation between state and market it is important to be aware of the different routes especially as some of them are often hidden and not very openly described.

Table 4.3 Tax expenditures as percentages of personal income tax revenues and percentages of GDP in selected countries

	% of personal income tax revenues	% of GDP
Germany (2008)	5.7	0.6
Spain (2009)	34.6	2.4
France (2008)	6.7	0.8
Italy (2009)	40.4	4.7
Denmark (2006)	1.7	0.5
UK (2007/8)	20.1	2.2

Source: European Commission (2011).

Note: No data available for Sweden, Hungary and the Czech Republic.

4.5   Choice and equality/inequality

The welfare state can have different roles with regard to equality and inequality (the more precise impact of difference in level of equality and questions on inequality are considered Chapter 9). One role is often labelled 'the Robin Hood effect', which is taking from the rich and giving to the poor. In most welfare states this takes place when most of the benefits and services are provided to those with the lowest income. The degree of redistribution depends on the concrete organisation of the welfare state, the size of benefits and progressivity in the tax system.

Another role is to help in redistributing income over a life cycle. This has been labelled 'the welfare state as a piggy bank' (Barr, 2001). Individuals receive benefits when they are children and young people in education, pay when they are on the labour market, and then receive again when they reach the age of retirement.

Equality and equity can also mean being able to ensure that similar cases are treated similarly. This is, for example, the case if all families with children get the same amount of money. In this case a transfer from families with children to families without children takes place. However, this can come into conflict with the situation that low income families without children might then have to participate in the financing of a benefit to a family with a higher level of income. Different principles of equality can thus conflict with each other.

The welfare state thus has a role with regard to the degree of equality by redistribution over the lifetime and in each year so that the outcome of the market's activities is not the only aspect having an impact on the degree of inequality. The impact of financing will further be explored in Chapter 5.

The impact on equality and inequality also relates to whether there is equality in access to welfare services. Not only as part of direct decided service levels, but also as part of the introduction of choice for citizens, sometimes relabelled as consumers, in welfare states. Increased choice, it is argued, should enhance the service users' position against the bureaucracy.

A reason put forward for using markets is therefore that they give more choice and hence make the public sector more responsive to the needs of the citizens. Thus from a neoliberal perspective choice increases competition, and from a New Left perspective choice empowers users. Arguments for a new balance between individual and collective responsibilities have also been part of the debate.

In general, six conditions need to be fulfilled in order to ensure free choice without a negative impact on equity in a society (Greve, 2010, p. 8):

1   competitive market forces
2   sufficient and precise information
3   low transaction costs
4   precise incentive structure
5   avoidance of incentives for 'cream-skimming'
6   trust in providers.

These six elements show that many and varied conditions need to be fulfilled if a negative impact on equity is to be avoided. The implication being that not all areas of welfare states can be used when allowing individual citizens to make choices. Furthermore it also reflects that choice is possible for persons in some circumstances and specific types of decisions. For some, choice might increase their individual welfare by making it possible to make a choice in accordance with their preference, whereas for others choice might imply that they do not get what they need (e.g. they might decide to buy an expensive good when they need more medicine). For some this can even increase their level of stress, as it can be very stressful to have to choose and to fear making a choice that is regretted later.

Furthermore, for those services where there are user charges, the individual or family income can also have an impact on their ability to make choices. High levels of user charges that might be expected to ensure higher revenue and better exercise of preferences by users might at the same time have a negative impact on the equality of access to welfare services. Here there can thus be a trade-off between different approaches, as what might be gained in one way can be lost in another.

Theoretically, it is not possible to argue for a precise and specific level of equality. The overall acceptable degree of inequality is then, at the end of the day, a normative political issue where analysis can inform on the consequences related to equality by choosing one or another policy instrument.

4.6   Summing-up

There are many and often interrelated ways to finance and deliver welfare. Looking at public welfare only would not present the full picture of the welfare state. Occupational and fiscal welfare also need to be included in order to gain full insight into the support from the state to the financing and delivery of welfare.

Different welfare states have different balances between the different approaches to welfare, and also different levels of public sector spending related to core welfare state areas. The way chosen to deliver welfare also impacts the degree of equality. Whereas public welfare tends to redistribute, the opposite is the case for fiscal and occupational welfare. The overall level of spending on welfare, when including all approaches, is not as much as first indicated if only looking into the direct public provision.

Even if there are arguments for public sector intervention, it does not imply that the public sector should be the provider. Financing and decisions about who has access to benefits and services are more important than the specific provider, although when a private provider is used, clear conditions need to be set down to ensure that quality as well as access will be the same for all. The private sector is therefore also in many aspects dependent on the demand from the public sector for delivery of goods and services.

Choice has been a relatively new development in the welfare states. When choice is possible it is presented as giving citizens better options. However, despite this, choices are possible only in some instances, not necessarily in all, and therefore choice might influence the degree of equality in the ability to receive welfare services. The impact of choice on equality is, as with many other issues in relation to the welfare state, only possible to answer by an empirical analysis and it might even vary from one area of the welfare state to another.

References

Barr, N. (2001), *The Welfare State as a Piggy Bank: Information, Risk, Uncertainty, and the Role of the State*. Oxford, Oxford University Press.

European Commission (2011), *Tax Reforms in EU Member States*. Brussels, EU Commission.

Farnsworth, K. (2013), Occupational Welfare. In Greve, B. (ed.), *Routledge International Handbook of the Welfare State*. Abingdon, Routledge, pp. 30-39.

Greve, B. (2008), *Occupational Welfare: Winners and Losers*. Cheltenham, Edward Elgar.

Greve, B. (ed.) (2010), *Choice, Challenges and Perspectives for the European Welfare States*. Oxford, Wiley-Blackwell.

Greve, B. (ed.) (2013), *Routledge International Handbook of the Welfare State*. Abingdon, Routledge.

Sinfield, A. (2013), Fiscal Welfare. In Greve, B. (ed.), *Routledge International Handbook of the Welfare State*. Abingdon, Routledge, pp. 20-29.

Titmuss, R. M. (1958), *Essays on 'The Welfare State'*. London, Allen & Unwin.

Chapter 5

Financing the public sector

Contents

5.1 Introduction

Taxes and duties are an important source of finance for public sector activities, but at the same time it is important to understand the impact of taxes and duties on issues such as incentives (especially work and savings) and equality. This chapter presents the principles and consequences of various ways of financing public sector activities and the role of the welfare state.

Section 5.2 describes the set of different instruments that in principle can be used to finance public sector expenditures. The focus is on advantages and disadvantages of various methods of payments seen from the perspectives of both the users and administrations, especially with a focus on the impact on equality. A few basic data concerning the structure of taxation will be presented and thereby the variety of ways welfare states are financed in different welfare regimes.

Recent years have seen tax competition in the area of company taxation including reduction in corporate income tax. The impact of globalisation through tax competition can therefore also be looked upon as one reason among others for changes in tax systems (Bernardi and Profeta, 2005). International initiatives in order to ensure compliance with the tax system and international cooperation related to transfer pricing and exchange of information is a new trend aiming at how sustainability in financing welfare states can be better achieved.

Historically, economists have had various ways of understanding the tax system. Economics was concerned with equality of opportunity until the last third of the nineteenth century. There was then a shift towards equality of material conditions which could be achieved by taxing the rich with high and progressive income taxes. For some systems, the focus then shifted towards potential disincentive effects and concentration of taxes on dependent workers, 'taxes lost some or much of their potential impact on income distribution' (Alfonso et al., 2007, p. 6).

Section 5.3 looks into regional and global development and the impact on the options to finance welfare states, whereas Section 5.4 examines the impact of demographic changes and the sustainability of financing welfare states. The principle differences between state and local level of taxation, and the degree of freedom for local provision of welfare will be discussed in Chapter 11.

5.2   Principles of how to finance the public sector

Taxes and duties are in general defined as payments which have to be paid without giving the payer reciprocal rights to a specific income transfer or service from the public sector.

The trend in Europe for the last 25–30 years has been to broaden the tax base by reducing tax reliefs, removing loopholes and so on. By broadening the tax base, it has long been recognised that it will be possible to lower the marginal and/or average tax rate without having to make reductions in public sector expenditure (see for an early description, OECD, 1988). This is an indication that the definition of the tax base is in itself highly important, and further that this most likely will vary from country to country. Omissions and loopholes within the system can make the overall level of taxes and duties, for those who will have to pay them, higher than if the systems mainly deal with how to guarantee the expected revenue. It also increases the risk of public sector debt and thereby a demand for lower welfare spending.

This section covers the principal ways to finance (directly as well as indirectly) welfare state expenditure, and core economic arguments about the different possible effects of using various ways to finance public sector expenditure. Different criteria need to be fulfilled in order to characterise a tax structure as good (see Box 5.1).

Box 5.1 What characterises a good tax structure?

Based on the classical textbook definition by Musgrave and Musgrave (1989), a tax system is a 'good' tax structure if it meets the following requirements:

a) adequate revenue
b) equitable distribution of tax burden
c) minimising excessive burdens
d) possible to use taxes in stabilisation policy
e) fair administration and open system
f) low administrative costs.

The list of requirements in Box 5.1 is, to a large extent, in line with what was also proposed by Adam Smith (Salanie, 2003). The list indicates how difficult it is to achieve a good tax structure as some of the points might contradict each other. Getting an adequate revenue might contradict minimising excessive tax burden and low administrative costs can be in conflict with equitable distribution of tax burden. So policy makers are left with a question of how best to combine various instruments in order to have an impact on societal development.

It is possible, again with reference to Musgrave and Musgrave (1989), to use taxes and duties to influence societal development with regard to:

a) allocation of resources
b) stabilisation of the economy, and
c) impact on equality.

It is normally not possible to achieve all three objectives at the same time using one instrument. Allocation of resources from one part of the economy to another part, for example, could be contradictory for reasons of stabilisation as well as distribution. Therefore, as part of the analysis of tax and duty systems it is also necessary to perform an empirical analysis given each country's specific economic structure and the way the tax system is operating, before being able to give a clear and concise answer to how the impact will vary in different countries. The possible contradiction also implies that it can be difficult to achieve, for example, a goal of a higher degree of equality, as this could be in conflict with the impact on allocation and stabilisation.

Using the tax and duty system to stabilise the economy implies, in a simple version, that in times of lack of demand taxes and duties can be reduced to increase demand and in times of high demand – implying inflation – increases can reduce demand. There are already in most welfare systems some so-called inbuilt automatic stabilisers such as income tax and duties increasing when there is greater activity in the economy and decreasing when the activity reduces. Using the financing of the welfare state to influence economic activity also implies that this is within certain boundaries due to the fact that in the global world open economies can have an impact on the level of employment, as the overall level of economic activity influences the level of employment.

The tax system, by use of different kinds of duties, can influence the allocation of resources. For example, a high duty on specific types of products will theoretically reduce the demand for them and thus employment in this area, and make it possible to increase activities in other areas.

In the following the focus is mainly on the impact on equality, but the impact on stabilisation and allocations are also important functions of tax systems.

For a good tax system it is also important to have as few distortions as possible arising from financing public sector expenditure. Almost all kinds of taxation will theoretically make some distortion as they are compared with a situation without taxes. Distortions can occur, for example, in the choice between work and leisure and between the use of capital and labour in the production process, but also on the impact on economic possibilities and options for individuals or groups of persons. Therefore, it is of interest to discuss how best to finance public sector expenditures if we want to minimise the distortions arising from taxation and achieve a more equitable distribution. Some kinds of distortion can be seen as beneficial even from an efficiency point of view. Examples are taxes and duties that reduce pollution, increase behaviour that will improve health and so on. The debate in recent years on sustainable environmental development can be seen as an issue where higher duties on energy could have been an aspect in reducing CO_2.

There is a variety of instruments available to finance public sector expenditure. A way to systematise them is:

1 *General taxes and duties*: This includes the main part of taxes and duties in most countries and it covers personal as well as corporate taxation and value added taxes (VAT).
2 *Insurance based*: Includes individuals who pay insurance either voluntary or obligatory in order to have some social risk covered.
3 *Social security contributions*: Includes compulsory contributions from employers, employees or self-employed or combinations thereof. They are sometimes earmarked, often levied on gross earnings and flat-rated. Sometimes voluntary social security contributions also exist. They can often be deducted from the income tax base.
4 *Others*: Includes user-charges, inheritance, taxes on gifts and bequests.

The choice between these different taxes and duties is not only a question of economic and social policy theory, but also of historical and national traditions and different understandings of the degree of equality acceptable in different countries. However, a starting point is the impact of different kinds of taxes and duties on incentives, level of revenue and overall impact on efficiency.

It is not possible, just from the way a tax or duty is described, to conclude what the effects are as it depends on different societies' economic structures and composition of inhabitants. Therefore, the following discussion presents the theoretical expected impact. The precise impact needs to be found by an empirical analysis, and it can change over time. When we become richer, for example, our preferences might change towards more spare time and fewer working hours, and this will therefore also change the impact of using different kinds of tax and duty if the aim is to increase labour supply.

Furthermore, the direct impact might not be the final outcome. It is thus not necessarily the person who first has to pay a tax or duty who will be the final payer. For example, employers will often pass social security contributions on to employees by reducing wages, or pass duties on to consumers by increasing the prices of products.

The impact will depend on the market structure for the different products, and the bargaining process in the labour market. In most European countries, there are some connections between the wages paid and the size of the tax and social security contributions. The implication is that in countries that rely more on social security contributions the nominal wages paid out to employees are lower as is the income tax.

Another important aspect is that it is not only the overall level of taxes and duties but particularly the marginal tax rates that might have an impact on the behaviour of individuals, and also on income distribution. Combinations of taxes and reductions in income transfers when people increase their income can have an impact.

> Marginal effective tax rates, which are one cause of these distortions, are typically high at both ends of the income distribution, and they may contribute to poverty traps among many individuals relying on benefits as well as to reductions in work effort, or attempts to escape taxation by individual's with high earning.
>
> (Förster and Mira d'Ercole, 2005, p. 30)

A poverty trap is defined as a situation in which people starting work or working more will not be able to increase their disposable income and still be living in risk of poverty. Changes in the tax system in recent years have, by various kinds of in-work benefits, tried to reduce the possible poverty traps arising from the combination of taxes and duties and income-related benefits or payment for welfare services.

Another possible effect of the tax system, it has been argued, could be that a high tax level would have a negative impact on labour supply and the growth of the economy. However, no clear evidence of this can be found, and the results of correlation seem to be that the hypothesis of a connection can be either 'true, false and spurious, and finally also indeterminate' (Bernardi, 2004, p. 496).

There are, as already mentioned, many and very different ways of financing welfare state expenditures. In the following a short presentation of the most used set of instruments with a discussion of how they might have an impact on the economic distribution will be given.

In many European countries, a very high part of public financing comes from income taxes and duties. These can be proportional or progressive income taxes or duties on a variety of areas. Flat-rate income taxes have been introduced in several EU countries. The most frequent duty is valued added tax (VAT), for which in the EU there is a common agreement on areas where it can be used and also limits to its level. The maximum level of VAT is 25 per cent and it is possible to have reduced VAT, for example, on foods and clothes for children. Otherwise, high duties are levied on goods such as liquor, perfume and other luxury goods. Cars are also often targets for a high level of duties, and recent years have seen increases in taxes and duties for environmental aims, such as on petrol, electricity, heating and water.

Seen from an equity point of view, progressive income taxes will transfer money or at least take money from people in the higher income brackets, and through direct public provision give lower income groups a relatively better position and hence reduce the level of inequality.

How progressive a country's tax system is depends on tax reductions and tax expenditures, for example, fiscal welfare. In general, tax-expenditure measures (Sinfield, 1993; Greve, 1994; Howard, 1997; Brixi et al., 2004) seem to be more favourable to higher income groups, thereby minimising the progressive character of the income tax system. Using tax expenditures to reach a goal also increases the likelihood of a more complicated tax system. Still, income tax, and especially a progressive scale on gross income, will tend to enhance a more just distribution of income. Income tax as head taxes or proportional taxes will have less impact on distribution and a head tax will have a negative impact, as this would imply a relatively higher burden among low-income earners. Furthermore, setting a relatively high amount which may be earned without paying income tax can increase the redistributive character of the income tax, and imply that it will be higher than otherwise expected.

Lower income tax on companies has been a trend in Europe (Eurostat, 2013), which might be seen in the light of tax competition among countries. The overall impact of taxes on companies' incomes depends, however, not only on the tax rate, but also on the often complicated and difficult issues related to global taxation, transfer pricing and so on. The international movement in recent years has been to try to eliminate risk of no tax payments by transfer pricing by international agreements and cooperation.

Duties might also work towards a more just society especially if the duties are imposed in such a way that they concentrate upon luxury goods. This is one of the areas where the more open economies and borders seem to imply a pressure, which has a negative impact on distribution by making it more difficult for an individual country to tax luxury goods higher than other goods if other neighbouring countries are not doing the same. Duties might be regressive if the proportion of income spent on certain items is higher in low-income deciles than in high-income deciles. If the aim is to influence the degree of equality there is an argument for concentrating on goods where the consumption depends on the amount of income. In the wake of the financial crisis that began in 2008 there has been an increase in the level of value added tax in many countries in Europe in order to reduce the public sector deficit (Eurostat, 2013).

Even without considering the impact on equality, duties might be important as they are more difficult to avoid paying – except for trading in the hidden economy. Therefore, duties are a way to ensure that all income groups contribute to the financing of public sector expenditures. Furthermore, they resemble payment for being in a country, and using the facilities. Countries with a large number of tourists might also use this as a way of deriving income from tourists, although the balance here naturally is whether this will make the country more costly to visit compared with other tourist destinations.

If the welfare state in itself is not providing economic security or access to services, this can be done indirectly by making insurance obligatory. Insurance can be seen as a special way of financing public sector expenditure. Using insurance can therefore be seen as a way of privatising the welfare state where each individual pays a fee, based upon the risk of a certain event occurring to them. Combinations can exist, of course, where the state pays the marginal expenditure and the claimant a specified amount. This is despite the fact that the welfare state in itself can be understood as a collective kind of insurance (Barr, 2001). If it should work as an insurance-based contribution then there must be a possibility of opting out of the system and choosing, for example, to be covered by either paying individually or reject having insurance.

There seems to be a high risk of inequality where the main part of the system is built on insurance. Inequalities will arise if the system is not regulated, because the good risks will go together leaving the bad risks to create their own system, for example, groups with low risk of unemployment having one type of insurance to a lower price than people with a high risk of unemployment. Furthermore, the high-income earners will be better able to pay for insurance cover than low-income earners. Therefore, systems based mainly (or at least relying heavily on) insurance will tend to be more unequal than other types of financing.

Seen from the individual perspective, and especially for low-income groups, the main advantage of an insurance-type system is that the stigmatising effects tend to be less. Seen from society's point of view, an insurance system might give more economic freedom to reallocate resources to poor people if the insurance means less pressure on public sector expenditure. By reducing the pressure on the public sector – without implying an overall expansion of the system as in the US health care system – it might be possible to avoid the worst and most negative impacts on the distribution. In practice, though, it seems insurance-based welfare systems create a more dualistic society with those who can pay to be in the insurance systems and those who cannot left on the outside.

Instead of using income tax, the welfare states of many countries, especially in central Europe, use social security contributions. These can be classified in the following way:

a) paid to institution providing social security benefits
b) levied as a function of earnings, payroll or the number of employees
c) earmarked to provide social security benefits and
d) made by insured person or their employer (OECD, 2012).

Traditionally the intention has been to finance social security by these contributions (cf. Musgrave, 1985; Owens and Roberti, 1985; Shibata, 1985). These can be a fixed amount or a percentage of the payroll/wages or combinations thereof. In some countries, the amount paid in this way goes into specific funds, which then pay out when a particular contingency occurs.

The many different ways contributions have been used shows that a variety of possibilities exist. It can therefore also be difficult to find a clear difference between a contribution and an income tax. Often the difference is that contributions are only paid by those actually on the labour market, whereas taxes and duties are paid by the whole population. How clear the difference is depends on how the whole system is structured. For example, what role does the tax threshold play, and in what ways are different contributions levied? Finally, how is access to social benefits and services managed, including whether there are derived rights for spouses and children?

The main problem from an equity point of view is that people without a job and those in more precarious positions in the labour market will not be covered, or at least not to the same extent as the rest of the population.

A further problem is that, at least in some countries, the benefit from contributions depends on staying with the same employer – as is, for example, the case concerning pensions in some countries. Finally, the risk of bankruptcy if the contributions are paid to a fund with a not well-developed administration could mean that the individual who thought he or she was covered was not. In the wake of the financial crisis this has been the case for some with regard to pension savings.

Concerning the overall impact on distribution, it seems therefore that social security contributions tend towards a more unequal society.

Naturally, a whole range of combinations exists, for example, contributions are deducted along with income tax. What one can expect of the combinations and possible effects on distribution, allocation and stabilisation can only be judged by looking at the precise structure of such combinations in each country. However, the argument as presented above concerning the individual elements can be seen as a guideline for how different types of tax and duty systems work.

Instead of financing through general taxes and duties, user payment can also be found in welfare states especially in relation to services such as day care for children and health. This is an indirect way of financing public sector expenditure. The main reasons for a user-pays system are to:

a) raise revenue
b) regulate demand
c) improve the allocative efficiency
d) prevent abuse.

User charges can be seen as an attempt to apply market mechanisms in order to improve efficiency in the supply of public services. The theoretical argument is that people's demands are higher when they do not have to pay for a good and thus by free provision the correct preference revelation does not take place.

The main problem concerning user charges is that people may decide not to use public services if they have to pay a charge, and this can lead – especially in the field of health care – to a lack of demand. This can be undesirable, for example, in the area of preventive medicine or patients visiting the general practitioner at a later phase of their illness. In the long run, this would increase expenditure due to more serious illness and higher mortality.

User charges and user payment have many of the same features as insurance and therefore the same problems arise in relation to equality. The final outcome depends on how the charges are calculated and if all citizens have to pay them. An issue with user charges has to do with the problems of high combined marginal taxes and reduction in social security benefits or increased payment for services. This might imply a combined marginal rate above 100 per cent and thereby also a risk of a poverty trap.

The distributional consequences of taxes and duties depend on the distribution of income, wealth and consumption in a given society. Direct taxation, including progressive income taxes, tends to work in the direction of a more just distribution. Duties on luxury goods tend to do the same. Duties on basic food tend to work in the opposite direction. Direct taxation, especially income taxation, if the intention is to increase the degree of equality, is therefore preferable to most forms of indirect taxation.

When it comes to environmental duties in particular, it seems that if they are levied on final consumption it is a priori not possible to describe the distributional consequences. It seems that many of the products will be basic goods and therefore such duties will work in the direction of a more unjust distribution. On the other hand, high-income earners often make greater use of heating, petrol and electricity and this counteracts the general tendency. This can further be counterbalanced by using the higher revenue to make special low tax rates for low-income groups or to transfer income to these groups. This contradiction shows that spending patterns must be known, and based on this knowledge the desired balance between distribution, allocation and stabilisation can be achieved by targeting the expenditure derived from tax revenue to vulnerable groups.

In using insurance-based systems to finance welfare state expenditure, their distributional effects depend on the way the systems are organised. The closer the systems come to a proportional (or progressive tax) the closer it will be to general taxation and in this sense minimise the negative distributional consequences.

Insurance-based systems organised purely by the market tend towards more unjust distribution. The reason for this is the connection between income and the risk of being unemployed, need to receive sickness benefit, etc. People with below-average life expectancy will have to pay higher insurance premiums than others. One will therefore need to combine change in different parts of the tax and duty system if one wants a more equal distribution and a just way of financing welfare state expenditure.

However, the overall societal impact also depends not only on how the tax and duty system is arranged, but also how the money is spent. One thus has to combine the analysis of taxation with the impact of public sector expenditures on the distribution. Thus it might turn out that even a proportional tax system, by combining it with public sector spending especially to the lowest income groups, in order to ensure both a horizontal and vertical redistribution, might end up with overall public sector redistribution in the economy. At the same time payment for childcare can be considered to be a kind of 'extra' tax on the wage earner, as it reduces the net take-home pay, and this might explain why many European countries today have a working tax credit and/or low payment for childcare (OECD, 2007).

Table 5.1 shows the main tax instruments available, including the expected advantages and disadvantages of the various instruments. The context and structure of each country is important in order to evaluate possible advantages and disadvantages. The types of welfare regime in which they are mainly used are indicative, as most countries use a broad variety of taxes and thereby all instruments are used in more or less all countries.

Table 5.2 presents an overview of the present ways of financing in broad categories of instruments in welfare states in Europe. It is possible to get more detailed information including more specific knowledge on the many and varied types of duties that exist in the different countries. Here the purpose is mainly to indicate the variety in the approach to finance the welfare state.

Table 5.2 is an indication of the diversity of financing welfare in Europe and also the difference in the overall level of taxes and duties. It ranges from high rates in the Nordic welfare states such as Denmark and Sweden to a lower level in the Czech Republic, Spain and Hungary – and the rest in between. Denmark has high income taxes whereas social security contributions are important in France and Germany. This reflects their different historical traditions. From 2000 until the financial crisis in 2008 there had been in Europe a downward trend in tax revenues from around 40.5 per cent of GDP in 2000 to 38.5 per cent in 2009 then again increasing to close to 41 per cent after the financial crisis.

Part of the development in the way of financing welfare states has to do with economic globalisation.

Table 5.1 Main tax instruments and their advantages and disadvantages

Main tax instruments	Advantages	Disadvantages	Used in – and reference to main welfare regime
Income tax	Can ensure a high level of revenue, and can be made progressive. Can be made both on wage-earners and companies	Risk of changing balance between work and leisure, especially with high marginal tax rates	All European countries, especially Nordic universal welfare regimes.
Value Added Tax	Relatively simple, and can vary between types of goods, e.g. low or zero on foods. Will also be paid by tourists and those not paying income tax	Might have a negative impact on distribution as persons with lower income tend to have a higher propensity to consume	All European countries, especially welfare regimes of southern and eastern countries
Duties	Can be targeted to luxury goods and might thereby have a positive impact on distribution. Can also help to enhance a better environment	Administration, and if not targeted an upside-down effect	To varying degrees in all EU countries, however southern and eastern to a higher degree
Social security contributions	Simple and effective, and ensure financing of welfare activities	Risk that those outside the labour market are not covered	Especially in the central continental and Liberal welfare model in Europe
User charges	Increase the information on consumers' preferences and are paid by those receiving the services	Risk that those with low income do not get the service or not at the right time	Especially used in the health care area, but also transport, day care for children in many EU countries. Liberal model countries to a high degree
Others	Can be a way to tax inheritance, wealth, housing	Mainly administrative, but also possible negative side effects in relation to mobility	Only more limited, and with a very varied structure

Source: Based on Greve (2010).

Table 5.2 Taxes and duties as percentages of GDP in EU28 and selected EU countries in 2012

	VAT	Other duties	Income tax	Social security contributions	Others	Total
EU27	7.1	4.2	12.0	13.0	4.4	40.7
Czech Republic	7.2	4.6	7.1	15.6	0.5	35.0
Denmark	10.0	4.8	27.6	0.9	5.8	49.1
Germany	7.3	3.4	11.7	15.8	2.2	40.4
Spain	5.5	3.3	9.9	12.0	2.9	33.6
France	7.0	4.2	10.7	17.0	8.1	47.0
Italy	6.1	5.1	14.6	13.6	4.9	44.3
Hungary	9.4	7.8	6.7	13.2	2.2	39.3
Sweden	9.3	3.2	18.1	7.5	6.7	44.8
United Kingdom	7.3	4.6	12.5	7.8	4.9	37.1

Source: Eurostat (gov_a_tax_main) (accessed 4 January 2014).

Note: Others include housing, inheritance, wealth, etc. in the dataset data on other EU countries are available, and also more detailed information on some specific taxes and duties.

5.3 Regional and global economic development and sustainable financing

Nation states have the right to impose taxes and duties on their citizens. On the other hand, citizens have the right to move, and with increasingly open economies this also implies that labour and capital can move around more freely (see also Chapter 12). A core argument is that globalisation and tax competition in the wake thereof imposes strong pressures on welfare states (Genschel, 2002).

Taxation of companies and capital, also labelled mobile factors, has thus been increasingly difficult and this partly explains the downward trend in corporate tax rates. When citizens have the right to move and to buy goods and services in neighbouring countries this makes it difficult for large differences in specific taxes existing in areas where cross-border trade is easy, such as on alcohol, but also a large difference in VAT might cause citizens to spend more money in another country. Within the EU there is a common VAT directive setting the rules for how to claim VAT, and there are also limits, so that, for example, the highest VAT rate possible is 25 per cent.

The increased openness of economies implies therefore that taxation of non-mobile factors will be more important in the future. Non-mobile factors include elements such as housing, energy consumption, water and local transport. How this can be done will vary from country to country, but searching for stability in the public sector income also implies a need for taxation in such a way that fluctuation in, for example, prices and income from stocks and bonds does not have a large impact on the revenue.

Globalisation, regionalisation and tax competition mean that the room for decisions on a national level has been reduced over the years. The recent attempts to agree measures for tax havens, transfer pricing and other attempts from companies and individuals to reduce what they have to pay in tax underlines that international cooperation is increasingly important in order to ensure sustainable financing of the welfare state.

5.4   Impact of demography on financing the welfare state

Changes in demography have two different types of impact on the welfare state: on the expenditure side and related to income. In Chapter 13, on further challenges, the impact of demography on welfare state expenditures is dealt with. Here the focus is on whether the greying of societies implies difficulties with regard to public sector income.

Elderly people have lower incomes from work than younger persons in most societies as it is often the case that annual income is highest at around 45–50 years of age. However, in many countries the pension system has developed towards increased use of saving while being in the labour market thereby producing a higher income among pensioners in the years to come. Still, the overall expected impact will be that the possible revenue from income tax will be lower with more people reaching the age of retirement which puts pressure on the welfare state's ability to be financially sustainable. This is also the case with regard to particular areas of consumption, given that elderly people typically have a consumption pattern different from that of young people, so from this there might also come a pressure in a downward direction. The overall implication is that there will be a need to restructure financing in many welfare states if they are to continue on the present level.

Change in pension systems takes time as individuals will need to know a long time in advance what their pensions can be expected to be. Therefore changes in pension systems are often enacted over a long time spell.

5.5   Summing-up

A broad variety of taxes and duties needs to be used in order to finance a modern welfare state. Furthermore, the combinations of taxes, duties and public sector spending are important parameters on which to evaluate the outcome of societal decisions in these areas.

How to combine the various instruments available further depends on the structure of income and wealth in different countries and also the given preferences for the degree of equality to be reached in the different countries. This finally means that decisions need to be based on sound empirical knowledge in the different countries.

As described in this chapter, many different ways of financing public sector expenditures can be found, and they are to a varied degree used in all European countries. This to a high degree reflects historical traditions, but also the differences in societal structure and efforts of the welfare states.

If the starting point is an intention to ensure a just income tax, then broadening of the tax base is advised – this means introducing a gross or close to gross income tax. By introducing such a tax, the system will move towards a more equal system, as the payment then depends more and more on earned income, and not the deductions available for different groups.

If the starting point is to reduce the problem of international mobility of labour and capital, then taxes and duties on immobile factors are important. This will mean taxes and duties on land, houses, electricity, water, etc. This seems a sustainable way of financing, and also has the feature that higher income groups spend a higher proportion of their income on immobile factors, and therefore they pay a greater share, and that taxes on immobile factors are more difficult to avoid when actually living in a country.

If the point is to combine public sector provision with achieving an equitable outcome, progressive user charges might also be used. By imposing higher charges on higher income groups, the main problem will be to avoid the combined taxes and charge rates being too high, as this can imply poverty traps or disincentives to work. A link between tax and welfare policies is thus important as the same goal, to a large degree, can be achieved in both systems. Taxes on wealth and inheritance could improve the equality of the systems, but still these will be difficult to enforce in a Europe with open borders.

The tax system thus has an impact on allocation, stabilisation and equality, but also the ability to finance the welfare state. Taxes and duties can be used to achieve goals in the welfare state; however, empirical analysis is needed in order to know the exact impact of the different taxes and duties.

References

Alfonso, A., Schuknecht, L. and Tanzi, V. (2007), Income Distribution Determinants and Public Spending Efficiency, papers.ssrn.com. Working Paper Series, No. 861/ January 2008, Frankfurt Am Main, European Central Bank.

Barr, N. (2001), *The Welfare State as a Piggy Bank: Information, Risk, Uncertainty, and the Role of the State*. Oxford, Oxford University Press.

Bernadi, L. (2004), Tax Reforms in Europe: Objectives and Some Critical Issues. Available at http://www.bancaditalia.it/studiricerche/convegni/atti/taxpolicy/iv/491-502_bernardi.pdf (accessed 6 June 2014).

Bernardi, L. and Profeta, P. (eds) (2005), *Tax Systems and Tax Reforms in Europe*. London, Routledge.

Brixi, H. P., Valenduc, C. and Swift, Z. (2004), *Tax Expenditures – Shedding Light on Government Spending through the Tax System*. Washington, DC, The World Bank.

Eurostat (2013), *Taxation Trends in the European Union*: *2013 Edition*. Brussels, Eurostat.

Förster, M. and Mira d'Ercole, M. (2005), *Income Distribution and Poverty in OECD Countries in the Second Half of the 1990s*. OECD, Social, Employment and Migration Working Papers No. 22, Paris, OECD.

Genschel, P. (2002), Globalization, Tax Competition, and the Welfare State. *Politics & Society*, vol. 30, no. 2, pp. 245–75.

Greve, B. (1994), The Hidden Welfare State, Tax-expenditure and Social Policy. *Journal of Scandinavian Social Welfare*, vol. 3, no. 4, pp. 203–11.

Greve, B. (2010), Taxation, Equality and Social Cohesion. In M. Zupi and E. Estruch Puertas (eds), *Challenges of Social Cohesion in Times of Crisis: Euro-Latin American Dialogue*. Madrid, FIIAPP (Fundacion Internacional y para Iberoamerica de Administration y Politicas Publicas), pp. 307–31.

Howard, C. (1997), *The Hidden Welfare State*: *Tax Expenditures and Social Policy in the United States*. Princeton, NJ, Princeton University Press.

Musgrave, R. (1985), Perspectives on and Limits to Public Finance for the Financing of Social Policy in Market Economies. *Public Finance and Social Policy*. Detroit, MI, Wagner State University Press.

Musgrave, R. and Musgrave, P. (1989), *Public Finance in Theory and Practice*. 5th edition, New York, McGraw Hill.

OECD (1988), Tax Reform in OECD-Countries: Motives, Constraints and Practice. *OECD Economic Studies*. Spring, pp. 185–226. Paris, OECD.

OECD (2007), *Babies and Bosses*: *Reconciling Work and Family Life*. Paris, OECD.

OECD (2012), *Revenue Statistics*. Paris, OECD.

Owens, J. and Roberti, P. (1985), The Financing of Social Security Systems. International Comparisons: Trends and Policy Issues. *Public Finance and Social Policy*. Detroit, Wagner State University Press.

Salanie, B. (2003), *The Economics of Taxation*. Cambridge, MA, The MIT Press.

Shibata, H. (1985), Financing and the Politics of Financing Social Security Programs: An Analysis and Proposals for Reform. *Public Finance and Social Policy*. Detroit, MI, Wagner State University Press.

Sinfield, A. (1993), Social Security through Taxation. In D. Pieters (ed.), *Social Security in Europe*. Antwerpen, Maklu, pp. 119–153.

Chapter 6

The role of the market

Contents

6.1   Introduction

The state, the market and civil society have been presented as the core institutions in the welfare state, with shifting responsibilities over time, and changed perceptions of why and to what extent they are involved in welfare state development. This chapter focuses on the role of the market.

In most countries the market plays a central role in relation to allocation of many and varied types of goods or services. The market's role depends on a number of factors, which will be described first. There are a number of situations where the market does not function, and there are arguments for government failure as well. Basic assumptions for when a market can work and the consequences of its failure are presented. Reasons for market failure will also be given. An essential question is why markets can work in some areas and the reasons why certain markets do not function in others. The financial market is touched upon as an example of how a specific market can influence both the individual economy and societal development, including how developments in the financial sector have had consequences for the development of many welfare states.

Finally, the chapter focuses on how marketisation has influenced the provision of welfare, and may do in the future, including impacts on who has access to welfare services and benefits and under what conditions. The use of market-type mechanisms within the public sector, such as incentives, is presented.

6.2   Market and government failure

The market has historically been used mainly to exchange goods and services (the following is the classic presentation of these arguments; for more details see, for example, Stiglitz, 2000). Since the writings of Adam Smith (1776/1970), it has been argued that an invisible hand helps to ensure that buyers and sellers meet and that thereby trade can take place at a price both buyer and seller are willing to accept. However, the market is not always perfect and sometimes state intervention is necessary to correct it. This requires knowledge of when a market functions and when it does not.

'The market' is the expression often used, as if there is only one market, although all societies have many and very different markets. These can be defined geographically. For example, often prices are higher in city centres and tourist areas. Markets can also be defined according to the type of goods traded (e.g. foodstuffs, non-food items or luxury goods). There are goods or services that can be traded through the Internet, and others require a shop. These differences contribute to explain why some products can be traded on a market more easily and effectively than others without the risk of negative side effects.

There are generally a number of conditions which must be fulfilled in order for a market to work efficiently, as listed in Box 6.1.

Box 6.1 The most important conditions to ensure the work of the market

1   Many sellers and many buyers, e.g. no monopolies
2   Full information
3   Transaction costs must be limited
4   Individuals and companies try to utility- and profit-maximise.

When these conditions in Box 6.1. are fulfilled the market will ensure that buyers are willing to pay the price for the good and the seller is willing to sell it. The price of the goods will thus reflect an equilibrium between the total supply and the total demand. There is no single buyer or seller who can decide the price. It is a general assumption that buyers are utility-maximising individuals, who are rational and behave economically. This includes that they balance their benefit (utility in economics) with a product with the price they are willing to pay as well as making an informed choice. Likewise the assumption is that companies are profit-maximising, and thus attempting to earn the highest possible profit. In a market with perfect competition there will therefore be equilibrium.

Problems arise when one or more of these conditions are not met. There may be conditions of monopoly or duopoly. If there is only one supplier (or very few) of a product this can mean that the seller can charge a higher price and buyers will have to pay more for their goods than under perfect competition. The risk that a monopoly seller requires higher prices and thus can secure a large profit explains why in market economies there is regulation in order to try to prevent monopolies or other types of cooperation between suppliers to fix higher prices than would be paid in a perfect market.

The risk of monopolistic or quasi-monopolistic dominance is greater in areas where there may be obstacles to entering the market. This applies, for example, to the production of medicines, which require high costs of research and development and evidence that the product works. Here, a new producer has difficulty in becoming established. It could also apply to a number of other areas (many consumer durables, for example).

There may be areas where there are not many who demand a variety of goods. When demand is limited (and thus it is more difficult to streamline production) the prices will be high, with the result that some parties will be unable to act in that market. This could be the case with very specialised products, such as those designed for the use of the physically disabled.

There are commodity markets, where there is not full transparency and therefore some buyers are going to pay too high a price for those products. Examples of areas where it is difficult to have full transparency is insurance and mobile phone subscriptions, where different combinations of coverage, co-payments, speed and additional payment means that it can be difficult for consumers to compare across different options. Lack of transparency also means that there is not necessarily a correlation between price and quality.

There is greater transparency in markets where there is a high frequency of transactions. Most people know the price of a packet of butter or a litre of milk, but not necessarily the differences in price and quality for consumer durable goods (e.g. computers or televisions). The market often works best in areas where there is scope for many purchases and sales, and less well in areas where there are few purchases and sales, and where the individual consumer only more rarely trades. This applies, for example, to health treatments where few will know how different treatments may have an effect on a disease given that they may use the treatment just once or only a few times over a lifespan.

Finding the best product is therefore often very difficult for an individual consumer. This therefore is an argument for government intervention.

Market failure is generally when the market, left to itself, does not generate an efficient output of goods and services. A common example is pollution, where the cost of pollution is not reflected in market prices. Different types of market failures occur: lack of production of certain goods; monopolies, including natural monopolies; disequilibria (unemployment, inflation, balance of payment deficits); and information problems.

Market failure has been a core argument for public sector intervention in the economy, and for having a welfare state. Most people accept some types of public intervention, such as defence, police, foreign policy and the administration of common rules for society's functioning (for an early expression of this see Box 6.2). However, there is greater disagreement about the need for social programmes and welfare state intervention.

Box 6.2 Adam Smith about the need for correction of market failure in 1776

The Third and last duty of the sovereign or commonwealth is that of erecting and maintaining those public institutions and those public works, which it never can be for the interest of any individual, or small number of individuals, to erect and maintain because the profit could never repay the expenses.

Smith (1776/1970)

Full knowledge and insight into how products work need not be the same for all consumers, and thus even if there is no market failure there may be inequality in access to different types of goods and services. There will also be a risk in certain areas of inequality if the market alone delivers a product. For example, a market for unemployment insurance will lead to a lower cost for people with low unemployment risk and a high – and perhaps even prohibitively high – payment for individuals with high risk of unemployment. In such situations where the risk is different, a common system of pooled risk, such as the welfare state, will therefore be cheaper both for the individual and society than an individual purchase, as the risk can be spread and the administration is simpler.

The assumption that consumers act rationally is not always met. There are impulse purchases influenced by advertising, and lack of insight into the impact of short-term and long-term care, including assessment of long-term needs. Lack of time can also cause people to buy more expensive goods and services than they would otherwise choose.

The buying and selling of products entails costs: the transport of goods, the cost of employees in shops and administrative transaction costs. Therefore, the distance to a market could also affect the price of the product.

The market can thus function well in a number of areas at allocating goods and services in accordance with user preferences, but in some areas there is a risk that some buyers are paying too much and others do not have access to the market. It requires therefore a concrete empirical analysis of each market in order to assess whether it is working properly. Confidence in the market, including the extent of corruption and the underground economy, may affect the transaction costs and the efficiency of market functioning.

The core arguments for public sector intervention thus revolve around the concept of market failure, that is, the market left to itself will not provide many types of welfare goods and services (including income transfers), or if it does provide the services or insurance to cover a social contingency many people will not be able to buy these. Market failure thus revolves around issues of monopoly, natural monopolies and public goods as being the central reasons for intervention. A public good is defined as a good where one person's use of the good does not reduce another person's possibilities of using the good. Public goods cannot be provided by the market as they are difficult to charge for the use of, such as air, for example. In the case of a road, as long as there is no traffic jam, one person's use will not be a hindrance for others, although it is possible to charge for using the road. Still, several of these types of goods and services will only be provided in a limited way if the market is left to itself. If the market is the main provider there will be differential access based upon the ability to pay for the goods, and this can be a hindrance for low-income groups, for example, buying the necessary products to help and be able to live as normal a life as possible in the case of a disability.

A further reason for public sector intervention is that in some areas it will be economically ineffective to leave the finance to individual households. The main example of this is care for the elderly. If an individual has to pay for care when needed later in life, he or she would have to save a large sum of money when younger. Yet people cannot foretell whether or not they will need such money as, for example, they might die before they need the care. A common pool of resources will thus be more efficient – those in need can receive the care and those not in need know they are covered in case they need it later without individuals having to put a large amount of money aside. To a large degree this is also the case regarding health care. Behind the veil of ignorance no one knows whether they will be in need of hospital or other health care treatment. The expression 'behind the veil of ignorance' comes from John Rawls's book, *A Theory of Justice* (1971), which discusses what we as individuals will prefer if we do not know our position in society, and thereby what level of social service we at least will prefer that all people should have access to notwithstanding their income and/or wealth. Therefore it would be economically irrational for society if all people save money in order to pay for care in old age. In this way, the welfare state works to share the risk of being in need of expensive care or unexpected lack of income or, in old age, no income. Thereby the welfare state is like a piggy bank (reflecting the title of the book by Barr, 2001) where society puts money aside and in case of need it will be there, and it helps to smooth levels of income and consumption possibilities over the individual's lifespan.

In principle, an insurance system in which all citizens are obliged to be members could also fulfil this function. However, the risk is the same as already outlined: some cannot afford to buy insurance, and some can only get insurance if they can afford to pay a very high price, for example, due to them having a higher risk than others of needing treatment. An insurance market can thus make access very unequal and highly dependent on the ability to pay, which can be different depending on the risk for the individual. The same is the case for unemployment benefit systems – those on the labour market with a higher risk of unemployment would have to pay a higher price than those with permanent stable jobs. Furthermore, the market might not ensure full employment (see also Chapter 7). Social insurance, such as in the continental welfare regimes, is thus a way to ensure that all citizens on the labour market are covered in case of a social contingency such as, for example, sickness or unemployment.

Public sector intervention and regulation can thus be a way of achieving certain societal development goals. Besides goals of higher levels of employment, public sector intervention can also have distributive goals (cf. also Chapter 4).

Even given the need to intervene in relation to market failure, this does not tell us how to intervene and on what criteria individuals will have access to benefits. For example, considering pensions, there is at present in most countries a mix of public, private and occupational-related benefits. An important question has been whether the level of pension should be based upon a defined benefit, for example, the level of benefit is known to beneficiaries when they fulfil the criteria for receiving the benefit (typically at a certain age), or whether it should be based upon individual contributions, for example, the amount one receives depends on what has been paid in or how many years one has contributed to a system.

There are also areas where the market works, but where use and demand is too low, thus warranting state intervention. This has been labelled 'merit goods' (Musgrave and Musgrave, 1989). The classic example is the case of lunch at schools in the United States. The argument is that many children would not get food without state intervention. The merit goods idea is used as an argument for ensuring a sufficiently high level of social capital: for example, without public sector intervention the educational attainment level would be lower in most countries. Merit goods as an argument for intervention in the way markets work is thus a paternalistic way of justifying state intervention in societal development. Investment in education is also arguably a way to see the welfare state as a social investment state.

However, even if there is market failure, government failure is also possible, and therefore the question is whether government failure or market failure is the greatest. Government failure refers to situations in which government intervention in society and the expansion of the public sector becomes larger than is optimal. The public choice theorists especially argue for the possibility of government failure and therefore they are in favour of less government and using at least some types of market mechanism within the public sector. The public choice approach also refers to the Leviathan monster of the Bible, implying that the public sector may be crowding out the private sector.

Other arguments for government failure revolve around the impact of pressure groups and the bureaucracy. The impact of pressure groups is that they can put pressure on policy makers, who want to be re-elected, to spend more on their specific area. Given that the impact for those in need can be large (benefits are concentrated) and the cost is spread among many, this is an argument for an asymmetrical pressure on public sector spending. The impact of bureaucracy, it is argued, is due to the tendency to expand its own area and thereby its own influence. It is not possible to measure the possible size of government failure, but it is obvious that as long as market failure exists so too may government failure and this needs to be taken into account. The development of welfare states in recent years seems to indicate that not only might there be pressure for higher spending, but also government finance departments wishing to curb the level of public sector spending and reduce the size of the public sector.

Even when the market functions there might be moral issues at stake, implying that even if it is possible to have a market our norms imply that we do not prefer it, as examples from Michael Sandel's (2012) book show. There might be a market for human organs, for sex, for adoption of babies, or for hunting endangered species. As Sandel asked: 'Are there some things that money can buy but shouldn't?' (2012, p. 95). The question also arises in core areas of the welfare state, such as whether those who can afford it should be allowed the right to buy faster access to medical care, or be allowed to pick up their children from day care later if they pay more. Another classical discussion has been whether companies if they can afford to pay should be allowed to pollute.

Even in areas where it is possible to establish a market with full information and willing buyers and sellers we might see that, based upon moral considerations, society is not willing to allow it. Based on different kinds of arguments, ranging from ethical to equality issues, this can be reason for state intervention. Where this should be used as an argument is not something one can decide based upon objective criteria, as it also reflects different opinions on individual liberty versus societal influence.

Finally, even if there is market failure, it may be possible to reduce the impact either through legal regulation, for example, by setting norms and standards, or by direct intervention and public sector provision of the goods and services. There can thus be many and varied ways to reduce the possible impact of market failure.

6.3   The financial market – a case history

The financial market can have an impact on the lives of many individuals and families, and as the 2008 crisis has shown, also for spending in welfare states. Therefore even if it is in many ways a perfectly functioning market it has implications for the overall development of society. The price of the financial market is interest and fees for borrowing money (both deposit and lending). Interest rates are fixed on one side as a result of supply and demand for money, but are also influenced by central banks and in Europe in particular by the European Central Bank.

Financial markets are important because changes therein can affect the development of a number of areas of society. This applies, for example, to firms' ability to borrow money and thus their investments and overall economic activity (and thus indirectly also the number of jobs in a community and thereby the level of unemployment).

Historically, there has been a series of financial crises and financial changes. The financial crisis of 2008 was mainly due to a combination of a housing bubble, the development of a range of financial instruments and a stock market bubble. When these bubbles burst and the financial systems are as closely related as they are today, there is a risk that many banks will fail at the same time because everyone will try to withdraw their money at the same time. To avoid a financial collapse, many countries allocated vast amounts of public sector money to ensure banks' survival and provide liquidity to ensure that normal financial activities could continue, including loans for the development of new investments in private companies. This created a public sector deficit and it has therefore also created pressure to make cuts on public sector spending or raise taxes in order to reduce this deficit, especially given that in many countries the level of public sector debt implies a high burden of interest payments which increases public sector spending.

The financial market, although working in principle like any other market, can thus have an impact on welfare states as imbalances in the financial market can influence public sector income and expenditure, levels of unemployment and options for investment in a country.

6.4   Marketisation of welfare provision

The management of the public sector can be undertaken in many ways. In recent years a development has taken place in the use of market or market-like mechanisms for the management and development of the public sector, often labelled marketisation. Marketisation not only uses the market to deliver welfare goods and services, but there has also been a focus on using market mechanisms such as competition inside the public sector, so that different public providers are obliged to compete with each other on price, quality and amount of production.

A key theoretical principle here is principal–agent theory. In simplified terms, the issue is how the principal (state, municipality or the head of an institution) is able to get the agent (municipality manager, the employee) to be effective and do the best job and meet the desired objectives. The difficulty is that the principal does not necessarily have the same information as the agent (asymmetric information), and at the same time the agent, as a practitioner in the field, may have different opinions of what may be the best to do. There might even be combinations where the agent also has an interest in providing demand, such as the case with regard to general practitioners both providing services and upholding the interests of the client. There is also the risk that providers in a marketised system in a principal–agent relation try to cream-skim, that is they will try to get those cases, clients or customers which maximise their own income, implying a risk that those in need of more expensive care or support will not be given the proper treatment, or that the public sector will have to provide for the most difficult cases, whereas the private sector takes over the easiest cases.

To ensure that the provision of necessary services is available to the required quality there is a need for different instruments, such as tools to measure output. To promote this aim, different financial or other types of incentives are often also used.

There may be a number of problems with the use of incentives in the public sector, such as:

1   It is expensive to measure the effort and quality of the work, as this implies need for registration and collection of data.
2   Errors in measurements may occur, so that the principal does not know whether or not the stated aim has been achieved.
3   Tasks are best solved jointly, making it difficult to ensure all are doing what they should.
4   There may be a desire for professional autonomy, for example, among doctors and social workers.

Freedom of choice has also been introduced in many welfare state areas, for example between different providers of health care, dentistry, day care for children or certain types of old-age care. In several of these areas there might also be a relatively high charge for users. A high user charge can be a negative element of free choice systems, since it implies that the free choice is really only for some groups, but not for everyone. A free choice also requires that the individual can grasp the freedom of choice and that there is full understanding and transparency in a market.

Freedom of choice can have both advantages and disadvantages (Greve, 2010; see also Section 4.5 on conditions related to when choice is possible). It is considered an advantage because it makes the user stronger in relation to the supplier, and thus there is an opportunity to have a product that is tailor-made for the individual's need. It is considered a disadvantage because not everyone is able to grasp the freedom of choice and for some having to make choices is experienced as stressful.

Thus allowing free choice and use of market-like reforms can lead to greater inequality in access to a range of welfare benefits, but can also help to ensure that citizens are stronger and better able to reveal their preferences through their choices. It requires a concrete analysis of an area to assess the advantages and disadvantages, but is an example of the use of a market-type mechanism. Another market-type mechanism is to open direct competition between public and private providers by competitive tendering.

Competitive tendering of public activities can have both advantages and disadvantages. There are advantages if the private provider is able to deliver the goods to a higher quality and/or lower cost than the public sector, and this is done without deterioration of wages and working conditions for employees. It is also necessary to ensure that there is security of supply, so that even in a market system older people can continue to be cared for if a private provider goes bankrupt. It also requires that the transaction costs of supply do not exceed the benefits, and that ongoing monitoring of performance and compliance with the agreements is not very costly.

Another type of approach has focused on how to increase productivity in the public sector. In both the public and private sectors there is a constant desire and demand for increased productivity and more efficient production. In the private sector the calculation of changes in productivity is easier than in the public sector as there often are more standardised products and activities.

It can be very difficult to measure productivity in the welfare state when a service involves the relationships between people, including, for example, whether increased productivity by each childcare assistant caring for more children can be achieved without having a negative effect on the quality of care. There is also an expectation of increased production and efficiency in the public sector, for example, by the use of digital or other types of new technology.

The relation between market and state is not always a simple either/or. A large amount of goods are purchased from the private sector by the welfare state, and without income transfer many citizens would not be able to buy goods and services in shops. Public sector demand can also be a way of supporting development of the private sector by ensuring a certain demand for production. For example, the hearing-aid industry has developed because the public sector has supported individuals in buying hearing aids. Also in relation to medicine the public demand can be seen as necessary to provide sufficient demand. Thus a reduction in the welfare state's activities can also imply less private sector activity due to a fall in the demand for privately produced goods and services, and an increase in unemployment. In this sense there is a close connection between activities within the private and public sectors.

6.5 Summing-up

The chapter has illustrated a number of strengths and weaknesses in using markets and market-type mechanisms in the welfare state. The market is, in a number of areas, able to distribute goods and services cheaply and in accordance with individual preferences. In a number of other areas, and when the conditions for perfect competition are not met, the market mechanism implies high prices and lack of supply of certain goods and services. It can also imply that not all individuals have the same access to all goods and services. There might also be moral limits to the market's operation.

The different markets (such as markets for goods, labour and finance) all have different roles and importance to societies as well as individuals. Without regulation and intervention there would in some ways be a risk of higher prices and lower quality and poorer wages and working conditions. On the other hand, in several areas the market works as an effective allocator of resources. It is an empirical issue to find out where best to use the market and where to use public sector intervention; and if coping with market failure whether this should be done by regulating and/or by public sector provision or by use of taxes and duties. This is also due to the fact that there might be government sector failure.

The size of and areas for intervention in the market are based on both a theoretical argument for how to ensure that it reduces market failure, and reasons of justice even if the market is working. This also contributes to an understanding of why the welfare state looks different in different welfare regimes.

References

Barr, N. (2001), *The Welfare State as a Piggy Bank: Information, Risk, Uncertainty, and the Role of the State*. Oxford, Oxford University Press.

Greve, B. (ed.) (2010), *Choice, Challenges and Perspectives for European Welfare States*. Oxford, Wiley-Blackwell.

Musgrave, R. and Musgrave, P. (1989), *Public Finance in Theory and Practice*, 5th edition. New York, McGraw-Hill.

Rawls, J. (1971), *A Theory of Justice*. Cambridge, Cambridge University Press.

Sandel, M. J. (2012), *What Money Can't Buy: The Moral Limits of Markets*. London, Penguin.

Smith, A. (1776/1970), *Wealth and Nations*, London, J.M. Dent, Everyman's Library.

Stiglitz, J. (2000), *Economics of the Public Sector*. New York, W.W. Norton.

Chapter 7

The labour market

Employment and unemployment

Contents

7.1 Introduction

Chapter 6 presented the key elements of what a market is, including how it can fail. Unemployment and the risk that the market will not ensure full employment is one such possible type of failure. The importance of the labour market in most economies as a primary allocator of income, for example, is the reason for looking at the labour market here, specifically and in some detail. The centrality of the labour market implies a continuous need to try and grasp the varieties of and differences in policies related to it. Is the labour market a market at all, and what is the implication of describing it as a market? This chapter deals with a variety of aspects related to being employed or unemployed, ranging from issues around gaining an income, having social contacts and feeling included, to the impact and consequences for social policy of the increasingly strong demand for the unemployed to become active. The idea of the working poor and active labour market policy, which to a certain extent are contradictory, is also presented, including the relation to a demand-driven fiscal policy.

In recent years, several countries have witnessed a gradual reduction in the strength of industrial relations and the influence of trade unions. Furthermore, national labour markets have become weaker due to the more open labour markets that exist within the European Union. Here this chapter will also discuss cross-border mobility of labour and its possible impact on production structures, including global development and the impact on societal development. Finally, the chapter will present different kinds of labour market regimes including the interpretation of 'work-first' and 'workfare' approaches.

7.2   What is the labour market?

This section will answer a simple question: What is the labour market? The short answer is that this is the market where human resources are bought and sold, and the price is the wage paid for the work. However, there is not only one labour market. Employers and employees have different perceptions of the appropriate price of labour, but in a perfect market all those who are willing to work at the current wage rate can get a job. The labour market would therefore in the classical understanding of how a perfect market functions thus be clearing, that is there would be full employment. However, the level of unemployment indicates that this is not the case.

The labour market consists of many and very varied types of market. They may be distinguished based upon:

- geography (local, regional and national)
- qualifications (from highly specialised to unskilled workers), and
- types of production (from services to manufacturing).

There are thus differences in the labour market depending on how and where production is localised and also where people with the necessary qualifications are living. This interaction between numbers of jobs with specific requirements and numbers of people with these qualifications combined with the level of wages and existing infrastructure also helps to explain the concentration of different kinds of jobs and activities in specific geographical areas. It is, for example, easier to start up new production demanding highly qualified workers in areas where there already are many highly qualified people.

Location, relocation and change in production methods also play a role in the location of jobs. The overall structure of a country's economy and changes therein likewise influence the ability and possibility of getting a job in different locations. The outsourcing of jobs from Europe to Asian countries is just one example of this transformation. The constant restructuring of production and jobs implies a higher risk for some groups than others on the labour market.

Production structures have changed in many advanced economies. In general over the long time perspective there has been a shift from the agricultural sector to manufacturing and now to the service sector. This development has also changed the demand for labour, including, in many countries, a reduction in the demand for unskilled labour (although certain jobs in the service sector are unskilled), and an increase in demand for more specialised types of labour. These changes must be expected to continue.

Unemployment can be a result of these changes in the production system and relocation of production. Those people with qualifications for the old production structure become redundant and, unless they acquire new qualifications, will have difficulty in re-entering the labour market. Even after gaining new skills older people may have difficulties in getting a job compared with young people entering the field. Other types of unemployment relate to changes in the business cycle and seasonal changes in demand. With respect to the EU27, Figure 7.1 shows the trends in economic growth and unemployment levels,

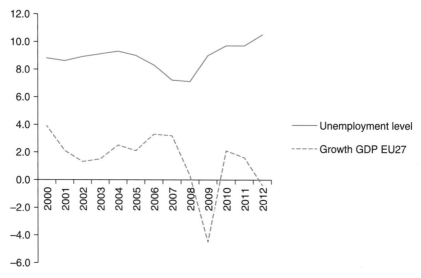

Figure 7.1 Unemployment and growth since 2000: GDP (yearly change) and level of unemployment as percentage of the labour force in the EU27.

Source: Based upon Eurostat data (online data codes: unemployment is une_rt_a; GDP is nama_gdp) (accessed 14 August 2013).

state, market and civil society

indicating how they interact with each other. Unemployment due to non-acceptance of the wage rate is often called classical unemployment.

As can be seen from Figure 7.1, the 2008 financial crisis was followed by an increase in the level of unemployment, so that a fall in economic activity had an impact on the number of people having a job. Sometimes it takes some time for growth in GDP to feed through into employment; even when the economy starts to grow it might take some time before the level of employment increases and unemployment decreases. Furthermore, in most economies there is a need for economic growth in order to ensure an increase in the number of jobs. This is due to the fact that there is often an increase in productivity, implying that the same amount of work can be done with fewer people and, therefore, in order to reduce the level of unemployment, economic growth needs to be greater than the increase in productivity.

The classical model of employment, whereby all who are willing to work at existing real wage rates can get a job, is difficult to achieve through public sector intervention (however, see Section 7.4, on some possible intervention, related to the ongoing wage rate). Cyclical unemployment, related to change in the overall level of economic activity, can be coped with if the necessary economic options, for example, financial means to expand economic activity, are available in a country. Economic policy might thus be able to support job creation to a limited extent.

Welfare states have had different ambitions related to full employment. The Nordic welfare states such as Denmark and Sweden, for example, have had a long-term aim of full employment through Keynesian demand-management intervention, that is spending more money or reducing taxes in times of recession, whereas the more classical understanding in a liberal welfare state such as the UK would not make any intervention, but would instead wait until the relative level of real wages has been reduced and thereby may increase the demand for labour.

Employment rates are in general higher for men than for women, although recent years have seen a movement towards greater equality in terms of labour market participation. This has been influenced by the welfare state providing day care for children (Thevenon, 2013).

On the other hand, the level of unemployment is often higher for women than for men (see Table 7.1). This is often related to fewer years on the labour market and the historical differences in educational attainment, as those groups with higher levels of qualifications generally have lower levels of unemployment. This is partly due to the fact that many unskilled jobs are now undertaken outside Europe given the outsourcing of the more traditional types of production to areas where the wage levels are very low. Recent years have seen in many welfare states a higher degree of gender equality regarding the educational attainment level.

Table 7.2 shows the employment rate for the population between the ages of 20 and 64 years. The employment rate is defined as those in employment aged between 20 and 64 years as a percentage of the total population of

Table 7.1 Unemployment in per cent and trends since 2000 in the EU28 and selected countries

	2000	2005	2009	2012	2012 Men	2012 Women
EU27	8.8	9.0	9.0	10.5	10.4	10.5
Czech Republic	8.8	7.9	6.7	7.0	6.0	8.2
Denmark	4.3	4.8	6.0	7.5	7.5	7.5
Germany	8.0	11.3	7.8	5.5	5.7	5.2
Spain	11.7	9.2	18.0	25.0	24.7	25.4
France	9.0	9.3	9.5	10.3	10.1	10.5
Italy	10.0	7.7	7.8	10.7	9.9	11.9
Hungary	6.3	7.2	10.0	10.9	11.2	10.6
Sweden	5.6	7.7	8.3	8.0	8.2	7.7
United Kingdom	5.4	4.8	7.6	7.9	8.3	7.4

Source: Eurostat (une_rt_a) (accessed 14 August 2013).

the same age group. The indicator is based on the EU Labour Force Survey. The employed population consists of those persons who, during the week when the survey was conducted, did any work for pay or profit for at least one hour, or were not working but had jobs from which they were temporarily absent. A high employment rate thus implies that more people are in the labour market.

Table 7.2 shows that there are differences among countries in relation to the employment rate. Three of the four south/east European countries (Italy, Hungary and Spain) have a lower employment rate than the EU average and the north/west countries, especially Denmark, Sweden and Germany, have a high employment rate. Table 7.2 shows the overall employment rate for both men and women. In all countries the employment rates are higher for men than for women, by on average 11.2 per cent, with Italy having the largest difference (close to 20 per cent) and Denmark the lowest at below 7 per cent. Over the last 20–25 years there has been a tendency towards a smaller difference, implying that both men and women are in the labour market. This has had effects on the work–family life balance.

The employment rate is one issue. Another central issue relates to the level and degree of unemployment. Table 7.1 shows unemployment levels in the selected countries since 2000; for 2012 a gender breakdown is also provided. The unemployment rate is calculated as the number of unemployed persons as a percentage of the labour force based on the International Labour Office (ILO) definition. The data represent those who are without work and actively searching for a job during the week sampled and able to start work within the next two weeks.

Table 7.1 shows that in 2012 Spain had the highest level of unemployment and Germany the lowest; this was despite the fact that Germany had the highest

Table 7.2 Employment rate in per cent (20 to 64 years) in the EU28 and selected countries since 2000

	2000	2005	2009	2012
EU27	62.2	63.4	64.5	64.2
Czech Republic	65.0	64.8	65.4	66.5
Denmark	76.3	75.9	75.3	72.6
Germany	65.6	65.5	70.3	72.8
France	67.8	69.4	69.4	69.3
Spain	56.3	63.3	59.8	55.4
Italy	53.7	57.6	57.5	56.8
Hungary	56.3	56.9	55.4	57.2
Sweden	73.0	72.5	72.2	73.8
United Kingdom	71.2	71.7	69.9	70.1

Source: Eurostat (lfsi_emp_a) (accessed 14 August 2013).

level in 2005. The higher level of unemployment in general in 2012 reflects the impact of the financial crisis on the welfare state and thereby also that change in economic activity influences welfare state spending and income by changing levels of unemployment. Historically, women used to have a higher level of unemployment than men. This is no longer the case, and there is no clear pattern among the countries. Unemployment is higher for women in the Czech Republic, Spain, France, Hungary and Italy and lower in Germany, Sweden and the UK, and equal in Denmark. At the EU27 level, unemployment among men and women is close to equal.

Unemployment can also be measured in ways other than as overall percentages. This includes differences in the level of unemployment depending on skill levels and education. Unemployment is frequently higher for unskilled workers. In recent years, many European countries have had very high unemployment rates for young people below the age of 30. Workers above the age of 55 who lose their jobs also have difficulties in getting re-employed. Native workers often have both a higher employment rate and a lower unemployment rate than migrant workers. Reasons range from discrimination to the lack of acceptance of migrants' qualifications. In addition migrants may lack the linguistic and cultural competences necessary for getting and keeping a job. Thus unemployment patterns can differ from country to country and from region to region depending on the availability of jobs and demographic changes, such as how many workers are exiting the labour market (through early retirement, pension, etc.) and how many newcomers are entering the labour market.

Not only is short-term unemployment a problem. Increasingly a specific problem is long-term unemployment, which is defined as having been unemployed for more than a year.

Having a job might be one issue. Another is the quality of the job both on a daily and lifelong basis. It can be difficult to measure the quality of a job, as this might be related to individual preferences, and depend on other available types of jobs. Box 7.1 shows seven possible features of job quality.

These issues will be returned to later, for example, with regard to family life, flexicurity and equality. The dimensions relating to job quality indicate the job's importance. Dimensions of job quality also indicate that there can be different important related issues involved. For example, a job with poor safety standards and thereby a high risk of work injury may be less interesting than a stable job without risk of injuries where one can stay for a longer time. A high income for a short period of time can also be less important than a long-term stable income.

In general the focus is often on employment or unemployment. However, there is also underemployment. This is defined as when an employed person is willing and able to work more hours than the employer is willing to offer. A recent estimate suggests that in the UK underemployment was as high as 9.9 per cent in 2012, up from 6.2 per cent in 2008, and even higher for young persons (Bell and Blanchflower, 2011; National Institute of Economic and Social Research, 2013). This has two implications: it reduces job quality and, with a lower income than the worker would like, the underemployed may join the working poor.

7.3   Consequences of being or not being in the labour market

Not being in the labour market usually implies a lower standard of living. The replacement rate, that is the economic compensation of unemployment benefit for those eligible for it, is often low compared with actual income before becoming unemployed. The calculation of the rate also takes the impact of the tax system into consideration. So, in the short run there is a direct negative impact on consumption possibilities and individual welfare when moving from being employed to being unemployed.

Table 7.3 shows the replacement rate for a person earning the average income, comparing single persons with married persons receiving unemployment benefits. The data use the net replacement rate; the impact of taxes on benefits and previous income has been taken into consideration, when comparing across countries. This type of calculation can also be used to compare the generosity of different benefits within a country. Possible supplements of housing benefits or other social benefits are not included, thereby showing the direct impact of the unemployment benefit.

Table 7.3 shows a different picture than expected, with the highest replacement rate being in the Czech Republic, France and Germany, and the lowest in the UK. Part of the explanation for the UK's position lies in the fact that economic support to the unemployed is higher regarding cash benefits to pay for accommodation, although also here the UK, with the exception of Australia within the OECD countries, has the lowest level. The often higher level of replacement for a married person than for a single person lies in the way the tax and benefit systems in many countries are organised. There is thus often an option to use the spouse's personal tax allowance, and further, when calculating social benefits, the household income and the number of persons who share[1] the income are relevant to the level of benefits available.

Being unemployed for a short while might not have a long-lasting negative social impact, but being unemployed for longer periods in most welfare states also reduces lifetime income dramatically. This can include the level of pensions as this also often depends on the number of years on the labour market and the money paid into a pension fund. The labour market not only influences welfare

Table 7.3 Net percentage replacement rate in 2011 for a single person and two-earner married couple with average income and without children in selected EU countries

Country	Single	Two-earner married couple
Czech Republic	65	84
Denmark	57	74
France	66	80
Germany	59	83
Hungary	54	73
Italy	55	74
Spain	58	75
Sweden	46	68
UK	13	49

Source: OECD, Tax-benefit models (www.oecd.org/els/social/workincentives) (accessed 14 August 2013).

in the short run, but might also have longer lasting impact, including the degree of social inclusion/exclusion.

An issue often discussed in relation to the level of economic compensation due to unemployment is whether it pays to work, sometimes labelled the unemployment trap or poverty trap. The argument is that there should be a clear economic incentive to take up a job, and if the economic incentive is too little, then too many will not actively be searching for a job in all welfare states. However, as the data in Table 7.3 show, there is a clear economic incentive to take up a job. This is also the case in other liberal welfare states such as Australia and the USA. In the USA access to other types of welfare, such as medical insurance, is an incentive to stay on the labour market. Besides economic incentives, it is important to be aware that having a job also helps reduce the risk of social exclusion. Most people prefer to have something for which to get up in the mornings, and people in the labour force are often happier than those who are unemployed.

Furthermore, those not on the labour market have a higher risk of living in poverty and in addition might have fewer social contacts. The lack of a position on the labour market, at least until reaching the normal age of retirement, can thus in itself have negative repercussions on living standards and social integration in many societies.

Access to welfare benefits and services can also be dependent on being on the labour market, including the ability to pay for certain services. Depending on the welfare state system, having a job and an income can have an impact on access to health care and childcare, but also wider implications for being socially integrated into society.

Unemployment might thus have a wider impact than just lack of money for a period of time. This further relates to the often negative perception of the unemployed, especially in times of low levels of unemployment. Longer spells of unemployment can imply a higher risk of divorce, loss of self-esteem, risk of personal bankruptcy, pressure to move to cheaper accommodation and so on. Unemployment is thus not only a cost for society (loss of possible production), but also has a high impact on individuals' welfare.

7.4   Active labour market policy – stick or carrot?

In recent years the focus has been on how to activate people to ensure that they can get a job again. A core issue has been whether the rhetoric of active labour market policy has the same meaning and implications in all cases and all countries. Historically, Active Labour Market Policy (ALMP) was developed in Sweden in order to cope with a lack of jobs in times of recession. The core argument for implementing ALMP is that there is market failure, that is without intervention there will not be a balance between supply and demand for labour. The main reason for this relates to lack of transparency among the different markets, a possible rigid wage structure and a low level of investment in employability.

Activation is often demanded by the state, related to individuals receiving, in particular, unemployment benefits and social assistance. Those who want to receive these benefits are thus obliged to be active in order to be eligible for these benefits. This is to a high degree the relation and balance between rights and duties when receiving support from the welfare state: you will have to show you are trying to get a job.

Four ideal types of active labour market policy are shown in Table 7.4, which gives an indication of the various possible instrument and types of ALMP. They vary between countries, regimes and over time (see also Table 7.7). Active labour market policy thus focuses on how to redress market failures related to not achieving full employment in an economy and therefore focuses on employment incentives, training, the integration of disabled people, direct job creation and start-up incentives. Various measures have been used in different countries. In the EU27 countries a varied emphasis on different kinds of these active labour market policies has been witnessed. There is, however, an ongoing debate as to whether they are effective or not (Card et al., 2010). If the ALMP is not effective in ensuring a way back to the labour market this can be due to overall economic conditions, but also that the instruments used are not the best to get people back into work. If the effectiveness is not strong it can be argued that the welfare state could better use the money for other types of activities, whereas the counter-argument is that an ALMP that increases human capital, for example, can also increase the social capital of society.

Table 7.4 Four ideal types of active labour market policy

Type	Objective	Tools
Incentive reinforcement	Strengthen positive and negative work incentives for people on benefit	– Tax credits, in-work benefits – Time limits on recipiency – Benefit reductions – Benefits conditionality – Sanctions
Employment assistance	Remove obstacle to employment and facilitate (re-)entry into the labour market	– Placement services – Job subsidies – Counselling – Job search programmes
Occupation	Keep jobless people occupied; limit human capital depletion during unemployment	– Job creation schemes in the public sector – Non-employment-related training programmes
Human capital investment	Improve the chances of finding employment by upskilling jobless people	– Basic education – Vocational training

Source: Bonoli (2010, p. 11).

In principle the ambition of active labour market policy has been to ensure social inclusion on the labour market. A question here is whether the focus has been on commodification or inclusion and what types of welfare-to-work regimes have been used. Dean (2007) developed a typology with four different types of welfare-to-work regimes:

1 Human capital development (egalitarian and competitive in focus).
2 Coercive – work-first (authoritarian and competitive in focus).
3 Active job creation (egalitarian and inclusive in focus).
4 Insertion/right to work (authoritarian and inclusive in focus).

An important question concerning ALMP is whether it is a workfare regime or whether the focus is on ensuring social inclusion by focusing on the human capital development approach. Different countries have pursued different strategies in order to get unemployed people back in the labour market. In general it is assumed that in the last 10–15 years there has been increased focus on the 'work-first' approach, even if the consequence has been that people become members of the working poor, that is even when they have a job their income is below the poverty line. Dean's (2007) typology can be used when trying to understand labour market policy and reforms in different countries and different regions. The Nordic welfare states especially have historically focused on human capital development, whereas liberal and continental welfare states if pursuing an ALMP have focused more on 'work-first' and a more coercive approach. Thus many countries have ALMP, but they might be very different in scope and approach.

Active labour market policy can further focus on sticks and/or carrots. Sticks relate to reductions in benefits if someone does not take a job and or is not very actively searching for one, whereas the carrots relate to both the economic and social incentives to get a job, and provide help to get back in the labour market. Different countries have pursued different strategies which have changed over the business cycle. It can be difficult to ensure that an ALMP has a positive impact especially in times of high levels of unemployment. Change in the ALMP in different countries can be analysed by looking into the purpose of the activation and whether this mainly focuses on one of the different types of welfare-to-work regimes referred to above.

Table 7.5 shows spending on labour market policy (passive as well as active) as percentages of GDP and changes therein since 2005. Data on active and passive measures in the selected EU countries is given for 2011. Table 7.5 is a reminder of both the diversities among countries in relation to labour market policy, and the impact of the economic crisis with the consequent growing number of unemployed. Spending on activation is emphasised in countries like Denmark, Sweden and France, and less so in Italy, Hungary and the Czech Republic – again an indication of a Europe divided into two blocs. In relation to labour market policy, there might be differences in the degree of training, further education, placement in the private or public sector, support for people with

Table 7.5 Spending on labour market policy since 2005 as percentages of GDP, and for 2011 split between expenditure on active and passive labour market policy

	2005	2006	2007	2008	2009	2010	2011	Active	Passive
EU27	2.011	1.830	1.607	1.622	2.179	:	:	1.637	0.542
Czech Republic	0.471	0.473	0.446	0.418	0.712	0.700	0.558	0.276	0.282
Denmark	3.767	3.230	2.660	2.407	3.192	3.660	3.741	2.091	1.650
Germany	2.995	2.608	2.030	1.908	2.529	2.281	1.835	0.798	1.037
Spain	2.136	2.162	2.177	2.596	3.785	3.991	3.601	0.793	2.808
France	2.488	2.317	2.178	2.027	2.426	2.589	2.341	0.936	1.405
Italy	1.288	1.213	1.101	1.226	1.782	1.803	1.701	0.338	1.363
Hungary	0.721	0.702	0.713	0.721	1.170	1.359	1.015	0.357	0.658
Sweden	2.395	2.247	1.712	1.387	1.789	1.864	1.679	1.050	0.629
United Kingdom	0.621	0.512	0.480	0.518	0.715	:	:	0.674	0.041

Source: Eurostat (lmp_ind_exp) (accessed 14 August 2013).

Note: Active and Passive for EU27 and the UK is from 2009.

':' implies missing data.

disabilities or public employment services. This is partly due to different historical traditions, and partly the different labour markets. It also reflects different labour market regimes.

Changes in spending on passive labour market policy (unemployment and early retirement benefit) are influenced not only by the number of people unemployed, but also the generosity of the unemployment benefit system. Trends in recent years have been a reduction in the level of the replacement rate, this implies that despite increases in the number of beneficiaries, the overall level of expenditure might remain the same. This also implies weaker automatic stabilisers in the economies over the business cycle as unemployment goes up or down.

7.5   Changes in industrial relations

The regulation of labour markets is often based upon relations between employers and employees. The balance between employers and employees and the state differs from country to country. In some there is a strong tradition of integrating and using labour market partners in corporative or tri-partite negotiations, in others the market is to a larger degree left alone.

Wage bargaining and new collective agreements can either be centralised or decentralised and in some cases core issues are agreed at the central level (such as working time, holidays, leave, pension contributions, minimum income) whereas the precise levels of income can be agreed locally. This may depend on the sector and economic development, etc. So a combination of local and central wage bargaining often takes place. The increase in international labour markets and migration within the EU has increased the need for, but at the same time also the possibility of, making international instead of national collective agreements. As yet this has been limited. There are very few agreements crossing borders at the EU level.

The union density rate has fallen from 27.8 to 23.4 since 2000. From 2000 to 2008 the union density in Europe fell by 3 million people to 43 million. At present 140 million workers are not members of a trade union. There are considerable differences among the European countries, with the highest density rate being in Sweden, Denmark and Finland (close to 70 per cent) and lowest in Estonia, France and Lithuania (below 10 per cent) with the UK being close to the EU average of around 25 per cent (European Commission, 2011). The weakening of union density also implies that a large degree of the wage bargaining which takes place centrally has been reduced, increasing wage flexibility. Collective agreements often cover larger groups of workers than those who are directly members of the trade unions, however, they imply a bottom line which is used as a reference for wage bargaining.

Flexicurity has been an important issue in debates on industrial relations and labour market developments. It is defined as:

a policy strategy to enhance, at the same time and in a deliberate way, the flexibility of labor markets, the work organisation and employment relations on the one hand, and security – employment security and social security – notably for weaker groups in and outside the labor market, on the other hand.

(Wilthagen and Tros, 2004, p. 125)

Table 7.6, which shows possible combinations and different aspects of flexicurity, helps to explain why there are as many different understandings and interpretations of flexicurity as there are many and varied combinations of job security (related to having a specific job), employment security (related to being able to get and keep a job) and income security (often through unemployment benefits). This can be seen in combination with flexibility in the workplace and flexibility regarding wages from work. Flexibility is especially related to the debate on how to hire and fire people in the labour market. Employers want a high degree of flexibility whereas the employed would prefer a higher degree of security.

The degree of employment protection can be an indicator of how easy it is to hire and fire employees. This varies among the countries in Europe. In some it is very difficult to sack a person when once employed; in others the period for redundancy notice is rather short.

There has thus been an important change in the labour markets in Europe and a weaker position for the trade unions, implying a higher degree of market-oriented approach to employment and income, weakening the impact of collective agreements on developments in the labour market. The last 10–15 years have seen a reduction in economic security in relationship to redundancy, increasing the negative impacts on individuals who are made redundant and who are not able to re-enter the labour market, and also

Table 7.6 Trade-offs and interconnections between types of flexibility and types of security

Flexibility:	Job security	Employment security	Income security	Combination security
External – numerical				
Internal – numerical				
Functional				
Wages/variable pay				

Source: Tros and Wilthagen (2013, p. 128).

especially in southern Europe a tendency to make it easier to sack people as a measure to achieve a more flexible labour market. The change in industrial relations points to an overall weaker position of labour in the European labour market with 'flexicurity' moving towards more flexibility and less security.

In the wake of fiscal crisis and the tightening of wages and working conditions in the private sector as well as the public sector there has been a number of strikes and protests in Europe (European Commission, 2013).

7.6 Labour market regimes – new structuring of societies

There are different kinds of labour market regimes. The focus depends on how they combine welfare with labour market policies. Table 7.7 shows different combinations of welfare regimes with types of labour market policy (including goals and ideology) with a focus on European approaches and shows that there has been a stronger focus on a work-first approach in most EU countries despite the high level of unemployment. The focus on ALMP (see also Table 7.5), differs among countries in the EU. The table further highlights that people in different regimes can expect a variety in the emphasis and generosity of unemployment benefits and the state's ambition to create, or not, full employment. Table 7.7 is not meant to imply that all countries within a specific category display all the characteristics of that category and none of

Table 7.7 Combinations of welfare regime with labour market policy

Welfare regime	Coverage unemployment benefit	Focus on ALMP	Goal of labour market policy	Ideological approach
Nordic	Comprehensive – although replacement rate has been reduced	Yes – central	Integration, full employment	Equality, Keynesian intervention, however increased focus on work-first
Corporatist/ Continental European	Less strong – lower replacement rate	Relatively important	Reduce pressure on public sector spending	State with corporatist inclusion labour market partner
Liberal	Weak	Only limited	If, then focus on business	Efficiency, liberal non-intervention
Southern/ Eastern Europe	Very incomplete	Only weakly developed	To reduce use of benefit system	Emphasis on civil society

state, market and civil society

the others from other categories. It represents the typical case of countries within that specific category, like in the presentation of welfare regimes in Chapter 3. Thus, for example, we can expect a Nordic country like Denmark to have a strong focus on ALMP, that the corporatist countries such as France and Germany will do so to a lesser degree, even less so in a liberal country like the UK, and only rarely in countries of southern and eastern Europe.

Table 7.7 can be used to reflect upon which countries offer greater support for lifelong learning. The expectation would be that this will be the case in the Nordic and corporatist countries (Denmark, Sweden, Germany and France) given that this would increase the likelihood of people continuing to be integrated in the labour market and ensure employability, whereas it is less likely in the UK, the Czech Republic, Hungary, Spain and Italy.

Table 7.8 focuses on a combination of labour market policies and the degree of employment protection. This is a further illustration of the difference in flexicurity approaches. These different combinations illustrate various employment regimes and the degree of protection they offer, the extent of labour market policies used, and countries' approaches to labour market and labour market policy. They can thus also be seen as a mirror of the welfare regimes as depicted in Chapter 3.

In countries with weak employment protection and weak labour market policies, individuals face a higher risk of being among the working poor, that is having a job on the labour market and still having an income below the poverty line.

A focus on work-first as part of labour market policy, for example, having a job is better than no job at all, can for some imply that they will not be able to search for a job that matches their qualifications and will be forced to take up any job available. This may be despite the fact that it results in them having an income below the poverty line and that their competences are less used than in a job better matching their qualifications. This development has also been affected by weaker industrial relations.

Table 7.8 Different combinations of employment protection and labour market policies

		Employment protection	
Labour market policies		Strong	Weak
	Large	Continental corporatist countries (e.g. Germany)	Northern welfare states (e.g. Denmark)
	Small	Southern European countries (e.g. Italy)	Liberal welfare states (e.g. UK)

Source: Based on Eichorst et al. (2010).

7.7 Global and regional impact – free movement of workers

A nation's own labour market used to be the only consideration national govern- ments needed to be concerned with. However, the increasingly global and regional integration of economic policy and labour markets has meant that migration has also had an impact on the functioning of welfare states. Increasingly, the relocation of production and outsourcing of some activities also influences the development of labour markets, presumably implying a reduced need for unskilled workers in most of the Western world, and thereby also creating difficulties in helping people with few qualifications back into the labour market in case of redundancy.

Countries with high levels of unemployment face the risk that workers will migrate abroad in order to find a job in another country and perhaps return if and when they are needed. Countries with low levels of unemployment might benefit from this, but they also risk workers staying or becoming redundant when the economic business cycle changes. Countries with comparatively high wage levels risk an inflow of foreign workers who are prepared to work for a lower wage, placing pressure on the existing workforce to reduce their wages. Push (for example, a high level of unemployment) and pull factors (for example, higher wages) thus have an impact on the mobility and migration of labour. Migrant workers who lose their jobs might be more willing and prepared to work in the hidden part of society, often labelled the grey or underground economy, including doing jobs for a very low wage where they do not have to pay tax. Thus the hidden economy also plays a role in the way the labour market works in different countries.

The free movement of workers has been one of the cornerstones of European integration since the Treaty of Rome. Since the 2004 enlargement, many workers, especially from Poland and the Baltic countries, have moved to western Europe, including the UK, in order to take up jobs. This has led to debate on wage dumping, as those arriving have been willing to work for lower wages, and even below the agreed or decided minimum wage in different parts of the labour market. This has resulted in a debate on the working or not working poor and also how migration might be influencing national labour markets and national labour market policies.

Workers exercising the right to free movement also have access to social security, welfare transfers and services under the same rules as national citi- zens. In some countries this has placed pressure on the welfare system, while at the same time helping to ensure a sufficient labour supply to reduce the risk of bottlenecks, for example, that there is unemployment in some sectors, but lack of labour supply in others, on the labour market.

Whether the impact of free movement of workers implies social dumping or improved labour market efficiency is a matter for empirical analysis as it depends on the overall situation in the economy, the specific sector in question, and whether the actual agreed or legally binding rules for workers on the labour market are fulfilled.

The EU has employment strategies, which shows that this is no longer an issue for nation states alone and also that European integration has an impact on national options and development (see also Chapter 12).

Furthermore, there are global trends whereby some enterprises relocate to other countries with consequent losses and gains in employment. The relocation of production thus can have both positive and negative impacts on the employment situation and presumably will continue to influence the structure of the labour market.

7.8   Summing-up

The labour market has a central role in modern welfare states. It provides income and social relations to and for many people. The labour market can work both as an integrator and as an exclusion device. Having something to do is important for many, and in that context having a job is often very important to individuals' lives, well-being and happiness.

Countries pursue different kinds of labour market policy according to their various welfare regimes. They have different approaches, ranging from an active intervention to help make the labour market function, to almost leaving the labour market to itself. Active labour market policies can focus on using a work-first approach or on ensuring the necessary qualifications to stay in the labour market. Sticks and carrots are employed differently in various types of labour market systems. The generosity of unemployment benefits varies between countries and thereby income security, job security and flexibility differ. The trend has been towards lower levels of both income and job security.

Labour markets have become gradually more international and the free movement of workers in the EU has had an impact on this development. This has had repercussions on the more affluent welfare states in Europe with increased inflow of labour. Consequently there is an expectation that working conditions will converge over time. One example is that wage levels within Europe are often, on average, relatively close to each other.

Note

1   Thus the first person counts as one, and the second, for example, counts as 0.5. Thus an income of 15,000 euro will be seen as an average for such a household as 10,000 euro – compared with 15,000 for a single person, and benefits such as housing benefits will be higher for the couple than for the individual. The rationale of counting the second person as less than the first is the ability to share costs and it is often as cheap to be a two-person household as a one-person household.

References

Bell, D. and Blanchflower, D. (2011), Underemployment in the UK in the Great Recession. *National Institute Economic Review*, no. 215, p. r1–r11. DOI: 10.1177/0027950111401141.

Bonoli, G. (2010), *The Political Economy of Active Labour Market Policy*. REC-WP 01/2012, Working Pages on the Reconciliation of Work and Welfare in Europe (RECWOWE). Edinburgh, Dissemination and Dialogue Centre.

Card, D., Kluve, J. and Weber, A. (2010), Active Labour Market Policy Evaluations: A Meta-Analysis. *Economic Journal*, vol. 120, F452–F477.

Dean, H. (2007), The Ethics of Welfare-to-work. *Policy & Politics*, vol. 35, no. 4, pp. 573–89.

Eichhorst, W., Feil, M. T. and Marx, P. (2010), Crisis, What Crisis? Patterns of Adaptation in European Labor Markets. *IZA Discussion Paper*, No. 5045.

European Commission (2011), *Industrial Relations in Europe 2010*. Brussels, European Commission.

European Commission (2012), *New Skills and Jobs in Europe*: Pathways towards Full Employment. Brussels, European Commission.

European Commission (2013), *Industrial Relations in Europe 2013*. Brussels, European Commission.

National Institute of Economic and Social Research (2013), *Underemployment in the UK*. Press Release, 2 May. Available at http://niesr.ac.uk/press/underemployment-uk-11285#.Ukfh48fU9D8 (accessed 9 June 2014).

Thevenon, O. (2013), *Drivers of Female Labour Force Participation in the OECD*. OECD Social, Employment and Migration Working Papers No. 145. Paris, OECD.

Tros, F. and Wilthagen, T. (2013), Flexicurity: Concepts, Practices, and Outcomes. In Greve, B. (ed.), *Routledge International Handbook of the Welfare State*. Abingdon, Routledge, pp. 125–135.

Wilthagen, T. and Tros, F. (2004), The Concept of 'Flexicurity': A New Approach to Regulating Employment and Labour Markets. *Transfer*, vol. 10, no. 2, pp. 166–86.

Civil society

Contents

8.1 Introduction

The relationship between state, market and civil society, the welfare mix, has been a central issue in the discussion about welfare states for a long time. Previous chapters have dealt with the market and the state, without including the role of civil society. The discussion about the welfare mix includes questions about who is responsible for what, who will take over if another person or institution fails to provide welfare, and how to balance individual freedom with societal intervention. Thus this chapter will begin by presenting the welfare mix, in order to depict the boundaries between the three central institutional providers of welfare in welfare states.

Families are a central institution in most societies both in terms of social connections and as being essential for children's development and childcare. In most welfare states women now are engaged in the labour market at more or less the same rate as men (see also Chapter 7). However, this raises new issues concerning the balancing of work and family life – including who takes care of the children and how and, in some circumstances, who takes care of elderly relatives – which also refers back to the presentation of the social invest-ment perspective of welfare states, as shown in Chapter 3. This chapter pays particular attention to the balance between state and civil society. Furthermore, it discusses families' lives and roles in modern societies, including, for example, if having a close relative has an impact on daily life and whether the ability to have someone to talk with on important issues matters. The role of the volun-tary sector as part of civil society will also be presented and discussed.

Social capital is basic for societal cohesion and also the functioning of fami-lies and civil society. Trust in others can be seen as an issue that is important for modern societies. This is therefore the focus of Section 8.4.

8.2   The welfare mix

The balance between state, market and civil society is often labelled the welfare mix. This relates to the fact that services including care, but also some income transfers, can be financed and/or delivered by the state, the market or civil society.

The concept and understanding of what civil society is have been much debated historically, including whether or not to include the family in the under-standing of the civil society. Therefore, in some understandings of the concept, voluntary and other associations are part of the civil society, and it has also been used as a metaphor for the good society, and by this

> represents the institutionalization of 'civility' as a different way of living in the world, a different kind of society in which all institutions operate in ways that reinforce these positive social norms so that society *becomes* 'a society that is civil'.
>
> (Edwards, 2009, p. 47)

Box 8.1 World Bank's definition of civil society

The World Bank has adopted a definition of civil society developed by a number of leading research centers:

> the term civil society [refers] to the wide array of non-governmental and not-for-profit organizations that have a presence in public life, expressing the interests and values of their members or others, based on ethical, cultural, political, scientific, religious or philanthropic considerations. Civil Society Organizations (CSOs) therefore refer to a wide array of organizations: community groups, non-governmental organizations (NGOs), labor unions, indigenous groups, charitable organizations, faith-based organizations, professional associations, and foundations.
>
> (http://go.worldbank.org/4CE7W046K0 (accessed 15 August 2013))

There can therefore be many and varied definitions of what the civil society is. In Box 8.1 the World Bank's definition of civil society is presented to indicate an understanding of the concept where the focus is on organisations, although they are non-governmental and not-for profit organisations.

Here civil society is broadly understood as encompassing everything from family to voluntary organisations, and also voluntary work for or without profit, thereby including the family in civil society despite the fact that it has a different function than associations and other institutions. It can be useful to analyse separately the function of the family and the rest of civil society given that the family and also the extended family by social bonds often have a stronger commitment to support a person than might be the case of the rest of the civil society. For the purpose here it is sufficient to be aware that there is a distinction and this might have an impact on the way civil society works in the welfare state (although as discussed later in this section there is the risk of voluntary failure).

The balance between the institutions of the state, the market and civil society has never been and will never be stable. There will be changes in who is providing, who is financing and what the roles of the different actors are, and how they interact with each other. Historically, for example, most care has been undertaken by the family or at least within the extended family. The first poor laws laid down in England in the sixteenth century show that institutional support from outside the family was very low. This remains the case with the Catholic understanding of subsidiarity originating with Pope Pius XI in 1931. This Catholic understanding has had a strong impact on welfare delivery and welfare states especially in southern European countries such as Spain and Italy. Here the state is often seen as the lender of last resort, with only more marginal state support and intervention, and a stronger role for the family. In the Protestant countries the focus has also been on the role of the family, but less strongly, and with a strong emphasis on employer and state involvement to support those in need without fault of their own, for example, in a country such as Germany.

This is also a reflection of the way societies were organised, as most women worked at home or supported their men by working in the field or in the shop. Gradually there has been a movement towards more gender equality in access to the labour market with this being most profound in the Nordic welfare states as seen in countries like Denmark and Sweden. There has also been a desire from the states for both genders to be employed especially in recent years because of the demographic changes that are expected, e.g. the possible decline in the size of the labour force. These changes have left some elderly people and especially children without care or at risk of having little care, and have thereby paved the way for the welfare state to take over care from the family, especially for children during daytime. In some countries, especially in the Nordic countries within Europe, the state relatively early on provided affordable and high quality day care for children, whereas in other countries, such as the UK, childcare was mainly left to private initiatives. Gradually, most EU countries have shifted towards greater state responsibility for providing childcare, tipping the balance between state and civil society towards the state. Childcare is an example of a service that in principle could be, and has been, provided by the market or by voluntary activities. Still, in several welfare states there are also private and market-based solutions to the delivery of childcare. The focus on and increase in state-provided care can also be understood as using a social investment perspective on the role of the welfare states (see Chapter 3).

The welfare triangle of the relations between state, market and civil society is depicted in Figure 8.1. The 'welfare mix' refers to the way in which welfare provision is balanced between the three, and it might also sometimes be labelled the mixed economy of welfare. The balance may differ from society to society and within the same society over time. The mixed economies of welfare can, if splitting the civil society into more spheres, be understood as public, private, voluntary, mutual aid or informal provision of welfare (Spicker, 1995).

There is no theoretical argument for any specific balance being the best as normative values are involved concerning which of the three is favoured. This is, for example, at the core of the debate which is taking place in the UK about the Big Society. In many other European welfare states the roles of the family

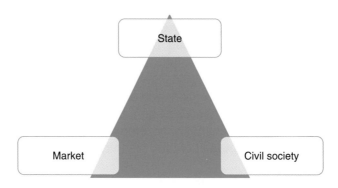

Figure 8.1 The welfare triangle.

and voluntary sector as important ways of delivering welfare have been ongoing issues. It is important to make a concrete analysis of the consequences regarding access, distribution, effectiveness and so on by choosing the specific balance between the three actors, as the theoretical presentation only can point to strengths and weaknesses of using the different actors. The welfare state therefore might have a different balance and interactions among the three sectors, and presumably an ever-changing balance.

The balance between the three sectors is often reflected in the way welfare states are organised within the various welfare regimes (see Chapter 3). Thus in the liberal model like the UK, the market has a greater responsibility than in the Nordic model, as in Denmark, where the state has a more central role, and in the continental model such as Germany and France, where there is an emphasis on both state and market. In southern and eastern Europe, families have a high degree of responsibility, and in the USA voluntary economic and in-kind support are seen as essential. This can naturally vary within the different countries and in various areas of welfare, but these variations are indications of how the mix can be balanced and how there might be change between state and market, market and civil society and civil society and state.

The market is often seen as one of the major institutions in modern societies, given its ability to circulate goods and services and establish contacts between buyers and sellers. The need for the market and market provision in the welfare sector is less obvious, as many of those who need welfare services have low incomes (see also Chapter 6).

In the UK, the growth in the voluntary sector was a central element of New Labour's vision of the Third Way in the late 1990s (Giddens, 1998). This changed only marginally from 2010 with the Conservative/Liberal Democrat coalition government's focus on civil society and the Big Society. For some this has been related to the ambition to expand social welfare, for others it is more strongly related to reductions in public sector spending. Taken together there is a line from Giddens's Third Way with a focus on creating the '"enabling state" with a firm emphasis on the individualised duties and responsibilities of citizens' (Jamieson, 2012, p. 451) to the present debates on the Big Society and the inclusion of other actors.

In the UK, Prime Minister David Cameron's introduction of the idea of the Big Society is an attempt to place greater emphasis on civil society's role in providing welfare. This is reflected in a speech he gave in 2011, quoted in Box 8.2. It revolves around the ideas of decentralisation, a higher degree of user involvement and individual responsibility, and philanthropy taking on and financing more welfare. Voluntary work is further expected to take on larger responsibility, thus once again the issue of the correct balance between state and civil society is raised. Both the USA and the UK are examples of countries which have placed greater reliance on voluntary social contributions than have other welfare states. However, in most European countries the civil society is also expected to participate in caring and support including economically within families.

Quote from David Cameron's speech on the 14 February 2011:

> First of all, we have got to devolve more power to local government, and beyond local government, so people can actually do more and take more power. Secondly, we have got to open up public services, make them less monolithic, say to people: if you want to start up new schools, you can; if you want to set up a co-op or a mutual within the health service, if you're part of the health service, you can; say to organisations like the Big Issue: if you want to expand and replicate yourself across the country, we want you to.
>
> The third part, but it is only a part, is yes, I think it would be good if we had more philanthropic giving, more charitable giving and more volunteering in our country, so that all of those three things need to happen.
>
> (http://www.number10.gov.uk/news/pms-speech-on-big-society/)

'Civil society' does not just refer to the family, as shown earlier, but also voluntary activities and organisations. Some see voluntary organisations as an option for avoiding the possible stigmatisation related to contact with the public sector and for avoiding contact with bureaucracy. Still, there is a tension between the independence of voluntary organisations and their need, sometimes, for state support in order to function. Voluntary organisations have thus been seen as a possible way of reviving democracy in the public welfare system.

The core debate has a link to what has been labelled 'voluntary failure', reflecting that there is not only market and government failure, but also possible failures by other types of provision and delivery. Voluntary failure is related to classical issues in integrating or using the Third Sector, which is part of civil society, in the provision of welfare. As Salamon (1987) argued, the Third Sector

> is limited in its ability to generate an adequate level of resources, is vulnerable to particularism and the favouritism of the wealthy, is prone to self-defeating paternalism, and has at times been associated with amateur, as opposed to professional forms of care.
>
> (Salamon, 1987, p. 42)

It is also in the light of these continuous and varying problems that the change in balance of the welfare mix has to be understood, including different perspectives of the best balance. Problems relate to the fact that not all citizens will be supported by the voluntary sector and also that it might have a tendency to self-defeating paternalism, that is that those individuals or groups providing the support have their own agenda and understanding of how to live life which could be in contrast with the wishes of those in need of support. A further issue is whether the voluntary work can be assumed to be stable or changing over time, when voluntary workers' interests and preferences change, or if fewer people are willing to spend their spare time doing voluntary work.

The role of civil society in the welfare state is therefore also often disputed. The dispute includes a wide range of issues ranging from the belief that the family is and should be the main provider of welfare, supported by friends, to that more voluntary work can help to ensure better welfare, to a question of the possible negative consequences of leaving more to the family and the voluntary sector. In relation to the last issue, one problem is that voluntary organisations might not be stable providers, and are in principle not obliged to help all who are in need. Thus relying upon voluntary work can imply new types of inequalities in access to welfare, and with a high risk of instability in provision.

Furthermore, there has often been a balance between the role of the state and voluntary organisations, where these organisations to some extent have been dependent on economic support from the state, and thus they are co-opted by the state. This is in many ways contrary to the possible role the voluntary sector sees for itself, as being independent and able to make its own decisions, including whom to support and under what circumstances. Therefore voluntary organisations may also see their relation to the state as a challenge.

The number of people doing voluntary work varies among countries and can be difficult to measure exactly. This is due to the fact that voluntary work can vary in terms of length of engagement; it can be very frequent, or just one hour a year, and therefore the total impact and size of the voluntary sector is difficult to estimate. Voluntary work can range from supporting the local sports club by training children, to visiting elderly lonely people, to sitting at a person's deathbed. This variation also adds to the debate about the role of the voluntary sector. A core issue concerns the fact that some functions can be supported by the voluntary sector, whereas others cannot, given that people might stop doing voluntary work if other supporters no longer want to be active in an organisation.

Civil society's role is thus still under discussion and is changing over time, including the changed roles of the family, and the balance of work and family life, to which we will turn in the next section. Furthermore, new risks in welfare societies which include the breakup of families and changing relationships between men and women mean that the family may not exist for all people in a society and therefore the family cannot support every individual in times of need. Changing family types can thus also reduce the option of using the family and civil society as central actors in welfare delivery.

8.3   Work–family balance

The employment rate of women has gone up in most welfare states (see Chapter 7). This has raised new issues on how to balance work and family life, including who shall take care of children during working hours and how both men and women can be in the labour market and also responsible for getting children to and from institutions. Care for the frail members in the family has also been an issue, especially concerning the importance of care during working hours. The increasing percentage of working women raises questions about responsibility for care. Most Western welfare states now see it as the state's responsibility, although the coverage rates are still higher in the Nordic welfare states than in the rest of Europe.

Historically, the family has delivered care and food and been the giver of security and love in all countries. The norms and traditions of family life go beyond being a caring institution; it is also a place for recognition, love and tenderness. It is often conceived of parents and children, and in some societies the family is seen as those responsible for providing income, shelter and food for all. The welfare state only intervenes as the lender of last resort, especially in countries like Italy and Spain. Therefore, in several countries' social systems the household is the unit of the provision of social benefits and often parents have a legal obligation to finance and take care of their children and in some countries (for example, Germany) also for their parents.

Historically, care has mainly been the province of the family. Although this has now to a higher degree been taken over by the state, the family still plays the major role in caring in several countries, as is shown in Table 8.1, where the focus is on the percentages of children cared for by parents alone, indicating that they are not in day care.

As Table 8.1 shows there are large differences among the countries. However, there is also a tendency for older children, over 3 years of age, to be taken care of outside the family, with Hungary and the Czech Republic being the exceptions. Part of the explanation for this is the leave systems in different welfare states that make it possible for parents (mainly mothers) to stay at home in the first year of a child's life. The opposite picture arises when we examine public support and activities in the area of care for children. Table 8.2 shows

Table 8.1 The percentages of children in the population of each age group cared for by parents alone in relation to age in 2011

	Less than 3 years	From 3 years to minimum compulsory school age
EU27	50	11
Czech Republic	60	12
Denmark	26	2
Germany	66	8
Spain	49	11
France	41	3
Italy	45	4
Hungary	72	20
Sweden	47	2
United Kingdom	46	4

Source: Eurostat (ilc_caparents) (accessed 15 August 2013).

Table 8.2 Percentages in public day care in 2011 in relation to the age of the child and length of time in care during one day

	Less than 3 years		From 3 years to minimum compulsory school ages	
	1–29 hours	30 hours or over	1–29 hours	30 hours or over
EU27	15	15	37	47
Czech Republic	4	1	29	45
Denmark	5	69	11	87
Germany	9	15	46	44
Spain	20	19	45	41
France	18	26	43	52
Italy	9	17	20	75
Hungary	1	7	16	59
Sweden	19	32	31	64
United Kingdom	30	5	66	27

Source: Eurostat (ilc_caindformal) (accessed 15 August 2013).

that for selected EU countries the number of children in public day care depends on their age and number of hours in the institution.

As can be seen from Table 8.2, children above the age of 3 are more likely to be taken care of by the welfare state. However, the number of hours spent in an institution varies among countries. The figures in the table mask the fact that in some countries the relatively low number of hours spent in institutions is due to the way data are categorised – those children in formal education are not counted as being in childcare. For those below 3 years of age there is a lower rate of coverage. This reflects the fact that especially maternity but also paternity leave for children below the age of 3 can be rather long in some countries. Thus this implies that there is a substitution between care in an institution and leave to take care of one's own child(ren), that is if there is a right to take leave when having a child and either state or occupational welfare benefits (e.g. full wage income throughout maternity/paternity leave or at least part of the leave time). This reflects a balance between state, market and civil society that can and will vary between countries. Box 8.3 shows the main policy instruments available in order for the welfare state to support families with children.

Box 8.3 Main policy instruments in welfare states' support to children

■ parental entitlements to take leave from work after childbirth;
■ the provision of childcare services for working parents with children of pre-school age;
■ transfers through tax and benefit systems which affect the financial advantages for women and their families of being in paid employment.

(Thevenon, 2013, p. 12)

In addition to formal care, we find informal and private paid-for childcare in some countries. This might be supported directly or indirectly by transfers through the tax and benefit system. The mix between state, market and civil society in this area has been and is seemingly also under constant change. User charges for day care also vary among countries. However, the level of user charges for day care has an impact on the net take-home income for a family, and thus might influence the choice of whether to work or not and who will have to stay at home to take care of the children.

Besides the possibility of children being taken care of in an institution, there is also the option of someone working less than full time. The high proportion of women working part time in some countries reflects the fact that this is one of the ways to balance work and family life. Seemingly this has a gender bias, as it is often the women who ensure that the balance is possible. This can reflect norms and traditions, but also that men still often earn higher wages than women. A higher number of women than men think that they have to do more than their fair share of the housework. This is highest in France (65 per cent of women), but also high in the UK (38 per cent) and low in countries like Denmark (12 per cent) (Eurofound, 2012).

Analysis suggests that the state has to help in the reconciliation of work and family life by providing care, especially affordable and high-quality day care for children, and leave opportunities following childbirth, and taking care of close relatives in cases of severe illness (Greve, 2012a). The employers' role is to ensure flexible working time, and in some systems also to pay wages at least part of the time when parents are on leave.

The other side of the coin is the family's role. Having a close family member to care for could imply a responsibility which could entail reduced access to the labour market. This is particularly the case for women in some countries where it is the expectation that they take care of the family members, including the children, although these roles seem to be changing in many countries (see also Chapter 10).

Table 8.3 shows that in eastern European countries such as Hungary and the Czech Republic more people find that they are unable to spend the necessary time at work compared with western Europe where the availability of support for families is more common. Thus the relation between welfare state and individual support also forms and has an impact on family life.

Developing affordable and high-quality day care has also been part of the EU employment strategy, especially as a means to ensure equality between men and women, but also in relation to demographic trends, as a large workforce will be necessary to meet the demands of an ageing population (for more on the European Employment Strategy see: http://ec.europa.eu/social/main.jsp?catId=101).

This has also formed the background for change in family models. Historically the male-breadwinner model was the main family model – men worked and women cared. Gradually more women have entered the labour market (see also Chapter 7), and thus a development towards a dual-earner

Table 8.3 How often do family responsibilities prevent you from giving the time you should to your job? (2010)

	Czech Republic	Germany	Denmark	Spain	France	United Kingdom	Hungary	Sweden	Total
Never	27.4	48.9	49.1	62.3	60.8	43.8	45.8	40.5	47.4
Hardly ever	36.7	29.8	35.4	24.3	19.7	33.2	31.7	38.1	31.1
Sometimes	29.1	16.6	12.8	11.2	13.8	18.9	20.2	18.4	17.5
Often	6.1	4.3	2.2	1.8	5.2	3.4	2.2	2.9	3.6
Always	0.7	0.4	0.4	0.3	0.4	0.7	0.1	0.1	0.4
Total	100	100	100	100	100	100	100	100	100
N =	824	1,449	804	873	781	1,139	684	795	7,349

Source: European Social Survey, 2010, http://www.europeansocialsurvey.org (accessed 15 August 2013).

Note: No data available for Italy. These are the latest available data, since the same question was not used in the 2012 Survey.

model has taken place in most of western Europe. In some countries, especially the Nordic welfare models, a dual-carer model also seems to have developed, that is both men and women are carers in the family. Changes in family models and family formations thus have also changed the role of men and women in the work–family balance.

One example also related to welfare benefits has been that fathers now often have a right to leave in case of the birth of a child, whereas previously only mothers had this right. Parental rights to leave from the labour market often with a generous benefit following the birth of a child thus also influence the development of the welfare mix, including the responsibility of civil society in the first year of a child's life. This parental leave, as well as family allowances, supports families with children economically. This is important for many families and reduces the risk of living at risk of poverty.

The care of frail and/or elderly people also raises problems. This is the case if the welfare state does not have a set of instruments available to help elderly people who either live alone or in homes for the elderly, or do not have the money to pay for one of the two alternatives. In most welfare states it is still the expectation that a spouse or partner will offer support with care if possible before the state steps in and supports the person in need of care.

Intergenerational issues are further an important aspect of welfare states, and this also includes whether one generation is prepared to pay for another generation's welfare. If there is a fear that this intergenerational solidarity is on the brink of being reduced, this might reduce the willingness to support the welfare state.

Finally, families also have an important role in offering people someone with whom to discuss important and personal issues. This is illustrated in Table 8.4 which shows that living with a husband/wife/partner increases the likelihood of having someone to discuss intimate and personal matters with, in all the welfare states sampled. Thus the family also plays a role in establishing social contacts and thereby also fulfilling other functions in people's everyday lives.

The picture is the same when people are asked about their level of happiness. Those having a close relationship and living together with others have a higher level of happiness. Elderly people, despite being widowed, are able to say that they are happy and this indicates that people also can value their life generally even though they have lost a close relative. Civil society thus has a role to play in order to achieve a high level of welfare and well-being, this includes establishing social contacts and thereby supporting social cohesion. Being a member of a family and having someone to share daily living expenses can also help people to avoid living in poverty. Family life can thus also in some instances increase economic security. Social contact, economic security and trust also relate to a high level of social capital, an issue to which we now turn.

Table 8.4 Percentage of people having someone to discuss intimate and personal matters with dependent on whether living or not living with partner (2010)

Someone to discuss with	Lives with husband/ wife/partner	Czech Republic	Germany	Denmark	Spain	France	United Kingdom	Hungary	Sweden	Total
Yes	Yes	44.8	59.7	61.5	56.8	48.3	50.4	55.8	57.9	54.2
	No	35.9	37.0	31.6	35.6	37.9	41.6	36.6	34.2	36.6
No	Yes	7.0	1.4	3.9	2.9	6.5	1.9	2.6	3.8	3.6
	No	12.3	1.9	3.0	4.7	7.3	6.1	5.0	4.1	5.6
Total		100	100	100	100	100	100	100	100	100
N =		2,338	3,026	1,563	1,878	1,725	2,413	1,553	1,496	15,992

Source: European Social Survey, 2010, http://www.europeansocialsurvey.org (accessed 15 August 2013).

Note: No data available for Italy. These are the latest available data, since the same question was not used in the 2012 Survey.

8.4 Social capital

Social capital has been seen as an important concept since it was introduced by Coleman (1988) and received international attention with the publication of Robert Putnam's book, *Bowling Alone* (2001), referring to a tendency for more people to be alone and lacking connections in modern society. Naturally, social capital and related issues have been discussed for centuries. Putnam defined social capital as: 'connections among individuals – social networks and the norms of reciprocity and trustworthiness that arise from them' (2001, p. 19).

Social capital includes a variety of resources ranging from economic and cultural capital (Bourdieu, 1986) to human and other types of capital. Presumably it was called 'capital' to connote other uses of the word, such as economic and human capital, which imply investment in the future. The word capital thus signifies that social networks have a value, albeit it is not so simple to measure this as it is to measure the capital to invest in factories and machinery, where we can use money as a measure. Still, attempts are made to measure social capital in societies, including key elements such as trust and having friends to talk with on personal matters (see Table 8.4).

Social capital is thus related to trust in and connection with other people, but also reciprocity, norms and sanctions related to these norms. There is a distinction between bonding and bridging social capital. Bonding social capital refers to strong ties, for example, within the family, with friends or in specific ethnic or religious groups. Bridging social capital refers to looser social networks. These might be useful in working life and, for example, might help one in searching for a job. Bridging social networks also exist within organisations, voluntary work, hobbies and so on. Given that they are looser, the ties are not so strong. However, they can be important for individuals in everyday life. They can be an important tool in a welfare society helping to increase social cohesion. This is also the case for bonding capital although the interaction with other networks might be weaker and there is a risk of strong social control.

Figure 8.2 shows an example of elements included when calculating social capital in different countries, and thus being able to compare across countries. The focus in Figure 8.2 is on volunteering, helping strangers, donations, perception of social support, trust, marriage rate and religious affiliation. The ten top-ranked countries are:

1 Norway
2 Switzerland
3 Canada
4 Sweden
5 New Zealand
6 Denmark
7 Australia
8 Finland

9 The Netherlands
10 Luxembourg.

Appendix 8.1 shows, for the nine countries studied in this book, the indicators used to calculate social capital and also the overall position of these countries among others worldwide.

The rankings and the data in Appendix 8.1 indicate that the Nordic welfare states score well with regard to social capital, but so do liberal welfare states

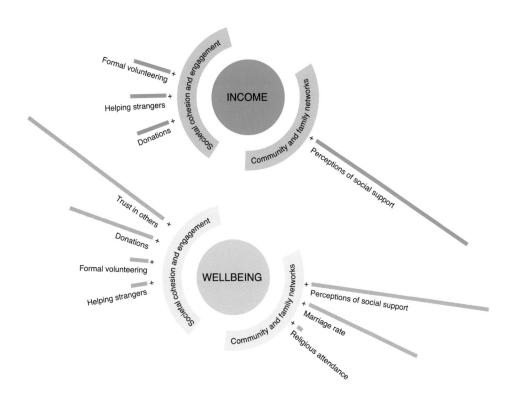

: and : Darker lines indicate a variable that is included in both income and wellbeing regressions.
and : Lighter lines indicate a variable that is included in only one regression.

Figure 8.2 Elements to calculate social capital.

Source: http://media.prosperity.com/2013/pdf/publications/Methodology_2013_FinalWEB.pdf page 12 (accessed 6 August 2013).

like New Zealand, Ireland, the USA and Canada. The eastern European countries perform less well in this area.

Putnam's definition, as given above, resembles that of the OECD. Therefore the development and measurement of issues related to social capital and well-being can be found in international statistics, enabling a discussion of whether and how social capital is linked to welfare, the welfare state and welfare regimes. One would, for example, expect that bonding social capital would be strong in southern European countries like Italy and Spain where there is a strong emphasis on the family. Bridging networks presumably are prevalent in countries like the UK and Denmark. Another expectation is that the welfare state could eliminate the need for social capital. However, social capital is important for the social cohesion in a given society. If there are social links between members of a society they give rise to positive interactions and social contacts; and further, as an example, social contacts have a positive impact on the level of happiness in a country (Greve, 2012b), and thereby on the overall level of welfare in the country.

A way to measure social capital is to examine trust in other people. Table 8.5 shows degrees of trust in selected welfare states. Trust seems to be higher in the universal Nordic welfare states, such as Denmark and Sweden, and lowest in central and eastern Europe, like in Germany, Hungary and the Czech Republic, with the UK and Spain placed in the middle. This indicates a higher level of social capital and social cohesion in the small Nordic countries. This can have an impact on the way societies function, and also the pressures on the welfare state, as a high level of trust could imply that the civil society has a strong role at the same time as the welfare state is able to support those in need of support. The development from 2010 to 2012 seems not to indicate any strong impact of the financial crisis on the trust in welfare states.

Strong welfare states seem to support trust (Box 8.4).

Table 8.5 Average level of trust in selected EU member states in 2010

	Czech Republic	Germany	Denmark	France	United Kingdom	Hungary	Spain	Sweden
2010	4.5	4.7	6.8	4.4	5.4	4.5	5.2	6.3
2012	4.4	5.0	6.9		5.4	4.8	5.2	6.0

Source: Calculated based upon European Social Survey, 2010 (accessed 4 January 2014).

Notes: No data available for Italy. Data for France not available for 2012. The calculation is based upon people answering whether 'Most people can be trusted' or 'You can't be too careful'. Possible answers ranged from: 'You can't be too careful' through 1 to 9 to 'Most people can be trusted'. The two extremes are given the value 1 and 9 respectively.

state, market and civil society

The relation between welfare states and social trust can be witnessed by the two following quotes, supporting the idea that social welfare expenditures help in increasing social trust in societies:

> Centralized social trust is correlated with increased levels of civic engagement, lower crime rates, and greater economic growth. Many scholars believe that equality provides the conditions in which social trust can flourish. Thus, welfare programs might be one way to generate social trust. (p. 61)

> As policy makers throughout the developed world debate the relative benefits of broadening welfare provision (e.g. universalizing health care) or of reducing the welfare state as part of austerity measures, this study suggests that increased social spending might enhance levels of generalized social trust and, by extension, the positive externalities associated with a cohesive society. (p. 68)
>
> (Brewer et al., 2014)

Social capital can be seen as an important element in welfare states. The state, if possible, should try to support and help to create social capital, as countries with high levels of social capital work and function better than societies with a low level of social capital. Social capital also makes civil society stronger and thereby better able to help in achieving the goals of a high level of welfare.

8.5   Summing-up

Welfare states and the balance between state, market and civil society vary over time and between countries. Thus the balance between the actors in the welfare mix is never stable and is constantly undergoing change. However, it seems to be important to be aware of the differences and the balance among the three sectors and how they can vary over time. The welfare mix has implications for who has the responsibility for welfare and who will finance and deliver welfare in different countries, and also for who has access.

The family is still an important institution in modern welfare states, with a function both as a provider of care, and also as a place for reciprocity and traditions. However, the state has taken over care for children to a large extent in many welfare states. The ability to combine work and family life is thus influenced not only by civil society, but also by the initiatives of welfare states.

Social capital is a way of describing the degree of social cohesion in different societies – a high level of social capital is expected to increase the degree of cohesion in society as well as in families. There is in general a relatively high level of trust in many countries, including in the aftermath of the financial crisis. A large welfare state seems to enhance social trust, not reduce it.

Overall civil society can therefore have a central role in ensuring welfare in a given society; however, there are also risks including failure of the voluntary sector, whereby access to welfare is skewed and uncertain for some groups.

References

Bourdieu, P. (1986), The Form of Capital. In Richardson, J. (ed.), *Handbook of Theory and Research for the Sociology of Education*. New York, Greenwood Press. pp. 241–58.

Brewer, K. B., Oh, H. and Sharma, S. (2014), 'Crowding In' or 'Crowding Out'? An Examination of the Impact of the Welfare State on Generalized Social Trust. *International Journal of Social Welfare*, vol. 23, no. 1, pp. 61–8.

Coleman, J. (1988), Social Capital in the Creation of Human Capital. *Journal of Sociology*, vol. 94, pp. 95–120.

Edwards, M. (2009), *Civil Society*, 2nd edition. Cambridge, Polity Press.

Eurofound (2012), *Third European Quality of Life Survey – Quality of Life in Europe: Impacts of the Crisis*. Luxembourg, Publications Office of the European Union.

Giddens, A. (1998), *The Third Way: The Renewal of Social Democracy*. Cambridge, Polity Press.

Greve, B. (2012a), Reconciliation of Work and Family Life in Four Different Welfare States, Neujobs Working Paper No. D 5.5.

Greve, B. (2012b), *Happiness*. London, Routledge.

Jamieson, J. (2012), Bleak Times for Children? The Anti-Social Behaviour Agenda and the Criminalisation of Social Policy. *Social Policy & Administration*, vol. 46, no. 4, pp. 448–64.

Putnam, R. (2001), *Bowling Alone: The Collapse and Revival of American Community*. New York, Touchstone.

Salamon, L. (1987), Of Market Failure, Voluntary Failure, and Third-Party Government: Toward a Theory of Government–Nonprofit Relations in the Modern Welfare State. *Nonprofit and Voluntary Sector Quarterly*, vol. 16, no. 1–2, pp. 29–49.

Spicker, P. (1995), *Social Policy: Themes and Approaches*. Hemel Hempstead, Harvester Wheatsheaf.

Thevenon, O. (2013), Drivers of Female Labour Force Participation in the OECD. OECD Social, Employment and Migration Working Papers, No. 145. Paris, OECD.

Appendix 8.1 Countries' social capital ranking in 2012 and the seven indicators used to calculate it

Country	Social capital ranking, worldwide in 2012	Donated money to charity in past month? (% yes)	Have you helped a stranger in past month? (% yes)	Are you married? (% yes)	Attended a place of worship in past week? (% yes)	Can you rely on friends and family for help? (% yes)	Do you think that most people can be trusted? (% yes)	Have you volunteered your time in past month? (% yes)
Denmark	2	70.0	54.6	51.5	19.6	96.2	62.0	22.6
France	40	28.7	44.1	47.3	21.3	92.1	19.9	29.3
Germany	15	43.1	48.5	53.6	32.8	95.1	31.6	24.2
Italy	38	37.2	44.7	62.1	47.6	91.3	20.7	18.0
Spain	34	25.7	49.1	56.0	34.2	94.4	22.4	12.6
Sweden	9	56.2	48.1	49.2	12.0	92.1	56.1	11.4
United Kingdom	12	70.2	55.2	45.2	18.2	95.6	35.8	25.9
Czech Republic	45	26.7	30.7	56.4	15.3	91.4	25.4	13.6
Hungary	79	26.2	38.3	46.3	19.6	89.4	13.3	7.6

Source: Based on http://www.prosperity.com/ExploreData.aspx (accessed 12 August 2013).

Part III

Equality and specific groups' position in the welfare states

Equality and inequality

9.1   Introduction

> The unequal distribution of resources like income, wealth, prestige and power is termed social inequality. These unequally distributed resources yield further advantages or disadvantages and accrue to individuals as a result of their position in the social structure and in social networks.
>
> (Mau and Verwiebe, 2010, p. 193)

This quote illustrates how equality can be understood and what it means for societies. In this chapter the focus is mainly on economic inequality. Issues surrounding equality, or various degrees and types of inequality, have been at the centre of debates in most welfare states and societies for centuries. This chapter will examine the way we understand equality and inequality and measure degrees thereof. How this relates to inclusion/exclusion will be considered in Chapter 10.

Section 9.2 will present theoretical understandings behind our understanding of equality, inequality and poverty issues, including a discussion of Amartya Sen's concept of capability. This will be followed in Section 9.3 by a discussion of different ways of measuring inequality, including the pitfalls and dilemmas. Finally, Section 9.4 will examine the welfare state's possible role and options relating to equality and inequality.

9.2 Theoretical understandings of equality and inequality

There are several questions related to understanding equality and inequality, including different normative positions of whether it is something the welfare state (see also Section 9.4), should deal with or whether it should be left to the market, or indirectly to the family if we are looking at the individual level. There are also ongoing debates about inequalities among countries, for example, in the developed and developing worlds. This kind of inequality is not included here.

The first important question is how we should interpret equality and inequality. This includes the issue of whether or not one should understand equality in terms of outcome or equality of opportunities. Our understanding has different implications for the measurement of equality and possible types of intervention that can be used. This also relates to different understanding of justice. Box 9.1 shows how three different understandings of justice can be interpreted in a concrete example.

Box 9.1 Three types of justice – presented by an example

Three children all claim a flute, and none of the other children is in disagreement with the others' argument. Who should have the flute on the basis of the arguments they present?

A – argues she is the best at playing the flute
B – argues she has fewer toys than the other two
C – argues that she has made the flute.

Child B would get support from an economic egalitarian, Child C from the libertarian and a Utilitarian will presumably support Child A.

It is then as argued by Sen (2009, p. 13):

> The general point here is that it is not easy to brush aside as foundationless any of the claims here based respectively on the pursuit of happiness, or the entitlement to enjoy the products of one's own labour. The different resolutions all have serious arguments in support of them, and we may not be able to identify, without some arbitrariness, any of the alternative arguments as being the one that must invariably prevail.

A second important question is whether one should look into a short time spell or intergenerational differences. A person might thus be poor for one or two years, but not for the rest of their lifetime, which then raises the question whether this is an issue for the welfare state to deal with. Intergenerational issues and life cycle approaches to welfare, at least implicitly, involve questions of how just a given society is.

The question of equality might be split into four different approaches (Fitzpatrick, 2011):

a) equality of opportunity for welfare
b) equality of opportunity for resources
c) equality of welfare
d) equality of resources.

One problem is that these might intersect and using just one approach it can be difficult to understand fully the way a welfare state is working. The first two deal with opportunities, the last two with outcomes.

An approach that emphasises equality of opportunity would argue that there should be equal options for all individuals in a society and would thus focus on how to provide opportunities, for example, by providing education, so that the individual will be able to choose the best life for him- or herself. One issue that can arise from this is that an individual's decisions at one point in time can affect the options open to him or her at a later date. Thus those who have saved up for a pension, other things being equal, will be in a better financial position when retiring than someone who has spent all his or her money. This does not necessarily mean that the state does not have a role here. There may be grounds to give welfare to those who have little income due to previous spending. One might, for example, argue that dire poverty should be eliminated whatever the cause.

The criticism of this approach can be that if the starting point is already unequal, for example, due to the fact that some have inherited valuable property while others have nothing, there would still be high levels of inequality in income and wealth. Equality of opportunity further might not reduce the existing degree of poverty.

A focus on outcomes rather than opportunities would examine the degree of inequality, for example, in income and wealth, what types of equality can be measured, and how they can be understood. It would then try to depict these and analyse their causes and the reasons for differences in degree of equality. Based on one's viewpoint on the role of the state, the market and civil society, this can give rise to different suggestions for intervention in the way society is working.

Instead of looking at one year, there could be a focus on the opportunities or outcomes over a whole life. A focus on lifetime would look into whether options and differences are equal over the life course. The main reason this approach is only used to a limited extent is that it is difficult to wait until the end of life to find out whether one has been treated unequally or not. However, the argument is used in relation to poverty, for instance, how the low income of students is not seen as a reason for welfare state intervention as the expectation is that later in life the same individuals will have a higher income.

There is also a distinction between vertical and horizontal degrees of equity. Vertical equity is the element often discussed in relation to equality as it deals with redistribution between rich and poor, sometimes labelled the Robin-Hood redistribution. The horizontal degree of equity focuses on those situations where the same should be treated equally, and relates thereby to issues of equality of access and opportunities. This is, for example, an analysis of whether all people with the same disease receive the same treatment or those who are better able to argue and/or to pay a user charge receive better treatment.

A broader approach to equality looks not only at these different kinds of distribution. The Nobel Prize-winning economist Amartya Sen has focused on what he has termed capabilities. Poverty is then defined in terms of capability deprivation, from

> elementary physical ones [such] as being well nourished, being adequately clothed and sheltered, avoiding preventable morbidity, and so forth, to more complex social achievements such as taking part in the life of the community, being able to appear in public without shame, and so on.
>
> (Sen, 1995, p. 15)

Sen has thereby sought to move the discussion away from the actual and directly measurable situation in relation to the distribution of income and wealth, towards whether the individual has a set of functionings, that is opportunities to take part in society, and has real freedom including multiple dimensions of well-being, as discussed in Chapter 2.

Capabilities are the options or opportunities individuals have available to them for achieving and choosing among a set of possible options. If you do not have sufficient resources your chance of making informed choices in welfare states will also be lower than other people's options and abilities to make choices. The ability to choose one's way of living is thus an important element in how we should understand equality in different societies, but also for our under-standing of processes and issues regarding inclusion and exclusion.

Capabilities are thereby the real opportunities, not just those on paper, to achieve certain functions (valued doings or beings). Sen (1995) argues that in terms of inequalities, capabilities are the correct evaluative space, as if one simply measures resources, such as incomes, two people can have the same income but have very different capabilities. Thus, for example, someone in a wheelchair needs many more resources to get around (a wheelchair, special transport, etc.) compared with an able-bodied person. If we measure inequality in terms of income alone, it does not capture such differences in opportunity. If, on the other hand, we measure functionings, actual doings or being, we also leave out important information. For instance, someone on an extreme diet and someone in a famine may have the same calorie intake (their functioning) but very different opportunities (capabilities).

There might be differences in complexities (Burchardt, 2006) and thus having more complex capabilities has an impact on one's ability to make the choice related to using the freedoms they confer. Capabilities when related to functionings can thereby have a broader interpretation, like, for example, the ability to make an informed choice in the work–family life balance (see also Section 8.3).

Capabilities, in Sen's understanding, is not a theory of justice, but a way to assess an individual's well-being (Sen, 2009), and therefore it does not indicate the necessary capabilities people should or ought to have. A criticism of the capability approach relates to the difficulty of measuring it, and thereby using the approach in welfare state policies, beyond relatively general notions of ensuring elements such as education and reducing discrimination. Furthermore, like the argument related to opportunity, even if there is equality in capabilities, previous types of inequality will not be redressed.

Given the problem with how to understand justice and capability, welfare state analysis has often used a narrower approach when trying to understand equality and poverty. Historically there has been a clear focus on how to measure and describe poverty. One question has been whether or not we should measure poverty in absolute terms or see it as relative.

The basic needs approach has sought to define poverty in absolute terms. This can be done in terms of what can be labelled survival needs: literally those goods, such as food and shelter, that are needed to survive. This was the approach taken by Rowntree in 1901 when he argued that a family was poor if 'their total earnings are insufficient to obtain the minimum necessities of merely physical efficiency' (cited in Saunders, 2013, p. 60). People who did not have such means were entitled to poor relief, later labelled social assistance (see also the different approaches to welfare in Chapter 4).

In terms of policy this approach implies a recommendation that individuals should have the necessary means to avoid living in poverty. It does not take the living standards of others in a society into consideration. This is in contrast to the relative approach, where to be living in or at risk of poverty means having an income below a certain threshold. This is the most commonly used definition in European countries and in the EU today (cf. also Section 9.3). However, even absolute poverty lines can change if what is necessary in the basket of goods and services changes over time. This is also reflected in Peter Townsend's definition:

Individuals, families and groups in the population can be said to be in poverty when they lack the resources to obtain the types of diet, participate in the activities and have the living conditions and amenities which are customary, or at least widely encouraged or approved, in the societies to which they belong.

(1979, p. 31)

Whether poverty should be viewed as relative or absolute depends on the approach, however, if the focus is on options for being involved and socially integrated (see also Chapter 10 on social inclusion/exclusion), then the relative approach is the most appropriate given that this indicates the ability to participate actively in society. In this way there is also a link to Sen's understanding of poverty that income is only a means for an individual to achieve his or her goals and set of functionings. Furthermore, for some there might be a need for a higher income in order to be actively part of society, as described in the case of disability above.

Still, the level and acceptance of the degree of poverty and level of equality/inequality is open for discussion and involves normative issues on what is the acceptable standard and degree of inequality. Research shows that unequal societies have more crime, less trust and several other problems compared with more equal societies (cf. Wilkinson and Pickett, 2009), and furthermore social cohesion is weaker in unequal societies. Still, this does not inform us where the exact borderline is, for example, where social cohesion will be dramatically reduced in case of an increase in the level of inequality.

However, even having established a theoretical understanding of equality or inequality there is a long way to go before we know how to measure it. This is the focus of the next section.

9.3   Measuring equality/inequality

Classical ways of measuring equality take as their starting point access to economic resources; however, non-monetary resources are also important given that they too have an impact on individuals' well-being (cf. Chapter 2). Inequality in, for example, access to health care and health care outcomes (such as average life expectancy) are issues that are in need of analysis given that factors might reinforce other inequalities or reduce equalities. If an individual has to pay for access to certain welfare services in some countries, but not in other countries, it also influences the equality in access to basic levels of welfare goods and services. Thus measuring equality/inequality needs to define in what area of life and in what relation this is to be measured.

Traditional analysis examines monetary inequality in the form of difference in income, disposable income and wealth. However, the impact of the welfare state by offering access to different kinds of services also influences the degree of equality. For example, a person might have a low disposable income but if all welfare services are provided by the welfare state their disposable income

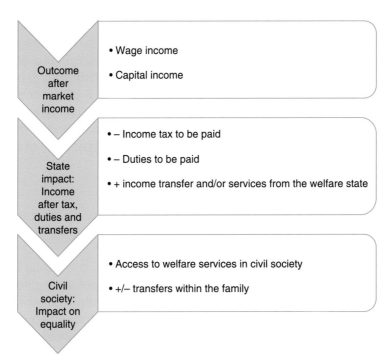

Figure 9.1 Different levels that can be used to measure inequality.

might be higher than that of a person who has to pay for extra insurance, health care, etc. in another country to get access to the same type of services. Furthermore, the tax system may have an impact. A move from inequality based upon market income to disposable income is indicated in Figure 9.1.

Frequently, the two first levels in Figure 9.1 are used to measure inequality in different countries, and thereby the impact of state and market on equality. Therefore analyses will often use data on market income and/or income after taxes and duties paid, and receipt of transfers. In many countries, pensioners – who have left the labour market – depend on transfers as their main source of income. Therefore only looking at income based on market activities will imply a higher level of inequality and more people living in poverty than when the impact of the welfare state's activities and income transfers (pensions, unemployment benefits, etc.) are included. Redistribution of resources in welfare states also takes place across generations. However, a person's living standard is not only dependent on income transfers as other factors such as access to welfare services, especially if free or a limited charge, also have an impact on quality of life and thereby well-being.

Civil society, the third element in Figure 9.1, also plays a role in relation to equality and reduction of poverty. Some individuals, for example, students, get income transfers within the family, which are not registered in the official economy. This has an impact on their daily life, that is they might appear to be poor in the official statistics, but in reality they are not poor due to economic support from their parents. Thereby the way civil society works also has an impact on individuals' living standards and to what degree the consequence of being below a poverty line is influencing everyday life. The availability of free housing in civil society can also have important consequences for daily life. Given the difficulties in measuring access to services such benefits are usually not included in official poverty analyses, and the influence of the state on the degree of equality and poverty.

Even when having gathered the data on market income and/or disposable income there are a variety of ways of presenting degrees of equality or inequality. Three types of measurements often used are:

1   the Gini coefficient
2   risk of poverty (at different levels, and in different numbers of years)
3   80/20 rule.

The Gini coefficient measures the degree of inequality by comparing the actual distribution of income with a hypothetical situation where everyone has the same share (often by decile) of the typical income (before or after taxes and duties). The size can vary between 0 and 1, where 0 is absolute equality and 1 absolute inequality (e.g. where one person has it all), the implication being that the closer to zero the more equal the situation is. Graphically it is described using the Lorenz curve (Figure 9.2).

The benefit of using the Gini coefficient is that the measurement of the degree of inequality only changes if the total area of inequality changes. The data are thus not influenced by, for example, a small change among either high- or low-income earners in a society.

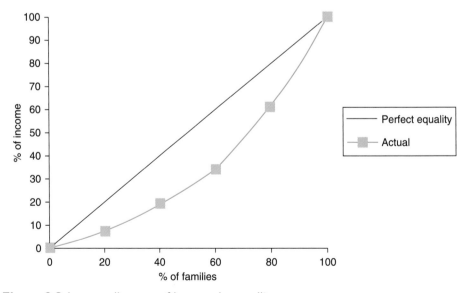

Figure 9.2 Lorenz diagram of income inequality.

A specific issue that needs to be discussed, and this also relates to the debate about poverty, is whether having a low level of income reduces the possibilities of being actively involved in social life and society's development, for example, by being able to have guests, go to see a movie, or be active in a sports club. This also revolves around the issue of social inclusion/exclusion and a society's degree of social cohesion (see also Sections 8.4 and 10.6), as this is influenced by the level of inequality.

In principle, as indicated earlier, measuring lifetime income would be the preferable way of comparing inequalities as not just one year with good or low income but the situation over a whole lifetime could be studied. This is a good idea in theory; however, in practice it is very difficult given the fact that one needs to use data for many different years, and only a limited amount of data might be available. Furthermore, if one first compares differences at the end of a person's life, it will be difficult to do anything to redress the inequalities. This therefore is an argument for using a variety of measures to describe social inequalities in a given year.

Whether richer or poorer societies have a higher or lower level of equality can be discussed. Figure 9.3 shows the relation between equality (using the Gini coefficient) and the GDP per capita for 2011, showing that there is no clear correlation between the degree of inequality and the level of income in a country. Both the richest and the poorest countries (e.g. Sweden and Denmark, Hungary and the Czech Republic) have low levels of inequality. Countries like the UK

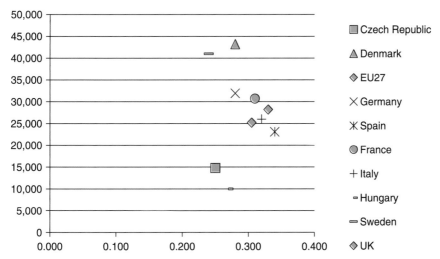

Figure 9.3 The relation between equality and income for selected EU countries in 2012.

Source: Based upon Eurostat data (online data code for Gini is ilc_di12).

Notes: Gini coefficient is from 2010 for EU27, Italy and the UK. The x-axis is the Gini coefficient and the y-axis is income per inhabitant in euro.

and Spain in Figure 9.3, as well as the USA and Australia, have high levels of inequality. This indicates that the degree of equality is to a large degree related to national decisions and due to differences in welfare states, and is thereby influenced by political preferences in various countries.

Another measure is the 80/20 rule, which refers to how much the richest 20 per cent earns compared with the 20 per cent with the lowest income. If, over a year, the richest 20 per cent earns 40 per cent of total income and the poorest 20 per cent earns 8 per cent, then the 80/20 would be: $40 \div 8 = 5$. There is thus a higher possible dispersion in the 80/20 than in the Gini coefficient as it ranges from one (completely equal) to infinity (fully unequal).

There are also several other kinds of measurement issues related to the degree of equality. Several of them are shown in Box 9.2. The elements listed in Box 9.2 are useful when one wants to discuss and analyse equality and trends. These can give different results, but they might also point to varieties in our understanding of equality. Income before and after tax, for example, is an indication of the inequality in the market when looking at before-tax income, but after-tax income shows how the welfare state through the tax system influences the distribution of money in a society. The question of one year or several years refers to the fact that a person might have a low income in one year, but a high income in the next, and thus this raises the question whether the welfare state should try to address this problem. The distinction of individual/household has to do with the fact that, for example, two persons earning the same income might have different living conditions if one of them can use all the money by him/herself, whereas the other has to support a spouse and children.

Box 9.2 A list of possible issues related to measurement of equality

Income – before/after tax
Hidden income – hidden economy in general
Are statistics reliable?
Are all countries included with the same type of information (e.g. China, India)?
Wealth?
One year – several years – students/pensioners
Other elements than income
Purchasing power parities
Individual or household income.

Some of the issues in Box 9.2 also relate to whether and how it is possible to make cross-country comparisons. This includes whether or not one has the necessary, and reliable, data. For example, it might not be a big problem to be poor in one year (perhaps as a student) when one has a high income the following year. Therefore a comparison based on lifetime income would be preferable; however, this is very difficult to obtain for many reasons (e.g. inflation, increase in societal income, availability of statistical data).

Furthermore, differences in level of income and wealth have an impact on the price level in different countries, so in order to make a comparison one needs to have a common type of measurement. This is done, for example, by using purchasing power parity which tries to account for differences in price levels and thereby buying power.

Equality/inequality is one issue, poverty is another issue. Poverty can be absolute or relative, as argued in Section 9.2. The level of poverty in the world can be examined by asking how many people have, for example, one dollar or two dollars per day to live on. However, in Europe the most frequent way is to measure poverty by those people who have an income below a set percentage (40 per cent, 50 per cent or 60 per cent) of the median income. The EU uses a threshold of 60 per cent of median disposable income. The median income is the income of the person in the middle of a distribution. For a team of 11 football players this would thus be the income of the sixth player if they are presented by size of income from lowest to highest. In Table 9.1 the poverty situation is shown before and after social transfers using a cut-off point of 60 per cent of median income.

Table 9.1 shows a clear difference among countries, with eastern European and Nordic countries having the lowest degree of inequality and countries from southern Europe and the UK having the highest level of inequality. Germany and France lie in between. This partly reflects history, and partly different approaches in the welfare states to the use of the tax and duty system and level

Table 9.1 At risk of poverty before and after social transfers using 60 per cent median income, 2012

	After social transfers (%)	Before social transfers (%)
European Union	16.9	23.7
Czech Republic	9.6	14.9
Denmark	13.1	16.9
Germany	16.1	21.4
Spain	22.2	28.4
France	14.1	22.7
Italy	19.4	25.6
Hungary	14.0	18.9
Sweden	14.2	17.5
United Kingdom	16.2	25.8

Source: Eurostat (Code: tsdsc350) (accessed the 4 January 2014).

Note: In the datasets figures for a longer time span and other EU member states are also available.

of welfare services and income transfers. This also reflects the different welfare regimes' approach to poverty: the universal Nordic model tries to reduce poverty to a larger degree than countries in the liberal model and in southern Europe, whereas the continental countries are in the middle.

In relation to measuring poverty, as in the discussion on equality, there is the question of whether one should look at the household or individual level. One person might have a high income but needs to support a large family, another having the same income may be single without dependents. Another can have a low income, but receives support from the family or civil society, and thus has a higher living standard. This can clearly lead to different levels of inequality. A further complication concerns whether one should just take a single year or several into consideration. A self-employed person might have a very low income one year, but a high income the next year. A pensioner might have had many years with a high income, but not have saved for pension purposes and now has a low income. A student whilst studying might have a low level of income, but often a high income later on. This is also one of the reasons why we talk of living in risk of poverty and further that persistent poverty is defined by examining whether or not a person has been below the poverty line for three consecutive years or more. A student with an income below the poverty line might in some instances receive economic or other types of support from his or her parents thereby either increasing income or reducing expenditure. So again, there is a strong influence from state, market and civil society, which also can be mixed in a variety of ways. The role of the market is due to the impact of the labour market (having/not having a job, high-income/low-income earners); the state through tax, duties and transfers; and civil society by support within the household or family.

Again there might also be a need to include the value of public services. The way welfare services are distributed and their scale also has an impact on the level of poverty in different countries. Therefore, a way to supplement the core economic data on poverty has been to look into the degree of material deprivation. In the EU being materially deprived is defined as the situation where a person experiences:

> at least four out of nine following deprivation items: cannot afford i) to pay rent or utility bills, ii) [to] keep home adequately warm, iii) [to] face unexpected expenses, iv) [to] eat meat, fish or a protein equivalent every second day, v) a week's holiday away from home, vi) a car, vii) a washing machine, viii) a colour TV, or ix) a telephone. People living in households with very low work intensity are those aged 0–59 living in households where the adults (aged 18–59) work less than 20 per cent of their total work potential during the past year.
>
> (Eurostat (Code T2020_50))

These indicators show that not only income, but other factors also are important for a good life and equality and, further, that there are other ways to examine

and measure poverty and inequality and the impacts related to material deprivation. Naturally, the examples also indicate a more normative stance. Further,
an issue for societal development is related to when one is poor or not. For
example, one can ask whether or not it is necessary in a modern society to
have a car, a washing machine or a colour television without being seen as
materially deprived. However, this list of items related to material deprivation
makes it possible to include factors other than money. This is also the idea
behind having other ways to measure equality, and as a way to understand
what welfare and well-being are – that they are not only related to monetary
aspects (see also Chapter 2).

Therefore other types of data are often included in poverty analyses and
used when describing countries' development and levels of equality. They
include, for example:

a) average life expectancy
b) degree of illiteracy
c) educational attainment level.

There are in most welfare states inequalities in average life expectancy between
high- and low-income earners and also inequalities in income between groups
with a higher or lower educational attainment level. The above-mentioned
measures are especially useful for making cross-country comparisons. The
United Nations Development Programme (UNDP) created the Human
Development Index as a composite indicator including two of these elements in
combination with the income component:

> The Human Development Index (HDI) is a summary measure of human
> development. It measures the average achievements in a country in three
> basic dimensions of human development: a long and healthy life (health),
> access to knowledge (education) and a decent standard of living (income).
> Data availability determines HDI country coverage. To enable cross-country
> comparisons, the HDI is, to the extent possible, calculated based on data
> from leading international data agencies and other credible data sources
> available at the time of writing.
>
> (http://hdr.undp.org/en/statistics/hdi/
> (accessed 16 November 2012))

The countries that rank highest in the HDI are mainly the richer countries in the
Western world and at the bottom are poor countries in Africa. There are many and
different ways of looking at poverty, equality and deprivation. These may include:

- satisfaction of basic needs
- capacity to afford basic leisure and social activities
- availability of consumer durables
- housing conditions

- appreciation of own personal conditions
- characteristics of the social environment
- ability to adequately heat home
- constrained food choices
- overcrowding
- poor environmental conditions
- ability to pay utility bills
- ability to pay rent/mortgage for accommodation.

These issues will not be discussed in detail here; they are included in order to illustrate other important issues and aspects related to the understanding of poverty and inequality, and can therefore be used when examining the different factors that have an impact on poverty and equality (see also Section 10.6 on social exclusion). However, many of the elements listed above are related to well-being and happiness, and are areas in which welfare states are involved and might be able to support individuals or certain aspects or groups in society in such a way that deprivations can be reduced. One example might be support for improvements to housing.

Intergenerational issues also relate to poverty and inequality. For example, an OECD study showed that the possibility of a person attaining a higher level of education is related to their parents having a high level of educational attainment (Causa et al., 2009). There is therefore the risk that inequalities continue generation after generation due to a relatively low level of social mobility, and not only within the educational system. This phenomenon may be labelled social inheritance. This does not imply that no social mobility takes place – in any direction – this is just an indication of a risk of persistent inequality if there is no welfare state intervention.

As already indicated there are many and varied types of initiatives welfare states could undertake, if they so choose, to influence inequality, poverty and deprivation.

9.4   The welfare state and equality

Most welfare states have several policies that can have an impact on the degree of poverty and inequality within society. They relate to the impact of the welfare state through taxes and duties, and the use of income transfers to people with low or no incomes. Higher levels of taxes and duties on high-income earners can thus help finance measures to alleviate poverty in the welfare states. The size of the welfare state and the degree of reduction of inequality it seeks is a highly contested area. Welfare states have several instruments they can use when trying to change this situation. Besides higher absolute or relative levels of taxes and duties on high-income earners, the welfare state can also target social transfers and/or make social services available for those most in need. This can then reduce the level of inequality based on the labour market and redistribute resources across generations. The welfare state can thus have a considerable impact on the level and degree of equality.

A possible reason for states being interested in and having policies aimed at reducing inequality relates to the possible negative societal outcomes of a high level of inequality (cf. Wilkinson and Pickett, 2009). Among these is the impact on children's lives, and the risk of children growing up with insufficient resources, and also the understanding of the welfare state as social investment as described in Chapter 3. In a situation of inequality, children might be at risk of not getting an education, not being included in society and thereby being socially excluded (cf. also Chapter 10).

New social risks, such as family breakups, might also have a negative impact on the economic degree of equality in distribution, with more people living at risk of poverty as single-income earners, including lone parents, as these households often have a lower level of disposable income. Lone parents further constitute a specific group at risk of poverty which might also have a negative impact on the lives of children.

The level of benefits and who is to receive them can therefore, on the one hand, be used to reduce poverty and inequality. On the other hand, there is the issue of the extent to which a high level of benefits might have a negative influence on people's incentive to take up a job (cf. Chapter 7), and/or try to be self-supporting. This further reflects a normative issue concerning who deserves income transfers and welfare services from the welfare state, and who does not. This also reflects whether it should only be those who are really poor who receive benefits or whether access to services should depend on need. Many welfare states have universal access to many health care services where the need for treatment is the priority, over the ability to pay for the services. In the area of welfare services and the influence on equality, one issue is whether the middle class uses these services to a greater degree and thereby that the welfare state instead of reducing inequality reinforces it. Whereas income transfers and the tax and duty system (with the exception of some tax expenditures, cf. Chapter 4) mainly reduce the level of inequality in welfare states, this is less clear for the welfare services. Empirical analysis of the precise impact and use of services is needed in order to find out the impact of distributional outcome on providing state welfare services.

Given that poverty and deprivation also relate to non-economic issues, welfare states can, by focusing on issues such as housing and the environment, reduce or reinforce other types of inequality. Further, given that differences related to equality often revolve around levels of education, access to the labour market, gender and so on (see also Chapters 7 and 10), the role of the welfare state can be to help alleviate poverty. However, it is difficult to say in theoretical terms exactly how much or to what extent this should be done. Still, the market left to itself will create inequalities. Due to different circumstances during the life cycle, these inequalities might have negative impacts on a society's development. State regulation that has an influence is, for example, the EU rules on equal treatment of men and women with the intention of avoiding wage discrimination between men and women doing the same type of job (see also Chapter 12).

One can question and discuss several of the ways that the welfare state could be involved in policies to reduce inequality and poverty and thereby social justice. As just one example, in Box 9.3 the ideas of a German political scientist are presented.

Box 9.3 Five priorities of social justice by Wolfgang Merkel (2004)

1   The fight against poverty – not just because of economic inequality itself, but on the grounds that poverty (above all enduring poverty) limits the individual's capacity for autonomy and self-esteem.
2   Creating the highest possible standards of education and training, rooted in equal and fair access for all.
3   Ensuring employment for all those who are willing and able.
4   A welfare state that provides protection and dignity.
5   Limiting inequalities of income and wealth if they hinder the realization of the first four goals or endanger the cohesion of society.

(Merkel, here from Diamond and Giddens, 2005, p. 109)

9.5   Summing-up

There are many and varied aspects one needs to take into consideration when trying to disentangle poverty and equality/inequality. One is how to define these concepts precisely and then to relate them to everyday life and functioning in modern welfare states. Poverty is now often measured in terms of a relative standard, and within Europe an income below 60 per cent of the median income is seen as living in poverty. Persistent poverty is defined as having such an income for more than three consecutive years. As people's living standards and understanding of the necessary level are different, instead of talking about poverty, it is often referred to as being at risk of living in poverty. This is then a further reason for also looking into material deprivation as another approach to understanding inequalities in different societies.

There are many and varied ways of measuring equality/inequality. The most commonly used methods are the Gini coefficient and the 80/20 measure. It is essential to know how the measure has been calculated and what kind of data is behind the various measures. It is further important to be aware that equality can be measured both in monetary and non-monetary items.

Welfare states can influence the degree of equality/inequality in different ways including both use of taxes and duties, and also by using income transfers and supply of welfare services. An important question has been whether middle-class people, due to their better ability to be in dialogue with the bureaucrats, receive more and better welfare services than those most in need. If the middle class is included in those groups that mainly gain from welfare services then the degree of redistribution in welfare states might be less than is often expected when comparing the situation before and after taxes, duties and income transfers. The overall impact seems also to depend on the routes and use of tax expenditures and occupational welfare seems to reduce the degree of equality in income and access to services in different welfare states.

Overall the impact of the welfare state depends on the precise nature and size of the chosen instruments and of services and transfers. It further also depends on the understanding of what justice is and the approach taken to justice in different societies.

References

Burchardt, T. (2006), Foundations for Measuring Equality: A Discussion Paper for the Equalities Review Panel. CSAE Paper 111. London, Centre for the Analysis of Social Exclusion, London School of Economics.

Causa, O., Dantan, S. and Johansson, Å. (2009), Intergenerational Social Mobility in European OECD Countries. OECD Economics Department Working Papers, no. 709, Paris, OECD.

Diamond, P. and Giddens, A. (2005), The New Egalitarianism: Economic Inequality in the UK. In Diamond, P. and Giddens, A. (eds), *The New Egalitarianism*. Cambridge, Polity, pp. 101–119.

Fitzpatrick, T. (2011), *Welfare Theory*, Houndsmills, Palgrave.

Mau, S. and Verwiebe, R. (2010), *European Societies: Mapping Structure and Change*. Bristol, Policy Press.

Saunders, P. (2013), Poverty. In Greve, B. (ed.), *The Routledge Handbook of the Welfare State*. Abingdon, Routledge, pp. 59–70.

Sen, A. (1995), The Political Economy of Targeting. In Van de Walle, D. and Nead, K. (eds), *Public Spending and the Poor*. Washington, DC, World Bank, pp. 11–23.

Sen, A. (2009), *The Idea of Justice*. London, Penguin.

Townsend, P. (1979), *Poverty in the United Kingdom*. Harmondsworth, Penguin.

Wilkinson, R. and Pickett, K. (2009), *The Spirit Level: Why Greater Equality Makes Societies Stronger*. London, Bloomsbury Press.

Chapter 10

Different groups' position in welfare states

Contents

10.1 Introduction

Welfare states have many and diverse dividing lines, and often these lines intersect with each other. This also refers to the fact that welfare states to varying degrees have been able to include all or most groups in society, and the risk that inclusion of some groups, at least implicitly, means the exclusion of others. The central issue for this chapter is whether and how welfare states are reducing, reinforcing or changing the possible integration of different groups in society. This can be along the lines of gender, ethnicity, age, disability or sexuality. Different types of inclusion/exclusion will be shown together with their impact and implementation. One reason for also looking at implementation is that even the best rules that are drawn up in order to ensure inclusion and equality might in practice be implemented in such a way that exclusion and social division occurs. Class used to be a central concept in the understanding of welfare states' development, including the struggle for better working and living conditions. Classes were often depicted by looking into people's structural position in the production (workers or capitalist), whereas today it is more along the lines of their position in the labour market and access to and/or ownership of assets. There are intersecting lines, and although this position has an impact on individual level of welfare the choice has been to focus on specific groups, which are or can be reinforced by their class position in society.

This chapter thus looks into how different groups in welfare states are included or excluded, and to what degree, and what kind of possible mechanism might support or reduce this. This will be done by looking into different groups' possible positions in relation to access to the labour market, welfare services and benefits, and the degree of economic and other types of inequality (see also Chapter 9). It can be questioned whether one can make this distinction in the analysis between different groups, or whether the analysis should be across the different issues, that is social exclusion/inclusion more generally. However, for the sake of presentation, and given that there are some differences, the analysis will be done by looking at these specific issues knowing that they are often linked together, and sometimes reinforce each other. There are therefore sections on gender, disability, age and ethnicity, followed by a presentation of possible mechanisms that influence position and links related to inclusion and exclusion in welfare states. These are seen as examples of how different issues can be influenced by different types of welfare state and further as typical groups with stronger or weaker positions in their society.

Social exclusion refers to a debate first presented in France in the early 1970s, where the socially excluded were those falling through the social insurance system, and who were thus not seen as included in society (cf. also Box 10.1. for a definition of social exclusion). Social exclusion can be understood as a narrow approach to social rights, whereas the broader understanding, which will be the one used here, takes a multidimensional approach (see also Chapter 9) and thus focuses on exclusion from standard living conditions within areas of social, economic and political issues in a society. Using these dimensions the following sections will present how different groups can be seen as included or excluded along different lines, and whether this differs in different kinds of welfare states.

Some overall trends at the European level are shown in Box 10.2. However, since 2009 more people in Europe have been living in poverty and at risk of social exclusion as a consequence of the fiscal crisis, so presumably the current situation at the time of writing is worse for many people within the European Union. The situation also varies among the European countries, for example, people in southern Europe and some countries in eastern Europe have had a much worse economic development in the wake of the financial crisis, with the impact that the number of people being socially excluded is higher than in other European welfare states.

10.2 Gender inequality

Gender issues and how to cope with and reduce gender inequality have been part of the development of the welfare state in many countries, often supported by international organisations. Gender issues also relate to the difference between men and women in several aspects of societal development. In the European Union, for example, gender equality indicators focus on issues such as education, labour market, earnings and social inclusion, health, childcare and elderly care. This reflects the areas where historically there have been, and still are in several countries, differences between men and women. The welfare state often has the aim of ensuring gender equality, albeit the factual situation is often that the actual outcome is not neutral. In general the Nordic welfare states are most gender equal, with southern European welfare states less so, and the continental and liberal welfare states are in between.

There is a need to make a distinction between sex and gender. Sex refers to the biological dimension and gender to the social element (Shaver, 2013). In relation to gender, some of the important aspects are the degree of care responsibilities, independence and 'defamilisation'.

Care refers to the activities for dependent persons (typically children and elderly people). It can be split between informal and formal care, and this implies different types of delivery from the state, the market and civil society. Formal care is delivered either by the welfare state or the market, sometimes for free at the point of use, other times for payment. Informal care is what takes place within the family and civil society and is unpaid work. Historically, it has mainly been women who have undertaken the care work in households, and still is, although more men now also take part in care for children, especially in northern Europe. This leads to the issue of independence and the goal that both men and women should be able to live an independent life. The goal of 'defamilisation' revolves precisely around the ability to maintain an independent and adequate life without having a family.

The issue of the role of the welfare state in different countries can also be seen in the description of different types of welfare states, ranging from the male breadwinner to the dual-breadwinner model, and further to the dual earner-dual carer model. The male-breadwinner model is characterised by the man being on the labour market and the woman taking care of the children and the household, whereas in the dual-care model both are earning income and taking part in care of the children. Different welfare regimes have different emphases and different approaches, although the tendency in Europe has been towards a dual-income earner model, whereas men being involved in care to the same degree as women is less strongly developed in some European countries.

A fundamental issue in the analysis of equality among men and women is whether measured differences are due to formal or informal discrimination. The reason for making this distinction is that in most countries from a legal perspective there is equality between men and women. The EU has had, since its start, a clear focus on and demand for equality between men and women, including equal pay for equal work, even if what is equal work is not simple to define. Furthermore, there might be differences due to different choices within the family or for the individual person. Historically, women have been the disadvantaged sex; however, in recent years, in some areas, for example, education, it now seems that men are at a disadvantage compared with women, at least in some countries, in that the level of educational attainment of girls, on average, exceeds that of boys. Furthermore, men in all countries have a lower life expectancy than women. There is therefore also more focus on men and masculinity as, in certain circumstances, they have more difficulties than previously, due in part to their changing role. This can be that the man is no longer the main provider (e.g. the male-breadwinner model has been changed), and also that women in some families earn more than their partner. Furthermore, men in several welfare states are now more actively involved in taking care of the children in the family. Therefore the roles and understanding of the roles of gender have changed.

These changed roles imply a need for an analysis to be aware of reasons for, and possible impact of, a variety of rules related to the way families and civil society functions. Gender analysis is thus no longer an issue dealing with women's relatively weaker position in society, but from case to case from area to area an analysis of men's and women's position in society, and also if possible what is the cause of the differences and inequalities.

Gender issues are especially the focus in feminist analysis. A distinction between three different approaches can help in understanding different feminist positions regarding the policy needed to reduce gender inequality. Three approaches are:

a) *Liberal feminism*: equal opportunities and rights are central.
b) *Social feminism*: women's disadvantage is related to the economic system favouring men.
c) *Radical feminism*: oppression of women is due to a male-dominated social, political and economic system (Johnson, 1999).

These approaches can help in explaining different approaches to welfare policies in different countries and whether, for example, parental leave on the birth of a child should be obligatory for both men and women, or whether it should be a free choice. Also, the focus is on whether there is a need for intervention to rebalance differences between the genders due to the outcome of activities in the market and in families.

Discussion and questions of gender can often be portrayed as an example of the fact that although the formal rules and conditions for equality are in place, they are not fulfilled when looking into what actually takes place in different societies. Two examples where women are disadvantaged can show this. The first is that in all countries within the EU (see Figure 10.1) there is a difference between wages for men and women, despite the principle of equal pay for equal work in the European treaty and also directives concerning equality. The relation to the kind of welfare state is not clear for the countries analysed in this book, with the highest gender pay gap in Germany, the Czech Republic and the UK, and the lowest in Italy.

Although there might be various reasons and explanations for the differences, for example, the different number of years in the labour market, different educational attainment levels, differences in the position in the labour market and more men than women working full time, some of the differences in most

equality and specific groups' position

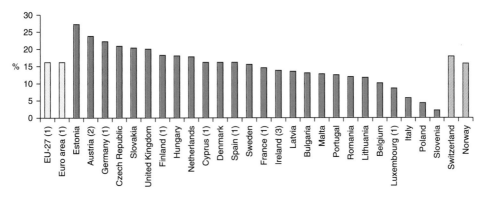

Figure 10.1 The unadjusted gender pay gap percentage in 2011.

(1) Enterprises with ten or more employees; NACE Rev. 2 Sections B to S excluding O; EU-27, EA-17, Germany, Cyprus, Spain, France, Luxemburg - provisional data.
(2) estimated data.
(3) 2010 data.
Source: Eurostat (online data code: tsdsc340) (accessed 9 June 2014).

countries remain unexplained. The different positions refer both to the number of people being promoted and that there is a vertical division of work in the labour market, for example, in most countries more men than women work in the private sector, and more women than men work in the public sector. Given that women often earn less than men, this also at least partially explains why women's labour force participation is lower than men's (see Table 10.1) in situations where the partners choose who will be working and who will be caring. Different uses of parental leave also have an impact.

Table 10.1 gives a clear indication of how there is a remarkably large difference in participation in the labour market between men and women when they have children. The differences are lowest in the Nordic welfare states, and

Table 10.1 Employment percentage rate for men and women between 20 and 49 years old in couples with children in 2012

	All	*Men*	*Women*
EU27	79.0	89.8	68.8
Czech Republic	79.3	95.2	63.5
Denmark	88.9	93.0	85.2
Germany	82.2	92.9	72.0
Spain	69.8	80.4	60.0
France	82.5	91.3	74.4
Italy	71.9	89.7	56.0
Hungary	71.8	86.5	58.3
Sweden	88.9	94.0	84.2
United Kingdom	81.1	91.1	70.6

Source: Eurostat (lfst_hheredty) (accessed 4 August 2013).

highest in eastern and southern Europe, but also high in the liberal and continental welfare states. When some women have children, at least for a few years after the birth of the child, they are away from the labour market, and therefore over the working life they have a lower participation rate than men, this is thereby also part of the reason for the difference in wages. A way for the welfare state to increase equality of access to the labour market has therefore been investment in day care for children. This provides equality in access to the labour market, increases the labour supply and also provides good facilities for all children. This has therefore also been reflected in the EU strategy of implementing affordable and high-quality day care. This is further also seen as part of the way to ensure a better work–family life balance (cf. also Chapter 8) and moving the welfare state more towards a social investment state.

Gender (in)equalities exist in various parts of society. This is the case in the labour market, in family life, in health care and also, for example, from another part of societal development, in participation in democratic decision making. There is thus a constant need for empirical analysis to find out the extent and development of gender inequalities in individual countries and in different areas, as well as the role of welfare states in relation to gender, in order to ensure a higher degree of equality.

10.3 People with disabilities

People with disabilities are a very diverse group ranging from people with minor problems to those who need 24-hour care. The central issue is whether and how they are able to live a life in the same way as others in the society. There is often a distinction between the social model of disability, focusing on the social, economic and environmental barriers to equality, and the individual model, which focuses on limitation in functioning and participation in society resulting from a medical condition. A further distinction is between impairment, which is an attribute of an individual, for example, reduced or lack of hearing abilities, and disability, which is the loss, or limitation, of equal participation in societal activities.

Box 10.3 shows some central principles related to the UN Convention on the Rights of Persons with Disabilities (UNCRPD), which was adopted in 2006 and came into force in 2008. This Convention was an attempt to focus on important issues related to both societal development and everyday life for people with disabilities. It has been signed by more than 150 countries around the world.

Box 10.3 Guiding principles of the Convention on the Rights of Persons with Disabilities

There are eight guiding principles that underlie the Convention and each one of its specific articles:

---

a) Respect for inherent dignity, individual autonomy including the freedom to make one's own choices, and independence of persons;
b) Non-discrimination;
c) Full and effective participation and inclusion in society;
d) Respect for difference and acceptance of persons with disabilities as part of human diversity and humanity;
e) Equality of opportunity;
f) Accessibility;
g) Equality between men and women;
h) Respect for the evolving capacities of children with disabilities and respect for the right of children with disabilities to preserve their identities.

(http://www.un.org/disabilities/default.asp?navid=16&pid=156 (accessed 6 December 2012))

The general principle of the UNCRPD is that people with disabilities should have the same rights, opportunities and options to live a life they themselves prefer and with a high degree of human dignity. However, formal rights and principles are one thing, and concrete implementation in the different welfare states is another, given the economic constraints and options available.

Thus in all EU countries people with disabilities have a lower rate of participation in the labour market and higher level of unemployment compared with those without disabilities. It is also often difficult to participate actively in societal development due to both physical and other types of hindrance. Physical hindrances can be difficulties in moving around, for example, buildings are not accessible. Other hindrances include the lack of personal resources or financial resources to support an individual's participation, for example, use of public transport is not always possible and if an individual cannot afford to use a taxi it leaves them dependent on someone to help with transport.

Social inclusion/exclusion for people with disabilities might thus range from direct or indirect discrimination in the labour market to difficulties in participation in society, including a lower than average income making it difficult to be able to afford the same types of activity as others in society. Children with disabilities are a specific disadvantaged group given that they might have more difficulties entering and/or continuing education and therefore have a higher risk of not being integrated in the labour market over their lifetime.

Policies to support people with disabilities are thus very diverse and include many of the welfare states' activities. This can range from income support (social assistance and/or housing assistance, disability pension) and support getting a job (various types of aids, positive discrimination, etc.) to accessing different kinds of services including, for some, 24-hour a day care. Furthermore, support to facilitate access to buildings and transportation, and adaptations in houses to enable independent living are some of the remedies available to support people with disabilities to a different degree in different welfare states.

Policies can also look at or focus on different approaches. A central approach in line with the UNCRPD has been to facilitate independent living by being aware of measures for support with housing, transport, access, personal assistance and so on. This also includes the options of individual people with disabilities being able to get a job and having a decent guaranteed income.

The welfare state thus has various options to support people with disabilities, although this area is also in competition with other areas of the welfare state in need of more resources. Formal rules banning discrimination are also an option, but their implementation might be difficult. Thus it is important to look into the forms of indirect discrimination, for example, why the employment rate of people with disabilities in most countries is much lower than for other groups. This furthermore also indicates the need to inform people with disabilities about already existing types of support and options in order to ensure, for example, their better integration in the labour market.

The market, and in particular private enterprise, might support people with disabilities by having policies of corporate social responsibility, which can include employment of people with disabilities, and retaining employees who become disabled during the course of their employment. These policies can be supported by the welfare state, for example, by financial or tax incentives.

Civil society's role is often related to supporting individuals within in the family, including care. Voluntary support to people with disabilities can also be found in most welfare states. Thus also in this area we see different roles and support from the state, the market and civil society.

10.4 Age discrimination

In principle, within the EU, discrimination on the grounds of age is prohibited, and this also relates to the issue of being or reaching a specific age. It is thus not permitted in the labour market, for example, to sack older people or to prefer to employ young people. However, minimum age limits for entering a night club, for example, or reduced prices for certain age groups are acceptable.

Even though it is unlawful to discriminate formally, discrimination still takes place informally. There are, for example, many and varied reasons that employers can give when they have to lay-off staff, and also when engaging a new employee it is possible to find arguments for the person an employer prefers. It is thus difficult to prove that discrimination has taken place. An example to illustrate this is the number of people in different age groups who have participated in lifelong learning within a certain specified time period paid for by employers. This is shown in Table 10.2.

Table 10.2 clearly shows that elderly people participate to a much lower degree than others in lifelong learning than younger persons in the labour market in all countries and in all types of welfare state. This therefore indicates that there is a risk that when reaching a certain age the continued improvement

Table 10.2 Percentages of people in the labour force who within the last four weeks participated in lifelong learning in 2012

	25–44	45–54	55–64
EU27	11.1	7.4	4.5
Czech Republic	13.4	10.3	4.8
Denmark	35.4	29.1	23.9
Germany	10.5	5.3	2.9
Spain	13.0	8.0	5.2
France	7.2	4.6	2.6
Italy	8.2	4.8	3.0
Hungary	4.0	1.3	0.5
Sweden	30.2	25.2	18.6
United Kingdom	17.9	15.4	10.2

Source: Eurostat (trng_lfse_01) (accessed 4 January 2013).

in competences is no longer supported by the employer to the same degree as for younger workers, and the decline seems to start from the age of around 45 years. Table 10.2 thus also indicates that the social investment perspective in relation to education is less strong for adults than for children and young persons.

The reasons for this can relate to both employers' and employees' positions. It might be that employers are less willing to pay for lifelong learning activities for older workers due to the expectation that they will leave the labour market relatively soon. It might also be because some employees do not find that they need more training, given their long experience in their field of work. Even though there might be reasonable explanations, this is still an indication that age discrimination takes place. Given the expectation of a future shortage of workers due to demographic changes (see Section 13.2), an increase in education for older workers might in principle be a way to use a social investment approach to reduce this problem.

People above the age of 55 also have a lower participation rate in the labour market than other groups, and sometimes also a higher level of unemployment. This again is also implicitly a type of discrimination, although not necessarily formal and direct discrimination. One explanation is that the risk of sickness, including as a result of an industrial injury or other type of accident, increases with age and thus participation in the labour market has become more difficult. Change in requirements for qualifications and new types of production and the constant change in employment structure also imply that older people who have been in the same job area for many years will have more difficulty changing their position in the labour market.

It is not only in the labour market that there is a risk of social exclusion. Elderly people outside the labour market have a higher risk of feeling lonely and a higher risk of living alone, with no close friend or relative to be in contact with. The elderly might also be less included in social life and participation in society in general. This is also because the ability to move around for some can become limited with increasing age. Mobility can thus be a hindrance to integration into the wider society.

Elderly persons are, to a larger degree, dependent on care (formal or informal) in order to cope with daily life, including cleaning, shopping and mobility. Such dependency increases the likelihood of being more marginalised in society. The role of the welfare state here relates to providing formal care. The role of civil society includes providing informal care and also voluntary work, for example, to relieve elderly people from feeling alone.

At the other end of the life cycle, there are some types of formal discrimination. This includes when a person is allowed by state regulation to buy cigarettes and alcohol, to drive a car or visit a casino, and age limits exist in relation to the classification of films. This kind of discrimination is a paternalistic type of discrimination in order to try to protect young people from harm, based upon knowledge of what might create problems for these groups or the actual norms in a society. Here the state is using mainly the legal approach and other measures to a lesser extent, although duties on cigarettes and alcohol also have an impact on young people's ability to buy the products.

10.5 Race and ethnicity

These are contested terms in social sciences and often relate to a discussion indicating 'us and them', which in itself implies a type of inclusion (us) and exclusion (them). The debate has for a long time reverted to issues of segregation based upon race in several countries, although a more modern approach to the issue of race and ethnicity tries to look into and disentangle various direct or indirect types of discrimination.

Ethnicity refers to self-identity and types of social construction and relatedness through culture and history. Race has a focus on common traits of genealogy or blood. Race and ethnicity are often used interchangeably, although today the focus is more often on variation in, and the impact of difference related to, ethnicity.

Three different positions on ethnicity can be distinguished (Mørck, 2011):

a) an approach based upon cultural difference
b) an approach based upon borders between groups, e.g. one group defines itself by its diversity from other groups
c) a position combining A and B.

Different positions also denote various types of impact related to inclusion/exclusion in societies. Further, for some ethnic groups it is simpler to define what is common and what is not common. Here the focus is on the implication of these differences.

The position of diverse ethnic groups in a society does not have to be the same. This is, for example, reflected in the fact that migrants from different countries have different positions in societies and in the labour market. Part of the reason for this may be discrimination; part may be due to different types of social network, for example, strong and weak networks (Granovetter, 1973). Strong networks might help in ensuring access to societal activities and especially the labour market, while at the same time carrying the risk of fragmentation into strongly differentiated groups, making it difficult to switch to being in contact with other networks. Weak networks also have both positive and negative elements. The negative aspects relate to the fact that it can be difficult to enter the labour market and be integrated into the wider society; weak networks can imply access to jobs in a wider group of sectors than being in strong networks which only offer access to a more limited set of options.

A risk of focusing on ethnicity is that it can, in itself, imply social exclusion. However, by not looking into it and analysing the possible types of segregation there is a risk that formal as well as informal types of exclusion are obscured. It is also important to be aware of the impact of diversity, and also for how long one can be characterised as being diverse and when this is just the way it is. Children of migrants, for example, and their children, might have lived for a long time or been born in the 'new' country, and whether or not to label these an ethnic group can be open to question.

Historically, foreigners have often been seen as a threat to the local work-force, and this includes the perception that they might, for example, have a higher crime rate and work for lower wages. Xenophobia has thus been an issue for many centuries. Integration of people from other countries in the labour market, and in society in a wider sense, might therefore be difficult with societal mechanisms that operate both to include some and to exclude those who do not 'look like' the others, and furthermore they might be used as a scapegoat by other groups. Immigrants and even refugees have thus often also had hard times in many countries, and most countries in Europe and the EU have rules making immigration very difficult for asylum seekers, including refugees, and also for economic migrants.

There might further be intersectionalities, that is a risk of social exclusion due to a combination of gender and ethnicity or other combinations. Therefore, it can be difficult to look into just one type of diversity, but there is a need to include and analyse several possible types together, and some elements might help in including, and others in excluding.

The role of the welfare state in relation to these issues can be to supply public information, and to try to ensure that discrimination does not take place. This might include support for integration in the labour market, given that having a job often helps in integration in the wider society. This also indicates that the market, and especially the labour market, can be an important force to reduce discrimination. Civil society, by reinforcing networks, might also offer support for individuals or groups in society.

10.6 Exclusion/inclusion and policies to combat exclusion

There are several instances in this chapter where we can see a variety of reasons why inclusion and exclusion take place. Some are cases of direct discrimination, while other types of mechanism work more indirectly. Some are directly against international and national agreements and law, whereas other types of discrimination are more hidden and indirect. Social exclusion can in principle be both voluntary and involuntary. The focus here is on the involuntary type of exclusion.

Mechanisms that imply exclusion from the options available in society at large are related to lack of economic options. For example, living at risk of poverty (cf. Chapter 9) increases the likelihood of being excluded from options and possibilities in societies, ranging from cultural and social aspects to the labour market. Having a lack of economic means might imply, for example, that a child cannot participate in the same activities as other children and therefore risks being socially excluded. It might also prevent adults having friends and social contacts. Therefore material deprivation can imply a higher risk of social exclusion. Box 10.4 shows the EU understanding of central elements related to material deprivation (see also Section 9.3).

Box 10.4 The European Union's definition of material deprivation:

The collection 'material deprivation' covers indicators relating to economic strain, durables, housing and environment of the dwelling. Severely materially deprived persons have living conditions severely constrained by a lack of resources; they experience at least four out of the following nine deprivation items: cannot afford i) to pay rent or utility bills, ii) to keep home adequately warm, iii) to face unexpected expenses, iv) to eat meat, fish or a protein equivalent every second day, v) a week's holiday away from home, vi) a car, vii) a washing machine, viii) a colour TV, or ix) a telephone.

(Eurostat, Code T2020_50)

Table 10.3 shows the number of people having some material deprivation in 2011 based upon the criteria shown in Box 10.4. Table 10.3 indicates that about half of the population in the EU do not have any kind of material deprivation as they are lacking none of the nine items listed in Box 10.4. At the same

Table 10.3 Number of people in percentages with no, three or more and five or more items lacking with regard to material deprivation in 2011

	No items	3 items or more	5 items or more
EU27	47.1	19.6	3.9
Czech Republic	44.1	16.8	2.7
Denmark	64.2	7.5	0.7
Germany	60.1	11.3	1.9
Spain	44.1	16.3	1.5
France	58.0	12.8	1.8
Italy	39.6	25.2	4.4
Hungary	16.2	44.0	13.1
Sweden	76.1	4.5	0.4
United Kingdom	49.1	16.6	2.7

Source: European Union Statistics on Income and Living Conditions (EU-SILC) (ilc_sip8) (accessed 4 January 2014).

time, many citizens also lack at least three of the elements in relation to material deprivation. Those with five or more can be described as severely deprived, and this is the case for more than one in ten of the population in Hungary, whereas it is less than that in the EU in general. The fact that the Nordic welfare states have the fewest persons with severe material deprivation confirms the picture from Chapter 9 on equality and the differences among welfare regimes. Among the countries with the highest level of risk of material deprivation is Italy, although Spain is on a par with Germany, France and the UK.

Being severely materially deprived can increase the risk of social exclusion. Hence, the role of the welfare state might involve trying to prevent people becoming socially excluded due to material deprivation. This might be, for example, efforts to reduce work accidents and ensuring work abilities by lifelong learning for people. Help in ensuring people's access to the labour market will also, in most welfare states, help to bridge the gap and increase the likelihood of social integration. Preventive measures are thus one option. However, when a person has one or more disadvantage there might be a need for various kinds of support to help the individual keep contact and be integrated into the wider society. This includes the right for people with disabilities to be interviewed in job selection procedures in some cases. This may be where the state imposes on employers' quota obligation, for example, to employ a certain amount of people with disabilities or otherwise forfeit an amount of money to the state.

Where the indications are that a person might be on the way to being socially excluded, this can also help to identify those who need support from the welfare state to avoid social exclusion. For example, a person losing his/her job and more or less at the same time becoming divorced might be an indicator that the person is at risk of becoming socially excluded. Furthermore, this can for some imply no home, and therefore the additional crisis of homelessness.

The degree to which it is the responsibility of the welfare state to ensure social contact with others and the responsibility of civil society can be debated, thus referring back to the issue and balance between state, market and civil society.

There are many and varied instruments the welfare state can use, ranging from different kinds of aids, ensuring that the workplace fits all, and requiring equal treatment and no discrimination, to economic support for different groups or persons excluded or at risk of being socially excluded. The welfare state thus, within the economic limits and options, has a role that varies from direct intervention and support to indirect creation of options and avoidance of constraints, helping to ensure a high degree of social inclusion.

The creation of certain locations where different groups in society live, for example, segregated housing areas, even though this is not a formal type of exclusion, will implicitly mean exclusion of those living in one area from those living in another area. Housing structures and dispersion in different areas can thus imply exclusion of some groups from other groups.

However, even when formal support is available either in kind or in cash, and when legal instruments require equal treatment, there might still be exclusion due to the fact that, for example, employers and employees prefer to work with people looking and being like themselves. Welfare state intervention thus might have a role in redressing the operation of the labour market, whereby people with disabilities have less access to jobs, women are sometimes not promoted, or men have difficulties getting jobs in certain sectors. This is because people might have different prior perceptions of how an individual might act or be, based upon certain characteristics. Norms and traditions might thus also imply the exclusion of some people in societies.

Exclusion from the labour market for people with disabilities, with the attendant risk of further social exclusion, might even in some cases, even when having the necessary available instruments, imply, as has been argued with reference to the UK case, that 'In other words, it is fine for employers to discriminate against disabled people if the economics of their enterprise can justify it' (Piggott and Grover, 2012, p. 9).

Finally, as to the role of civil society, voluntary organisations can by a variety of initiatives support those at the margin of society by helping with, for example, clothes, shelter and social contacts. Self-help groups and other activities supporting those who, for example, have become severely ill can help in reducing social exclusion and also in ensuring social inclusion.

equality and specific groups' position

10.7 Social inheritance – or the risk of reinforcing outcome generations after generations

This chapter has in various ways dealt with different groups' possible positions, including social inclusion. Social activities might intersect so that a person may have more than one disadvantaged position that may be interlinked in a variety of ways. For example, a disabled person may be at a higher risk of being unemployed. The risk may be increased if the person is older and without a long previous work record.

At the same time there is a risk that a child coming from a family with fewer resources is more likely to be at the margin of the welfare state. A child of an unskilled single mother might thus be at a higher risk of not getting an education than a child from a family where at least one member is a skilled worker. Naturally, this is not to say that this will always be the case and indeed many coming from disadvantaged homes get a job, an education and are socially integrated. Rather there is a higher risk of what is termed negative social inheritance. In comparison, positive social inheritance is often referred to when, for example, a child of a football player also becomes a well-known football player. As the proverb says: the apple falls close to the tree.

A possible risk when talking about negative social inheritance is that simply talking about it can lead to stigmatisation, so that, for example, social workers or others in contact with people who have a problematic social background from the outset believe that such people will themselves have problems. However, it might be important to be aware of the risk in order to, if possible, start a more preventive initiative, by, for example, ensuring better education for the children and/or support in more vulnerable and dilapidated housing areas.

This is also seen as referring to the impact of class on position in society, and the influence of social class on poverty, social exclusion and occurrence of social risk (Pintelon et al., 2013). It can be debated whether, with the increased fragmentation in society, class is still relevant as an analytical concept. However, when social class is seen as the social background influencing the possible life of different persons and thereby social stratification this might be used as a starting point for analysis. There is no clear and single definition, but it can be higher, middle and lower class, and it can also refer to position related to means of production. Today, position is often considered by either the level of education or occupation of parents.

The possible impact on life chances of the social background of the family can perhaps also be a reason for the EU focus on children living in households where none of the parents work (cf. Table 10.4). Living in a jobless household is seen as a risk that the children will have fewer opportunities in the future, as well as children living in poverty (Table 10.5) might have a larger risk of ending in poverty themselves.

As can be seen from Table 10.4, there is a higher risk of children living in jobless households in the UK, Hungary and Spain than in the Nordic countries,

Table 10.4 Children aged 0–17 living in jobless households

	2000	2005	2011	2012
EU27	9.7	9.9	10.8	11.1
Czech Republic	7.7	8.2	7.2	7.9
Denmark	:	5.7	8.2	8.2
Germany	9.4	11.4	8.8	8.5
Spain	6.6	5.6	11.9	13.8
France	9.3	8.8	9.9	10.4
Italy	7.6	5.9	8.3	9.2
Hungary	13.5	14.1	16.3	15.0
Sweden	:	:	8.4	7.3
United Kingdom	17.0	16.5	17.3	16.5

Source: Eurostat (lfsi_jhh_a) (accessed 3 January 2014).

Note: Data are the percentage share of persons aged 0–17 who are living in households where no one is working.

Germany and the Czech Republic. The figures have been remarkably stable despite the very varied economic development since 2000. The data also indicate that the traditional pattern among welfare regimes cannot be witnessed in this table. Part of the reason for the low rate in the Nordic countries might be that the labour force participation is higher, especially for women.

Living in poverty can have detrimental impacts especially on children. Table 10.5 shows the number of children below the age of 16 living in poverty. As can be seen from Table 10.5, children's risk of living in poverty is lowest in the Nordic countries, the Czech Republic and Germany. It is very high in Spain, Italy and Hungary, and in the middle in France and the UK. This is not fully in line with the welfare regime depiction of the countries, however, again the Nordic countries with the more generous and universal welfare states seem to achieve a lower level of child poverty than other less generous welfare states. They are at the same time, like the Czech Republic, in general more equal societies, which also influences this.

Figure 10.2 shows the relation between a person's education and the educational attainment level of their parents, there is a clear indication that a child of parents with a low level of education has a higher risk of also attaining a low level, whereas a child of parents with a higher level more often gets a higher level of education. Given the importance of having an education in relation to the labour market, social capital, income and social integration this highlights the risk of negative social inheritance. Still, it also shows that many in fact get a higher education. This is partly due to the fact that over time in most societies higher levels of educational attainment have been achieved.

Table 10.5 At-risk-of-poverty rate children below the age of 16

	2000	2002	2005	2011	2012
EU27	:	:	19.8	20.4	20.4
Czech Republic	:	:	17.7	14.4	13.6
Denmark	:	:	10.1	10.3	10.0
Germany	13	:	11.6	15.5	14.9
Spain	25	21	25.7	28.7	28.9
France	18	16	14.2	18.6	18.8
Italy	25	:	23.3	25.9	25.9
Hungary	17	13	19.7	22.6	22.2
Sweden	:	10	9.2	13.7	14.4
United Kingdom	27	23	23.3	17.6	18.1

Source: European Union Statistics on Income and Living Conditions (EU-SILC) (ilc_li02) (accessed 3 January 2014).

Note: The rate is the 60 per cent of median income after social transfers.

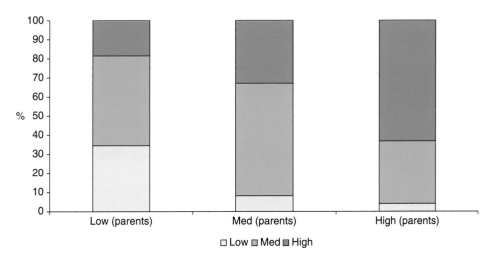

Figure 10.2 Relation between a person aged 25–59 and the parent's educational attainment level.

Source: Eurostat (accessed 12 January 2014) (http://epp.eurostat.ec.europa.eu/statistics_explained/index.php?title=File:Highest_level_of_education_of_the_parents_by_their_descendants_level_of_education,_shares,_EU-28,_age_group_25-59,_2011_new.png&filetimes tamp=20131209090234)

10.8 Summing-up

This chapter has focused on different groups which in different ways are or might be excluded from societal development. This is particularly important in the labour market, but also in a broader context related to being fully integrated into society.

Although there has been a focus on different groups, however, it is important to be aware that they might be reinforcing each other and thus intersect. Different groups might at different points in time be socially excluded or at risk of social exclusion.

Another important issue is that although it is in principle not acceptable, and often prohibited by law, to discriminate, this mainly deals with the formal types of discrimination and less with the more informal and not clearly stated types of indirect discrimination taking place in different welfare states. The lack of knowledge of types of support available to them also helps to explain the disadvantaged position of different groups.

The welfare state has several instruments available, and therefore sometimes the problem is not the lack of welfare state support, but more the indirect type of discrimination. The size of income transfers and access to different kinds of services might also in some societies be a reason why different kinds of discrimination take place. A low level of income transfer, for example, might make it more difficult for people in a disadvantaged position to take part in societal development and activities. It is a fundamental task in many welfare states to reduce the number of people who are socially excluded, as a high level of social inclusion also increases cohesion and sustainability in a welfare state.

References

Granovetter, M. (1973), The Strength of Weak Ties. *American Journal of Sociology*, vol. 78, no. 6, pp. 1360–80.

Johnson, N. (1999), *Mixed Economies of Welfare: A Comparative Perspective*. London, Prentice Hall.

Mørck, Y. (2011), Ethnicitet og kritiske hvidhedsstudier. In Greve, B. (ed.), *Grundbog i Socialvidenskab*. København, Nyt Fra Samfundsvidenskaberne, pp. 257–274.

Piggott, L. and Grover, C. (2012), Employment and Support Allowance: Capability, Personalisation and Disabled People in the UK. *Scandinavian Journal of Disability Research*, vol. 15, no. 2, pp. 170–184.

Pintelon, O., Cantillon, B., Van den Bosch, K. and Whelan, C. (2013), The Social Stratification of Social Risks: The Relevance of Class for Social Investment Strategies. *Journal of European Social Policy*, vol. 23, no. 1, pp. 52–67.

Shaver, S. (2013), Gender Issues in the Welfare State. In Greve, B. (ed.), *The Routledge Handbook of the Welfare State*. Abingdon, Routledge, pp. 94–104.

Part IV

New ways and international perspectives

Chapter 11

New ways of steering the welfare state

Contents

11.1 Introduction

Recent years have seen changes in the way welfare states are managed and organised. A simple hierarchical model is no longer necessarily the way of managing the welfare state. Networks, coordination and delegation are also used. In this chapter the focus is on new elements in the way welfare states are organised, managed and steered.

New types of governance are therefore examined in Section 11.2. These range from the impact of a changed role of the street-level bureaucrat (Lipsky, 1980) to the impact of using new types of steering. This includes demand for quality and effectiveness for the welfare state's activities in ways similar to how the market works, and trying to reduce possible government failure. The section also focuses on the fact that it might be preferable for the middle class to be in contact with the system given that they to a large degree share norms, traditions, meanings and the ability to communicate in a bureaucratic language. Therefore the organisation of the welfare state also has an impact on who is getting what and under what conditions, so even in universally financed welfare states there is a risk of inequality in access to services.

Decentralisation, devolution, but also recentralisation and delegation of power, have entered the way welfare states are developing. This is the focus of Section 11.3.

Given the scarce resources available, constant competition among users and interest groups in order to pressure for a development in their specific area, there has been a growing interest in social policy to know what works best as a way of maximising the impact when spending money in a certain area and ensuring the best results for those using it (cf. Section 11.4). This includes ambitions to make the public sector even more effective and increase productivity in public sector delivery. Social policy thus seems to some extent to follow the pathway already depicted by development in the area of health care.

Another new area of development has been an interest in new ways of trying to influence behaviour, not only with traditional instruments such as taxes and duties and legislation, but also by trying to nudge people in another direction, which is the focus of Section 11.5. Section 11.6 considers a growing issue, how to use technology in the delivery of welfare, including how welfare technology might be a way to solve the possible demographic pressure on welfare states. Section 11.7 sums up the chapter.

11.2 What is governance in welfare states?

> The concept of governance is notoriously slippery; it is frequently used among social scientists and practitioners without a definition all agree on.
>
> (Pierre and Peters, 2000, p. 7)

Governance thus has many and varied meanings. Despite this, governance revolves around how to steer and manage the welfare state, looking at it from both a process perspective and how to coordinate activities within the welfare state. Governance thus orbits around how to find ways to develop, organise and structure society, and here it is especially related to the welfare state. Governance is not only used in relation to the state, but is also connected to important issues such as corporate governance and good governance (openness, for example). Change in governance has also implied integration of market-type mechanisms within the public sector, such as use of demand for services, as a way of trying to improve effectiveness and reduce possible government failures (see Chapter 6).

Changes in governance have had an impact on the way welfare policies have been managed and steered at various levels, although in many ways this is a continuation of analysis and discussions on how the way the welfare state has historically been managed and administered. Governance focuses broadly on actors and how they are integrated in different ways in both decision making and the daily administration of the welfare state. It also focuses on how and in what ways different actors can be involved in many and very varied areas. Additionally, there has been a movement not only to consider national issues important, but also supranational and even global issues (see Chapter 12). Governance can therefore be seen as an overarching concept whose real and central importance lies in the direct application in different areas of welfare policies and how they are implemented. Thus the central question is not the definition of the concept, but the way in which it involves various actors and how it is used in the development of welfare policies.

There are varieties and changes in governance at local, national, supranational and global levels; however, governance and changes therein are not just simple concepts, but have been used differently, and one could argue that in fact the main point is that governance is a way of combining and changing the interrelation between the various actors involved in managing the welfare state.

Governance can be referred to as the coordination of interdependent social relations, and coordination is understood in three distinct forms: anarchy of exchange, hierarchy of command and heterarchy of self-organisation. The first type is especially prevalent in relation to and with regard to market forces, the second in relation to state steering and the last to networks, including civil society. In this way the distinction and interactions between the different modes of coordination and change imply a balance between classical agents in the welfare state's development: state, market and civil society (cf. also Chapters 2, 4–8). When governance changes so does the relation between the actors. Table 11.1 shows a systematising of types of governance.

Table 11.1 is an indication of the variety of governance types and the way they work. This ranges from law and rules to delivery and development with a focus on culture and co-production. They can also have different forms of control mechanism and be universal or more targeted, and also use different kinds of market aspects, such as price (often labelled user-charges in welfare states). There can be different types of logics, from a classical state approach to a more market-based approach, with networks in civil society as another type.

The use of different types of governance can vary across welfare states, and also within different parts of the welfare state's delivery, including a difference varying from service (which is the main focus of Table 11.1) to income

Table 11.1 Governance types

	Source of rationality	Forms of control	Service delivery focus
Procedural governance	Law	Rules	Universal
Corporate governance	Management	Plans	Target groups
Market governance	Competition	Contracts	Price
Network governance	Culture	Co-production	Clients

Source: Considine and Lewis (2003, p. 133).

transfers. It might also vary within different types of service, for example, more outsourcing and use of market governance within public employment and active labour market policy within health care treatment and hospital services. A country might thus use not just one type of governance but a variety, depending on the issues and aspects related to the different areas. However, looking at welfare regimes reveals differences. A more universal approach and procedural governance should be expected in the Nordic welfare state, such as Sweden and Denmark, and more targeted and market-based in the liberal welfare states such as the UK, with the continental type of welfare state somewhere in between.

Important questions of governance thus revolve around: Who are the actors and how do they interact with each other, and what are the consequences of these different ways of making decisions? Who takes the decision and is it top-down, bottom-up or done in various kinds of networked, multilevel or otherwise organised decision-making bodies? There are thus many and very varied combinations of governance, and they may vary from one area of the welfare state to another.

A new concept has been labelled delegated governance. This relates to the fact that one body has delegated the ability to make decisions for, administer or develop a specific public sector area. In the USA, this has been labelled the delegated welfare state, defined as: 'delegated governance is the delegation of responsibility for publicly funded social welfare provision to non-state actors' (Morgan and Campbell, 2011, p. 19). This is in a sense a continuation of the description of a hidden welfare state, and therefore the use of public, fiscal and occupational welfare approaches to the delivery of welfare (see Section 4.2). The state's role is to focus on ways of financing and enacting regulation, whereas the provision is left to other bodies. The term delegated governance to a certain extent resembles discussion in Europe on privatisation and contracting out of public provision and public production.

Use of the market and market-type mechanisms within the public sector also helps in explaining new trends in the way welfare states are managed.

new ways and international perspectives

Market-type mechanisms within the public sector include using free choice among providers of a welfare service for the users, who are sometimes even relabelled as welfare consumers: for example, by the issue of vouchers to users, who can then choose between different providers. It can also be competition for resources based upon the ability to set results from the principal towards the different agents providing services, so that those providers who promise to provide most output for the least resources will be awarded the right to provide the service, and these might also be providers from outside the classical understanding of the state, for example, private providers might compete with public providers. There are many and varied ways of enacting this kind of mechanism. The point here is just that the boundaries between public and private production might not always be as clear as they used to be. Governance might further vary across policy fields and across welfare state regimes.

11.3 Decentralisation, devolution – the changed role of the actors – and possible consequences

> Nonprofit agencies have taken over functions previously undertaken directly by public workers, and have assumed program responsibilities in new areas where government workers have never performed. The staff of nonprofit agencies are the new 'street-level bureaucrats': that is, workers who . . . act under the cloak of public authorities.
>
> (Smith and Lipsky, 1993, p. 13)

This is again another example of integrating new actors within the public sector and its administration and, especially, the delivery of welfare services. The citation also points to the role of civil society and in particular voluntary organisations. The number of analyses of different possible ways and types of welfare service delivery has increased in recent years. This is presumably because welfare services, including not only health care but also, for example, child care and care for the elderly, have been growing in most welfare states in Europe. Welfare services are often analysed and measured in terms of expenditure in a specific field or the number of people employed in the service area. However, aspects such as coverage (cf., for example, Section 8.3) or the number of children in day care could also be an indicator of the development of the service sector. Such analysis often overlooks the quality of the services. One reason for this neglect of the quality of welfare services is that it has been difficult to define and measure quality in service and this has also been part of the increased interest in evaluation and evidence.

An additional reason for analysing services and how to best deliver social services in more detail concerns the role welfare states have in social investment approaches (see Section 3.5), which have been increasing in the Nordic and continental welfare states. In the UK an increased focus on day care for children can be witnessed. This suggests that despite tendencies of retrenchment and pressures on welfare states, there has been, in some areas, an increased use of the welfare state in delivery of certain services.

Another issue relates to who is using the welfare services and whether they are used by those most in need or whether, for example, the middle class is also using the welfare services. This raises issues in relation to governance, and whether services and benefits should be targeted or universal. This is also a more traditional issue in welfare state delivery: What is the impact of street-level bureaucrats on who gets what and under what conditions? If access to a benefit or service is fully based upon a right when a certain contingency occurs then the street-level bureaucrats' influence over who will be given what kind of services is limited. However, if there is discretion and an opportunity to decide who will get what, bureaucrats can influence the distribution of public services. This is because middle-class people are often seen as better able to argue their case in front of service providers than low-income earners. In this way the expected goal of the welfare state might not be achieved. The degree of discretion could open up the possibility of a broader perspective concerning the needs of the individual family. This might contradict the principle of equal treatment of equal cases: that if a specific social contingency occurs for social claimants then if they apply they can get a benefit at a previously defined level.

Public sector civil servants are usually limited in their use of discretion, although this is not necessarily the case, at least to the same degree, for non-profit and other non-governmental organisations (NGOs) as they might have reasons for supporting specific groups in society, and they might have very limited resources. Thus including the non-profit sector in the welfare state also opens the possibility for new types and degrees of inequalities not present within the classical administration in welfare states. In some more clientelistic welfare states there still remains the risk that some citizens are, by paying gratuities, for example, better able to get benefits or services than others.

Decentralisation of welfare state activities from a centralised public sector level to local, regional or other kind of bodies acting on behalf of the government might thus influence who gets what. If the local authorities have the right to decide on the level and quality of benefits and services, regional inequalities in welfare support may arise depending on the local area in which the individual lives. The possible conflict between local autonomy and welfare state inequality in access to welfare services is thus obvious when decentralisation or devolution takes place. The degree of difference one is willing to accept in local provision and the degree of influence given to local administration can thus be an issue. Although local authorities might be those best able to judge the need for treatment and other provision.

The balance between central and decentralised provision, especially in the area of services, can depend on the more normative view of how equal or unequal a society can be, and to what extent resources should be transferred regionally from more affluent parts of society to the less affluent. This can also be related to different preferences in different parts of a country. So, differences might in this understanding on one hand be acceptable if they reflect variations in local preferences across a country. On the other hand they might not be acceptable if the deviation is due to the fact that some areas have better economic opportunities than others.

Developments in recent years in individual countries in Europe and the USA imply that part of regional and local differences are due to local decisions, whereas others are due to the fact that some parts of the country are richer than others. The degree of difference thus also depends on to what extent a local area has the option and possibility of charging its own local taxes. If the local entity has an independent right to tax, and differences in levels of service also reflect difference in level of taxes, then it can be argued that this reflects local preferences for welfare. If the level of services is high and the level of taxes is the same, then it can be argued that difference implies inequality which is not based on variation in local preferences.

In several countries there are different kinds of mechanism aimed at – as best at possible – making local differences reflect local understanding of how to balance taxes and duties with welfare services. The reason why this mainly concerns services is that the level of income transfers is often uniform across territories and set by central authorities. In large countries with relatively independent local entities there can, in principle, also be variation in the level and composition of social security benefits.

11.4 Evidence and evaluation as steering instruments

There has been a constant and growing pressure to ensure that the welfare state, in order to cope with increasing demand and expectation, changes in demography and new social risks, should be able to finance and deliver welfare services. This has raised the issue of how to ensure that society gets most value for the money available.

The ambition to have information and data available for the decision making and ruling of the public sector has therefore been developed to try to find out, given the context, what mechanism will give which type of outcome. This has been essential to the understanding of the aims of the intervention, and why it will work under which type of circumstances for the citizens (Pawson et al., 2005). This therefore also implies a need to know what types of analysis are the most precise and informative with regard to the provision of welfare services.

Evaluation can have different purposes and there are therefore different models of evaluation. They may be looking for results, that is comparing the results of an activity before and after the intervention. It can also focus on the process, including, for example, the viewpoints of the users and other stakeholders. It can be done by cost-effectiveness or cost–benefit analysis, or have a strong focus on the system's way of working. The central issues are thus who the evaluation is for, and what we wish to know and why. For example, when measuring an intervention it will be important to know what the expected outcome was and compare this with the actual outcome. Another question is: Why do we want to find out the outcome of a specific measure? This is besides the more general need for effective use of scarce resources, as it might be that some specific measures are only effective for a small group, where the question is why the impact is or might be rather limited. Furthermore, if different measures exist, which one will produce the best outcome for the least amount of money?

There can also be a need for evaluation at a certain time (before decision making), and therefore also a need to find the appropriate methodology to make the evaluation. Collecting and finding the right data to inform on the impact of an activity are therefore important, and often there will be a need before starting new activities to ensure that the right data to use for analysis are available or gathered during implementation.

It is also important to ask what the best evidence is. This can be depicted by using the evidence hierarchy as indicated in Figure 11.1, which shows that at the top of this is a systematic review, that is an overview of the data and analysis from other studies, trying to detect common patterns and knowledge from the studies conducted so far. They are based upon evidence syntheses, which again use the gold standard in collecting data, the randomised controlled trial (RCT). RCTs involve giving treatment, or different types of intervention, to one group and none to another, and then comparing the outcomes of the two groups. Box 11.1 shows the central issues of RCT in more detail.

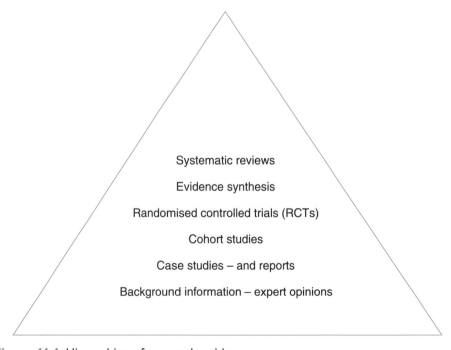

Figure 11.1 Hierarchies of research evidence.

Randomised controlled trials (RCTs) are the most rigorous way of determining whether a cause–effect relation exists between treatment and outcome and for assessing the cost-effectiveness of a treatment. They have several important features:

- Random allocation to intervention and control groups.
- Participants and trialists should remain unaware of which treatment was given until the study is completed (although such double-blind studies are not always feasible or appropriate).
- All groups are treated identically except for the experimental treatment or intervention.
- The analysis is focused on estimating the size of the difference in predefined outcomes between intervention and control groups.

Other study designs, including non-randomised controlled trials, can detect associations between an intervention and an outcome. But they cannot rule out the possibility that the association was caused by a third factor linked to both intervention and outcome. Random allocation ensures no systematic differences between intervention groups in factors, known and unknown, that may affect outcome.

Given that it is not always possible to achieve data from RCTs it might also be useful to use other types of evidence, as indicated in Figure 11.1. This sometimes implies that the best knowledge is background information and/or interviews with experts within the different fields. Even if this is not perfect it is better than no information, and every time information is collected this might also reveal what information is lacking and how more and better information can be found, making it possible to give those in need of treatment or different kinds of service the best available support.

Evaluation and evidence of the impact of different decisions have for years been part of decision making and approaches within health care, and there are strong demands to ensure that medicine has the expected impact without side effects before new medicine can be sold on the market. Welfare states often regulate the right to sell medicine by demanding systematised evidence of the impact of a new drug, how it works, for whom, and for whom this will not be a good medicine. Pharmaceutical companies that fulfil these demands then obtain a licence to distribute the medicine and thereby the possibility of selling it at a higher price as they might have a monopoly in the provision of the medicine.

Within the broader social policy area the use of evidence has been less strong given that it is often argued that the impact of a policy is so highly dependent on the people doing the work, the overall context and the relation between the user and the provider. However correct this might be, given the always scarce resources available there is a need to know whether there is the option of using different kinds of interventions and/or a need to prioritise different kinds of interventions as to which works best for the user for the lowest amount of money.

This may be criticised from an ethical point of view as it might reduce the support for specific groups due to the fact that they might be more expensive to help, but even for groups where services or benefits might be expensive there can be a need to compare the impact of using different approaches in order to ensure the best outcome. For example, one intervention might solve the problem for 85 per cent of the population at a considerably lower cost than an intervention solving it for 98 per cent of the population. The political decision makers will then have to consider the willingness to pay the amount of extra money to solve the problem for the extra 13 per cent of the population, also taking other possible areas in need of resources into consideration. The way to prioritise between different instruments can thus be enhanced with the knowledge of evidence, while at the same time increasing the likelihood of taking difficult ethical decisions.

Another criticism relates to the fact that given the large differences in cases it should be left to the service providers to decide what to do, given the legal framework and their professional knowledge of the impact of different types of intervention. The risk, however, is that the decisions can vary across a country, but also that the risk of making the wrong intervention might increase. Another counter-argument is that if some measure is better able to help the most vulnerable, this knowledge should be shared so that all in need in the welfare state could be supported.

11.5 New ways of steering individuals

Taxes and duties have for a long time been used in an attempt to change individuals' behaviour by making either luxuries or unhealthy goods more expensive and then by using economic incentives to try to steer individuals' consumption away from one area to another (see also Section 5.2). Direct legislation to interfere with the choice of individuals is also used. This is the case, for example, with the prohibition of drug use and banning of smoking in public places, but also rules regarding motorists' behaviour in the traffic system are examples of regulatory instruments used in order to try to influence behaviour. Information campaigns on what is a good and healthy lifestyle are another example of ways of trying to influence behaviour in society. These various types of 'sticks and carrots' are often used in an attempt to make people live a healthier life, thereby aiming to reduce public sector spending, but also to ensure a certain type of behaviour to make society work. Many of these interventions are based upon the fact that people are expected to be utility-maximising individuals who act rationally, in the same way that the market works.

Recent years have also seen the development of what has been labelled 'libertarian paternalism' to influence individuals' choice and living standard in a – seen from a societal perspective – better direction. 'Nudging' is another label. The idea is to push people in the right direction. The now classical example is that of putting a picture of a fly in a urinal for men in the airport at Amsterdam, which improved cleanliness as men were then better able to hit the urinal, reducing spillage by 80 per cent (Thaler and Sunstein, 2008). The idea is to try to find ways to make it easy for the individual, without taking away his or her options for choice, to behave in a way – seen from the perspective of either a company/individual or the welfare state – moving in the right direction. Therefore the strategy is to encourage people to voluntarily behave in, for example, a more healthy way, and especially using nudges in places where the traditional measures, such as information campaigns, have not been successful.

Obesity is one of the problems of rich countries, as it also places pressure on public sector spending on health care. However, despite many years of public information on how to live a healthier life, and fiscal duties that increase the unit cost and hence aim to reduce intake of alcohol, etc., there is still a growing issue related to the fact that too many people are overweight and/or consume too much alcohol. Lack of exercise and smoking are other health-related problems. Information campaigns seem to have an impact mainly on those already living a healthy life. Given the inequality in life expectancy between higher educated and lower educated groups in society, an issue has been how to reduce and improve the lifestyle of those most in need of the improvement, especially if traditional information campaigns and use of financial incentives are not working. An example using nudges can be given. People tend to fill their plates with food in a canteen. If the plates are smaller and if the healthier foods are the first available at the servery in the canteen, diners will fill their plates with less and healthier food, thus improving living standards without making it prohibitive to consume other types of diet. Making it easier to walk, to use public transport and to be active are other ways of nudging that can be used as a way of steering people's choice towards a more active life with at least some physical exercise every day.

Trying to make people behave healthily without interfering with their right to choose the life they want is seen by some as a positive option; others still see it as a negative intervention in everyday life for people. However, it shows that it might be possible to change individual behaviour by organising and orchestrating a specific choice architecture.

It is not only the welfare state that creates systems to nudge people in different ways. Companies also do it, by, for example, setting defaults if the client does not choose a specific option. This is often the case in an occupational-based pension system where the members might have choices to vary the terms, but there is a default choice already made available for them. Informing people of their options, and then presenting them with a particular option unless and until they actively choose an alternative, is also an example of how to work in a preventive way using default options as a steering device.

Nudging and setting default options are thus new instruments within the welfare state that can supplement the more traditional instruments. By combining this individualistic approach with a mild form of steering, individuals are more likely to take, for example, the healthy option.

11.6 Welfare technology and social innovation

New types of steering have been important in welfare states. Additionally new ways of providing goods and services, including various types of social innovation, especially in relation to the provision of welfare services, seem to be an important aspect of modern welfare states.

On the one hand this is due to the need to ensure provision at a reasonable price, but on the other hand it has also been argued that it is necessary due to the risk of having insufficient manpower relating to demographic changes in most societies. However, use of technology within welfare services is a new trend aimed at creating more welfare for less money – in a way a transition in the same way as industrial production has changed.

New welfare technology covers a broad selection of aspects ranging from robots that can be used in operations, to cleaning robots, to robots helping people with disabilities with food, and arrangements making it easier for the employed to lift elderly patients. It also encompasses help in rehabilitation and for those less able to move to come in better contact with other people by using modern communication means such as e-mail, Skype and other ways of using the Internet. Another example is telemedicine which can help those in more remote areas in gaining access to welfare services.

New organisational forms both within the public sector and in the relation between the public and private sector can be seen as innovative approaches to making welfare states more effective, without it necessarily implying new types of inequalities. However, for some, the use of IT communication is problematic if they are IT-illiterate. So, inclusion in the form of new technology can also create new types of division.

Social innovation includes aspects which are related to social well-being and social needs, often for users, producers and those financing the welfare. Hubert et al. (2010, p. 7) explains that social innovations are 'new responses to pressing social demands, which affect the process of social interactions. It is aimed at improving social well-being'.

Social innovation, as innovation in general, includes changes in processes, products, organisation and/or relations. Social innovation can thus be part of the new way of steering and managing welfare states (see also Sirovatka and Greve, 2014). It can also be a way of finding new balances between the responsibilities and involvement of state, market and civil society. Use of telemedicine, for example, can imply that individuals themselves carry out tests, making it possible to ensure that their medicine is better targeted or that wounds are better treated. Information technology and other welfare technologies might make it possible to stay for a longer time in one's own home, and even have easier access to support from nurses or social workers.

11.7 Summing-up

Welfare states are steered, managed and under constant change. New types of steering and managing the welfare state are constantly developing. This is also because new needs are arising and citizens have different and varying expectations of the welfare state's initiatives and support.

Welfare states are subject to change both from an upward and downward direction. In Europe this is through a stronger impact of the EU on the development of national welfare states (see Chapter 12). In some specific areas of welfare and in some countries changes are underway through the devolution and decentralisation of the management of the welfare state, that is in a downward direction.

Furthermore, the use of new types of market mechanism in the provision of welfare services, both within the public sector and by external providers, has changed the governance of welfare states in recent years. At the same time a stronger focus has developed on what works and under what conditions, not only in the area of health, but also in the broader approach of social and labour market policy. A stronger emphasis on evaluation and evidence of intervention will also come to be more important in policy making in the years to come due to resource constraints and the ambition to give the users the best possible help.

New ways of steering, for example, by nudging, is part of the new development of welfare states where individuals are pushed to act voluntarily in ways – seen from both the perspective of society and frequently also in reality the individuals' themselves – that are more positive, implying a better life and lower level of public sector spending.

References

Considine, M. and Lewis, J. (2003), Network or Enterprise? Comparing Models of Governance in Australia, Britain, the Netherlands, and New Zealand. *Public Administration Review*, vol. 2, no. 2, pp. 131–40.

Hubert, A. (2010), *Empowering People, Driving Change: Social Innovation in the European Union*. Brussels, Bureau of European Policy Advisers, Luxembourg, European Commission.

Lipsky, M. (1980), *Street-level Bureaucracy: Dilemmas of the Individual in Public Services*. New York, Russell Sage Foundation.

Morgan, K. J. and Campbell, A. L. (2011), *The Delegated Welfare State: Medicare, Markets and the Governance of Social Policy*. Oxford, Oxford University Press.

Pawson, R., Greenhalgh, T., Harvey, G. and Walshe, K. (2005), Realist Review – A New Method of Systematic Review Designed for Complex Policy Interventions. *Journal of Health Services Research & Policy*, vol. 10, suppl. 1, pp. 21–34.

Pierre, J. and Peters, B. (2000), *Governance, Politics and the State.* Basingstoke, Macmillan.

Sirovatka, T. and Greve, B. (eds) (2014), *Innovation in Social Services: The Public–Private Mix in Service Provision, Fiscal Policy and Employment.* Farnham, Ashgate.

Smith, S. and Lipsky, M. (1993), *Nonprofits for Hire: The Welfare State in the Age of Contracting.* Cambridge, MA, Harvard University Press.

Thaler, R. H. and Sunstein, C. R. (2008), *Nudge: Improving Decisions about Health, Wealth and Happiness.* New Haven, CT, Yale University Press.

Chapter 12

The role of the EU in the development of welfare states

Contents

12.1 Introduction

The well-being of citizens and welfare state policies have been thought about historically mainly in national settings and understandings. Thus the international impact has been mainly related to any one country's dependency on the economic development of other countries and how strongly their national economy was affected, and its impact upon the development of a national welfare state.

This chapter will look into recent changes, and how and if we might see a movement towards welfare states – taking all things into consideration – coming to look still more alike. Are they, due to growing international interdependence, as a consequence of globalisation and regionalisation, moving in the same direction, despite historical differences and the historically different pathways chosen in their development? The types of convergence and the understanding thereof will be presented in Section 12.3.

Before looking into convergence/divergence, Section 12.2 will present the role of the EU in relation to welfare states in Europe, as there has been growing influence from the EU on the way and understanding of what can be decided nationally. Furthermore, the distinction between the roles of the state and of the market have had an impact on the delivery of welfare services. The supranational impact on welfare states and possible implications thereof will further be explored in Section 12.4, before a summing-up in Section 12.5.

12.2 The role of the EU in relation to welfare state policies

In principle, nation states have responsibility for their own welfare policies. However, where the dividing line is and how they are influenced by regional organisations is less clear. The USA itself consists of many independent States, having some local autonomy, but with certain types of decisions made centrally in Washington. In Europe, in principle each member state can decide upon its own national welfare policy and, as seen in Chapter 3, they have diverse approaches to welfare and belong to different kinds of welfare regimes.

Nevertheless, the EU also influences national welfare policies and does so increasingly. The instruments available to the EU are directives, recommendations, decisions of the European Court of Justice, and also its possible role as agenda setter. The ability to act as agenda setter can influence member states' ability and choice in delivery of social services in modern welfare states.

The influence of the EU can further be distinguished between so-called hard law, such as EU directives, or soft law, for example, the Open Method of Coordination (OMC), which, by naming and shaming those not in line with or falling behind other countries within the EU, can put pressure on decision makers in member states. The EU can also act as agenda setter by pointing to and trying to make countries agree that a specific approach is important. This can be seen by the emphasis in the EU on flexicurity, and also in the area of social investment (cf. Box 12.1).

The EU can issue communications to try to influence member states. Here is an extract from the conclusion from one such document:

Member states are urged to reflect in their National Reform Programmes the guidance provided in this Social Investment Package with a particular attention to:

- ■ Progress on putting an increased focus on social investment in their social policies, particularly on policies such as (child)care, education, training, active labour market policies, housing support, rehabilitation and health services.
- ■ The implementation of integrated active inclusion strategies, including through the development of reference budgets, increased coverage of benefits and services, and simplification of social systems through for instance a one-stop-shop approach and avoiding proliferation of different benefits.

(European Commission, 2013, p. 22)

The extract given in Box 12.1 indicates how the Commission tries to frame a policy area and push EU member states towards these kinds of initiatives without being very specific or entering into national prerogatives to make national decisions in the area.

Historically, there are two areas in which the EU could have a particular impact on national welfare states: gender equality and the free movement of workers. Use of the social fund and support for regional development have also, although more implicitly, played a role in many regions' economic and social development.

On gender equality, the EU has a general principle of equal treatment of men and women. This should especially have had an impact on the way wages can be set and should reduce the differences between men and women within the European countries. The EU has legislated that in principle men and women should have the same wage for the same work, and discrimination among and between men and women is against the EU treaty. This was historically intended to avoid competition among member states if some had lower wages for women. The main problem with the rules is that it is difficult to define what is 'the same work'. There are, therefore, still differences between the EU countries in the discrepancy between wages for men and women.

The second issue – free movement of workers – has been one of the cornerstones in the European development. Mobility is still lower between EU countries than between States of the USA. However, free movement has given rise to several initiatives trying to make the position for workers the same so that they would not lose their welfare rights if they move around within the EU. In this area, initially the issuing of directives binding in all countries had the greatest impact, and later decisions of the European Court of Justice became important.

In order to ensure the free movement of workers, rules were laid down, with the former Directive 1408/71 (now Regulation 883/2004) as the core instrument. This, in combination with case law of the European Court of Justice, has opened up possibilities for more internal migration between EU countries, especially in the wake of the accession of countries in eastern Europe in 2004 and 2007 and the fiscal crisis of 2008. The general idea was that if a worker moved from one country to another, the legal rules, rights to benefits and calculation thereof, should not be a hindrance, but rather they should support the free movement of workers. For example, it should be possible to combine the earned right to pensions acquired when working in different countries, and the right to welfare benefits should also be given to migrant workers, such as child benefits, even if the child is not residing in the country where work takes place. In Box 12.2 is presented the debate on the risk of welfare tourism by the use of the free movement of workers and others within the European Union.

Box 12.2 Welfare tourism?

After the enlargement of the EU with countries from eastern Europe in 2004 and 2007, there has been an increase in the use of the rules of free movement. This has resulted in debates on whether individuals move in order to get a job or to use the higher levels of welfare provided in the more affluent parts of Europe.

Arguments have been revolving around whether they pay tax, take jobs away from others, imply social dumping and/or just move in order to get higher benefits. Furthermore, it is also argued that such movement has implied better supply of labour and a more flexible labour market.

Overall on a macro-economic level the free movement seems to have a positive impact, while at the same time it risks reducing the legitimacy of welfare states among part of the population.

There are also EU rules on safety at work and parental leave, for example, and other directives often setting minimum standards where it is up to each member state to implement and also decide the level.

With the enlargement of the EU, it has become difficult to reach agreement on new directives in the field of welfare policy. This is especially due to the fact that in most welfare policy areas there is a rule that all countries should agree on a specific proposal. This is part of the reason why the Open Method of Coordination (OMC) was introduced as a method making it possible for the member states to move in the same direction while at the same time respecting the national differences and traditions within welfare policy.

The OMC functions by setting goals agreed upon by the member states, and then the member states have the freedom to find out the best way to reach those goals, for example, having more people in jobs, etc. The OMC thus revolves around issues of recommendation, benchmarking, communication, peer review, opinion, guidelines and so on. The general aim is to try to reach a common understanding and common interpretation of societal development. The EU countries are at the same time expected to learn from best practice and good examples from other countries and thereafter develop them in their own way. In this way policy learning across countries is expected to increase convergence and the use of best knowledge on what works and for whom. There is OMC in areas such as employment, social inclusion, health care and care for the elderly (de la Porte, 2013). The first area to be covered was employment, pursuant to the Amsterdam Treaty of 1997, whereby all member states should make plans on how to achieve certain goals regarding employment rates, unemployment levels, etc. In 2000 OMC functions in the area of social inclusion also came into force.

A basic problem has been whether it is possible to measure and understand the impact of the EU on national welfare state policies, and how to understand the transmission of ideas from a supranational to a national level (Zeitlin, 2005). The learning outcome might also differ among the different welfare regimes (de la Porte, 2013). However, part of the agreement in relation to OMC has been that countries can interpret certain concepts differently. This is the case, for example, with activation of the unemployed, lifelong learning and flexicurity. The ambiguities of the understanding of different 'buzzwords' also implies that national interpretation and implementation can differ. The conclusion is that the EU does have an impact while, at the same time, national welfare states can be sustained.

Goals for EU countries' development has been part of the OMC process since the Amsterdam Treaty, and with the option that each country can use its own instruments to reach these goals. After the financial crisis, new goals were set for 2020. These are shown in Box 12.3.

Box 12.3 EU 2020 goals

The five targets for the EU in 2020:

1 *Employment*
   - 75 per cent of the 20–64 year-olds to be employed
2 *Research & Development*
   - 3 per cent of the EU's GDP to be invested in R&D

Box 12.3 shows the clear focus in the EU on welfare policy areas with the aim of targeting employment, poverty and social exclusion, and also that education and research and development have clear links to welfare policy.

Another area where the EU has been able to influence national welfare states is that of changing the confines of the role of the market and the role of the state. The European Court of Justice has, by referring to the free movement of goods and services, changed several borderlines between the state and the market, one example being where the court came to the conclusion that a person was entitled to have the cost of a hip operation reimbursed, despite the operation taking place outside the physical borders of the UK, as it would other-wise have taken too long to wait for treatment within the UK (The Watt case, available at http://ec.europa.eu/dgs/legal_service/arrets/04c372_en.pdf).

The Court has argued that medical services are within the scope and freedom with regard to the provision of service, and by this that a person in one country can buy, for example, medicine in another country. In this way at least some national welfare state services are more open to international competi-tion, and therefore also movement with regard to steering and governing the social services in these areas. The debate concerning the service directive within the EU has indicated the future possibility of a movement away from universal welfare states providing specific welfare services in view of the inherent difficulties. If a national welfare state, for example, cannot provide certain health-care services without a certain delay, then a citizen might also have the right to go to another country to receive the treatment at the expense of the home country.

The rules related to the posting of workers, and cross-border mobility of workers, is another example of a possible influence on national welfare states from the EU, as nation states might be forced to pay benefits to migrant workers and students only living for a short while in a country, and sometimes not paying the same taxes and duties as the long-term residents.

Finally, there will presumably still be more cases in the future where the borderlines between state and market, and therefore the role of the welfare state, may come into question.

12.3 Convergence or divergence in the development of European welfare states

A central question is whether the increased economic integration and the expected development in policy learning imply that European countries' welfare policies will gradually become more alike, and that the differences between their welfare states will gradually fade away – leaving little variety in welfare regimes or welfare typologies, and only one or two ways of delivering and financing welfare.

In order to answer this question it is necessary to find out what is meant by convergence in welfare states. Are we looking at the same level of spending, at the same level of employment in the public sector or at the same institutional structure or system? This type of analysis has therefore looked into different dependent variables such as goals, content, instruments, outcomes and style of policy making.

The coefficient of variation (labelled sigma convergence, calculated as the standard deviation divided by the arithmetic average) is a good measure, as it shows in a relatively simple way whether a group of countries have moved in the same direction or not. The measure can be used for comparing the development in various issues such as expenditure, taxation, employment and so on. The lower the coefficient the more alike the countries are.

There are many ways of interpreting whether or not welfare states are alike. As already explained earlier in the book, there are many different ways to welfare, and thus the comparison of welfare states and whether they are moving in the same direction is very difficult. However, at the same time looking at convergences even in a crude way by only comparing direct public spending can be an initial way of depicting whether changes have occurred.

Table 12.1 shows the development in the coefficient of variation with regard to welfare spending, measured as percentages of GDP for all EU member states.

Since the year 2000 there has been a slight movement towards convergence in spending on welfare in EU member states, and this despite the recent financial crisis. However, whether this is gradual convergence or cross-convergence (Aurich, 2011) is not the focus here. Despite this, countries still pursue welfare policies in different ways, indicating that there might be convergence in the spending approach, but not in the structural approach on how to deliver welfare. However, it is an indication that some countries within the same regional area and where economic integration takes place will have a likelihood of gradually looking more alike in the manner of financing and ability to finance

Table 12.1 Coefficient of variation (COV) in welfare spending in EU member states since 1995

0.23	0.24	0.24	0.23	0.22	0.25	0.26	0.26
1995	1996	1997	1998	1999	2000	2001	2002
0.26	0.27	0.27	0.27	0.27	0.25	0.22	0.22
2003	2004	2005	2006	2007	2008	2009	2010

Source: Calculations based upon Eurostat (spr_exp_sum).

Notes: Until the year 2000 data are missing for several of the new member states from eastern Europe. From 2000 until 2005 only data for Bulgaria is missing. When increasing the COV countries are moving apart, when reduced they are converging.

welfare state activities. Nevertheless, the overall level of benefits and services can vary if occupational and fiscal welfare are also included. Therefore a full picture of convergence/divergence needs to include these ways of providing welfare.

Analysis of convergence is also in line with looking at similarities and differences, which can then be used also for the purpose of policy learning in different countries. This is seen in the fact that this is not different from looking into and comparing different companies, regions, local municipalities, etc.

Reasons for moving in the same direction can be due to increased economic similarities, as would be expected among countries in an economic union. In this way the EU, to a certain extent, resembles the USA, although the EU's role at the central level in relation to welfare policies is rather weak. Albeit there is another part that might help explain convergence in European welfare states: the development and use of the Open Method of Coordination whereby policy learning makes the systems move in the same direction by learning from best practice and peer pressure.

Historically, in European development there has been a debate on whether the pressure towards convergence would increase social dumping in the EU (Alber and Standing, 2000). By social dumping it is understood that some countries lower the welfare benefits and services as part of becoming more competitive in relation to other countries, as payment of lower benefits implies that the taxes can be reduced. In 2002 it was concluded that: 'It is fair to conclude that these studies by and large do not provide empirical support for expectations of a general "race to the bottom," but emphasize the path-dependent resistance of welfare-state regimes to the downward pressures of economic competition' (Scharpf, 2002, p. 10). A question is whether recent developments and strong pressure from European and global development would now give another interpretation such as there is a race to the bottom.

new ways and international perspectives

12.4 Impact of Europeanisation and globalisation on the welfare state

Europeanisation and globalisation are having an impact on the welfare state as they imply changes in the labour market, the ability to finance welfare and the possible structure of the welfare state. Globalisation has led to increased free trade of goods and services, hence production has moved to countries with lower wage costs and also the outsourcing of some commercial activities to several countries. Many low-skilled jobs have disappeared and thereby certain types of manufacturing production no longer take place in many countries in the developed world, which has an impact on the welfare state. Globalisation also implies a pressure on the possible ways of financing the welfare state. First, let's consider what is meant by Europeanisation.

Analysis of European integration and understanding of the mechanism is not easy given that Europeanisation is not a specific theory, but more 'a way of orchestrating existing concepts and to contribute to cumulative research in political science' (Radaelli, 2004, p. 1). There are at least three different ways to understand Europeanisation:

1   by the development of a European level of governance
2   by the process of impact and influence from the supranational level to the national level
3   by processes focusing on the development of shared beliefs and norms that might then be transferred to nation states, but also in both a bottom-up and top-down understanding.

(Börzel and Risse, 2007)

However, in general Europeanisation can be understood as the impact of the EU on the member states as this implies a focus on the link between the supra-national development and national welfare state development. The impact can in principle be in both directions based on either uploading or downloading of ideas and policies.

The impact on a national welfare state of Europeanisation can further be direct or indirect. The OMC, as mentioned in Section 12.2, is an indirect way. The EU Economic and Monetary Union and gradual integration of European economies imply a pressure on national welfare states and can be argued to be in between direct and indirect. Direct as it implies restrictions, especially for those members of the Economic and Monetary Union, on the level of public sector deficit, debt and structural public sector deficit. The ability in the longer run to have a high deficit is thus not possible, and this is a restriction on nation states' ability to pursue the balance between willingness to pay for welfare and the size of the public sector. In the wake of the financial crisis this has been even stricter than before, and the new European Fiscal Compact also implies that countries will have to develop their welfare states with less economic freedom than earlier. At the same time, it can be argued that the free movement of goods and services and free trade, all other things being equal, implies a higher overall level of welfare by the increase in wealth as a consequence of European free trade.

An indirect impact is also that citizens are allowed to shop in other European countries and also do shopping on the Internet. This reduces the ability to have substantial higher duties than in neighbouring countries. Companies' ability to move around and also the easy way to move capital implies a restriction on the level of taxes in this area. Monetary policy is now mainly an issue for the European Central Bank. National economic policy, including welfare, is thus restricted by the overall development in Europe, making it more difficult to pursue national strategies.

The economic interdependencies also imply that, in the event of financial crisis, the impact will be stronger and, especially in the larger countries, economic performance is reduced; this will also reduce growth and employment in other countries. The economic problems of the financial sector in one country can also spread to other countries, as seen by the financial crisis in southern Europe, and thereby nation states' abilities to perform well and develop a specific type of welfare can be reduced as the room for manoeuvre might be very limited.

The more direct way is the EU agreeing a directive in relation to welfare issues. However, this is difficult to achieve given that in most areas either unanimity or a qualified majority is needed in order to impose a directive.

Another direct impact is that countries will have to follow decisions of the European Court of Justice. The court builds its jurisprudence in relation to welfare on the cornerstones of EU development, especially possible hindrance to the free movement of workers. So, if a rule seems to be a direct or indirect hindrance to free movement then the court will decide against it. One consequence is that it might be difficult just to ensure that a citizen in a country receives benefits or welfare services. The court also sees the free movement of goods and services as important, and the boundaries between what is state and market responsibility have been changed, so that health care now is seen more as a market service than a state responsibility, also implying that the state's role can be reduced (Martinsen, 2005, 2012).

One way to understand the Europeanisation of social protection is thus to look into how development at the EU level regarding policy processes, the internal market and so on is mediated by the welfare regime, country size, etc. – this then might imply different kinds of responses and welfare reforms. The conclusion is that, since 2000, the EU has had an increased influence on social protection, but also that 'in sum, EU developments have influenced national welfare reform, but in varied ways and to different extents' (Kvist and Saari, 2007 p. 238).

Recent years have seen a stronger impact from supranational developments also due to the gradually more integrated European economies, implying that an economic crisis in one country, especially the larger countries, also has an impact on many other countries in Europe. A financial crisis and constant difficulties, as has been witnessed in southern Europe since 2008, thus also influences welfare states in the rest of Europe.

12.5 Summing-up

A specific issue has been whether there has been a movement in the same or in a different direction among welfare states in the developing countries, and especially within regions such as Europe. Convergence among welfare states or possible convergence also among typologies has been an ongoing discussion in recent years, one argument being that the increasing interconnectedness among countries will also lead towards a growing resemblance in financing and delivering welfare. At least within the EU this seems to be the case when looking over a longer time perspective. Therefore the approach and consequences of different ways of delivering welfare become even more important. This is further necessary in order to know the outcome of welfare states' activities when choosing different routes to welfare.

Whether movement has been in the same or different directions also encounters the difficulty in getting good comparative data to make a valid analysis. However, there does seem to be an impact.

Globalisation and Europeanisation also challenge the role of the welfare state in relation to employment, including types of jobs, the ability to finance welfare and rules related to public sector spending. Thus the EU, in relation to welfare states in Europe, has had a gradually stronger role not through many direct routes, except for European Court decisions, but more as the room for national ways to finance welfare has been reduced. The global movement of companies and production also implies strong pressure on the types of jobs available and thereby also how to understand and grasp national welfare states in an international perspective.

References

Alber, J. and Standing, G. (2000), Social Dumping, Catch-Up or Convergence? Europe in a Comparative Global Context. *European Journal of Social Policy*, vol. 10, no. 2, pp. 99–119.

Aurich, P. (2011), Activating the Unemployed – Directions and Divisions in Europe. *European Journal of Social Security*, vol. 13, no. 3, pp. 294–316.

Börzel, T. and Risse, T. (2007), Europeanisation: The Domestic Impact of European Union Politics. In Jørgensen, K., Pollack, M. and Rosamond, B. (eds), *The Sage Handbook of European Union Politics*. London, Sage Publications, pp. 483–503.

de la Porte, C. (2013), Social OMCs. In Greve, B. (ed.) *The Routledge Handbook of the Welfare State*. Abingdon, Routledge, pp. 410–418.

European Commission (2013), Communication from the Commission to the European Parliament, The Council, The European Economic and Social Committee and the Committee of the Regions: Towards Social Investment for Growth and Cohesion

– Including Implementing the European Social Fund 2014–2020. Brussels, 20.2.2013 Com(2013) 83 Final. Brussels, European Commission.

Kvist, J. and Saari, J. (eds) (2007), *The Europeanisation of Social Protection*. Bristol, Policy Press.

Martinsen, D. S. (2005), The Europeanization of Welfare. *Journal of Common Market Studies*, vol. 43, no. 5, pp. 1027–54.

Martinsen, D. S. (2012), Welfare States and Social Europe. In Neergaard, U., Szyszczak, E. and Van de Gronden, J. W. (eds), *Social Services of General Interest in the EU*. The Hague, T.M.C. Asser Press (pp. 53–72).

Radaelli, C. M. (2004), *Europeanisation: Solution or Problem?* European Integration online Papers (EIoP), vol. 8, no. 16; http://eiop.or.at/eiop/pdf/2004–016.pdf

Scharpf, F. W. (2002), The European Social Model: Coping with the Challenges of Diversity. MPIfG Working Paper, No. 02/8. Cologne, Max Planch Institute.

Zeitlin, J. (2005), *The Open Method of Co-ordination in Action: The European Employment and Social Inclusion Strategies*. Brussels, Peter Lang.

Chapter 13

Is there a future for the welfare state?

Contents

13.1 Introduction

Will we seize the opportunity to restore our sense of balance between the market and the state, between individualism and the community, between man and nature, between means and ends?

(Stiglitz, 2010, p. 296)

The above quote from a Nobel Prize winner in Economics is a good starting point for the final chapter, given it raises many questions around the different kinds of balances in societies and the role of the state and market in providing welfare for citizens and also civil society, including the balance between individuality and collectivity.

It has been claimed for a long time that the welfare state is in crisis (O'Connor, 1973; OECD, 1981; Offe, 1984; Wilson and Wilson, 1995). Therefore the trend since the burst of the housing bubble and the banking crisis in 2008 is arguably just another and just a new, temporary slow-down given that welfare states since the Second World War seemingly have matured and expanded continually along with economic growth. However, what constitutes a crisis is not always clearly and precisely defined, and also whether this implies a discontinuity of the welfare state or just different tracks in its development or in some areas a paradigmatic shift in policy and approach is not always clear. Furthermore, the impact of a crisis will depend on the willingness to finance welfare, including in recent years how to reduce public sector deficits by what kind of combination of tax increases and reduction in public welfare spending and at what pace this is expected to occur. Finally, a crisis can also be a window of opportunity to make fundamental changes – and whether this is good or bad for the welfare state will at least to a certain extent depend on a normative stance towards these changes – and can therefore vary among countries.

As shown throughout the book, the welfare state is not a uniform phenomenon. The different ways of describing what welfare and a welfare state is and therefore also different pressures and crises might have diverse connotations in various societies at different times. Although the recent fiscal crisis looks like a window of opportunity to make fundamental changes in many welfare states, it might be that when the crisis is over, and fundamental changes have been made, the demand for more welfare will be even stronger than before and thereby expansion of welfare states will take place again. If one can increase both private and public consumption this may be an option.

This final chapter will focus on some of these issues challenging the future of the welfare state in a more explorative way while at the same time highlighting some of the central aspects of the future development of welfare states and whether we will need to talk about one or several types of welfare state.

13.2 Demographic challenges

The changes in the demographic composition of the population, the greying of societies over the next 40 years or so and the possible impact on public sector spending has already been touched upon in Chapter 5. Here the focus is not only on the direct possible impact on public sector spending due to the expected increase in elderly people in need of care and fewer young people entering the labour market. The changed composition of the population also implies a constant need for rebalancing and changing the organisation and structure of the welfare state. Pressure on the health care sector will be looming unless new technologies and new kinds of treatment in combination with healthier lifestyles reduce this pressure.

The future pressure on public sector expenditure will also be reduced if the ongoing pension reforms around the world continue so that pensions in principle are financed directly by the individual citizen (or his/her employer). Occupational-based welfare thus seems to be part of the answer for the future of the welfare state, at least in certain areas, where, for example, saving or insurance contributions over a lifetime can help to alleviate the risk of poverty in old age or the cost of treatment when it is needed. Still, this also implies that those who participate more marginally in the labour market during their working lifetime will also be at risk in old age of having a low living standard unless there is a welfare state or they have a family able to support them.

Changed demographic composition also alters the overall demand in society, as elderly people typically have more diverse consumption and saving patterns than younger generations – and again this has implications for the organisation and structure of production and therefore also jobs in the labour market. If more elderly people implies a decline in consumption, this can further reduce the possibility of economic growth in the years to come, and through this also reduce one of the elements that otherwise could help in job creation and reduction of the relative size of the public sector debt. The last issue is due to the fact that a constant level of debt in a country will decline in relative terms if there is economic growth and/or inflation – and otherwise, as seen during the last crisis, when countries are in recession the debt will, relatively speaking, increase and thus further imply pressure on the welfare state. So the change in demography can imply a triple pressure on welfare states through the risk of increasing expenditures, reducing income and slower economic growth.

A changed demographic composition can influence the voters' preferences and thereby influence the decision makers over what choices they might make. The elderly might, for example, create pressure for higher spending on support and care for the elderly, thus reducing the capacity for social investment of the welfare state by spending, for example, on children.

The positive side of the coin is that we not only live longer but we also have more years with a healthy life and are able to work longer than before, thereby reducing the pressure on the public sector for helping with a good living standard. An increase in the age when people can receive a retirement pension, as part of pension reforms in most welfare states, has been part of the answer to this issue. Furthermore, new technologies in the years to come might further reduce the need for welfare spending in several areas. If there is a need for more labour in certain sectors that is not directly available in a country there will in principle be an option open for increased migration to cope with the lack of workers, although increased migration will open up other challenges in several welfare states.

Finally, higher economic growth will increase countries' economic prosperity and therefore also make it possible to spend more money on welfare. So, if states can return to an economic growth strategy this will also reduce the pressure on the welfare state as there will be more money available for private as well as public consumption. However, there is a risk that this will not be the case in the first few years, thereby increasing the pressure on welfare states and reducing the scope for fulfilling the expectations of the citizens.

13.3 European and global challenges

There is not only a pressure internally in the different welfare states of Europe, although the Nordic welfare states and Germany seem under less economic pressure than the liberal, southern and eastern European welfare states, there is also a growing international perspective on how and to what degree welfare states can develop. The European and global challenges for welfare states revolve especially around two issues:

1 Will it be possible to finance the welfare state when capital and labour can move around the world so quickly?
2 How will change in the global production structure alter the labour market and variety in welfare states?

Welfare states have been financed in particular out of general taxation and duties, as shown in Chapter 5. These have come under pressure due to an increased risk of tax competition among countries which might imply what has been labelled a risk of social dumping in Europe (Alber and Standing, 2000). Capital can move rapidly around the world, and relocation of production is also now easier than it used to be. This has put pressure on states' employment and financial capabilities, including fewer unskilled jobs. Taxes on capital and production income are a competitive factor where countries might have to balance the wish to have jobs or tax revenue from companies.

Finding a sustainable way of financing the welfare state is thus also very important for the way it can be expected to operate and develop in the future. This includes, among other things, taxation of non-movable types of activity and income, such as housing, but also energy consumption, which at the same time might have an impact on the environment. A tax on capital should in principle be international, such as the suggested Tobin tax on international capital movement. This is, however, a tax that will only work if it is implemented by general agreement by most countries around the world as otherwise there is a risk that all capital transactions will take place in a country where there is no such tax. In Europe a similar movement seems underway, so at least a certain tax on some financial transactions will be implemented in several countries.

The constant change in production structure also has implications for the types of jobs available in different countries. Some types of jobs will be moving out and new kinds of jobs will be created. This, as discussed in Chapter 7, is a process that has already been underway for some years. However, many of the types of jobs disappearing in many welfare states are unskilled (with the exception of certain jobs in the service sector including tourism), often being replaced by jobs where there is a need for strong competences and a high level of skills.

Those working in sectors no longer in demand might therefore risk becoming redundant with a high risk of never re-entering the labour market and thus become dependent on the welfare state or relations in the civil society. Lifelong learning is part of the answer to this issue, although this might not be sufficient for all persons. It also creates new kinds of inequalities in different countries between those with permanent and stable jobs and those outside the labour market.

Movement of people searching for jobs and security in the form of international migration is also a challenge for welfare states. This movement might be easy for highly skilled workers, but can be less easy for low-skilled workers who lack also the necessary linguistic skills. Migration can also be a challenge for the cohesion of welfare states.

This movement is not only a global issue, including migrants to and from the relatively rich European countries. In a regional perspective it might be difficult, with increased free movement of workers, goods and services, to have very different kinds of welfare state models and a labour market flexicurity model given that in still more of the welfare states services seem to be perceived by the European Court of Justice as belonging to the area of free movement for goods and services (see also Chapter 12). Therefore it is more difficult for a country to know what it will have to pay for, and also universal support, for example, for health care will be even more difficult in the future unless there is some common understanding of what the task of the welfare state is. This might further change the welfare state towards a more market-oriented type of welfare state, giving higher emphasis to market delivery and use of market-type mechanisms within the public sector. The role of civil society and family in this development can be very varied, ranging from the ideas of the Big Society to a more limited influence in the core of social policy areas.

An economic challenge for the more mature welfare states in the developed world might be that the times of economic growth will be less strong in the future, thereby making the possible conflict in the development between public and private consumption stronger, and also making it more difficult to find economic resources to finance existing as well as possible new activities within the current framework of taxation.

Nation-specific types of welfare state might thus be less strong than they used to be, and thereby perhaps a movement towards a European kind of welfare state instead of the existing welfare regimes might occur. However, at the same time new kinds of risk, and continuation of the incidence of market failure, imply a need for at least some kind of public sector intervention either at a very local or at least regional level.

13.4 Future legitimacy of the welfare state

The welfare state's size, structure and development have always depended on democratic support in the different societies and also at elections, and the recent crisis seems to have made the approach to welfare in some countries even more ideological than it used to be. This varies from the right-wing argument for deep cuts in public sector spending as the only way to restore confidence in public sector economy, to the left-wing argument for an increase in taxation, and if not reducing welfare spending, then at least decreasing it more slowly, and also taking more care of the most vulnerable by using the welfare state as a vehicle for equality. The social investment perspective can be argued to be in between these positions.

The legitimacy of welfare states and support to different parts of the welfare states also varies among countries in different welfare regimes. 'Support for equality, redistribution and state intervention is strongest in the social democratic regime, weaker in the conservative regime, and weakest in the liberal regime' (Svallfors, 2012, p. 9). There is still seemingly a demand for welfare in Europe.

The issue of regulation and the impact on societal development has been especially strong with regard to the financial sector in the wake of the financial crisis given the fact that the public sector deficit in many countries has also been high due to financial support for the banking sector. Arguments have varied from the need for stronger regulation and capital requirements to the establishment of a more deregulated financial sector.

The legitimacy issue underlines that the welfare states' development is not only dependent on classical arguments such as the impact on the development of societies. Intervention should be based upon knowledge of what works and what does not have a positive impact on development (see also Chapter 11), as this can be part of arguments for welfare state intervention and initiatives. The need to interact with the market and civil society and to try to solve problems not solved in other areas of society, is still a strong argument for intervention, including how to reduce the negative impact on society of market failure.

The classical discussion of whether sticks or carrots should be used in the welfare state is also an important aspect of the discussion and has both academic and ideological connotations. In labour market policy, for example, using economic incentives and having strong means tests or other types of coercion policies have thus been seen as important means to reduce the expenditure of the welfare state in several countries. This builds upon the idea that the human being mainly acts on economic incentives, and therefore the lowering of, for example, income tax will make people work more, or a lower level of unemployment benefit will also ensure a greater willingness to work. In this way there is a link back to debates on who is deserving and non-deserving, where the deserving receive greater support from the population at large – the electorate in democracies. The majority consider that the non-deserving should either receive very little or at least be forced to try to do something for the money they receive. The movement of the active labour market policy more towards coercion is an indication of this trend.

The counter-argument to using economic incentives, exclusively or predominantly, is that individual persons, although also influenced by the economic development, also react for other reasons, such as social contact, the need to have something to get out of bed for and so on. Human beings are thus also social animals (Brooks, 2011). Well-being and welfare are thus not only dependent on the availability of economic resources. Social aspects and what increases social capital would also be important for the welfare state.

A balance between individualism and collectivism – and the middle-way approach – can thus be a battlefield for the future of the welfare state. The role of intervention against the right to live completely an individually determined life is thus open to interpretation in welfare states. This also includes the degree of paternalism and other ways to steer individuals (see also Chapter 11).

Another problem is whether intergenerational trust and balance still exist. This has been important as one generation is expected to pay for all, or at least a large part, of the next generation's welfare expenditures. If one generation does not believe that the next generation is willing to pay for their welfare they might also be less willing to pay for the present generation. Trust across generations, given that many of the welfare state's costs relate to children and the elderly, can therefore be an important aspect of having and continuing to have a welfare state.

Governance types will have to be open and transparent in order to avoid the risk of unequal treatment of users, but also as a way of ensuring an effective provision of welfare services and based upon the best knowledge available for the time being.

13.5 Summing-up – the future

The welfare state is here to stay, although in what form, size and structure in different countries is difficult to foresee. The balance between state, market and civil society is constantly changing. How and to what extent solutions will be based upon a more universal or selective approach is also open for interpretation and discussion. A core reason for this is that in several areas there is a need for collective solutions in one way or another, given it will not be economically rational that the individual saves alone or pays for all individual welfare solutions. Market failure will furthermore presumably still exist and thus also emphasises a need for public sector intervention; again this does not inform what type of intervention and to what degree the state will take over. This also implies that the role of the family and civil society will be there, but to what extent and how this can be balanced against individuals' right to live an independent life without families is not clear. A growing ambition for more equality among men and women can also change the welfare state landscape.

There will be pressure on the welfare state in order to ensure that it is financially viable in the future, including constant discussion and analysis on whether to cut/or reduce growth in expenditure, to increase or decrease taxation, and how to use economic growth for either public or private purposes.

Demographic transitions will also be expected in the future to exert pressure on the welfare state, although this might be balanced by economic and technological development.

The balance between individualism and collectivism, between state and market, and between state and civil society will be important in the future. A legitimate welfare state will have to be responsible, open and effective. It will need electoral support and therefore the steering of the welfare state should be able to support possible goals of the welfare state to help alleviate poverty, create jobs, ensure some degree of equality and be financially viable in the future.

References

Alber, J. and Standing, G. (2000), Social Dumping, Catch-Up or Convergence? Europe in a Comparative Global Context. *European Journal of Social Policy* vol. 10, no. 2, pp. 99–119.

Brooks, D. (2011), *The Social Animal.* New York, Random House.

O'Connor, J. (1973), *The Fiscal Crisis of the State*. New York, St. Martin's Press.

OECD (1981), *The Welfare State in Crisis.* Paris, OECD.

Offe, C. (1984), *The Contradictions of the Welfare State* (edited by J. Keane). London, Hutchinson.

Stiglitz, J. (2010), *Freefall: Free Markets and the Sinking of the Global Economy.* London, Allen Lane.

Svallfors, S. (ed.) (2012), *Contested Welfare States: Welfare Attitudes in Europe and Beyond.* Stanford, CA, Stanford University Press.

Wilson, D. and Wilson, T. (1995), Social Justice and the Reform of Social Security. *Social Policy & Administration*, vol. 29, no. 4, pp. 335–44.

Glossary

Active labour market policy: The term for initiatives related to trying to help people back to the labour market. This includes among other things employment services, job support and labour market training.

Cash benefits: Benefits paid out such as unemployment, sickness and maternity benefits or pensions.

Child benefits: Benefits given to families with children. They can be means tested, dependent on the number of children and age of children.

Citizenship: Individual's legal position within a country. Citizenship is connected to social, political and civil rights.

Coefficient of variation: The ratio of the standard deviation divided with the average of a distribution. The lower the value is the more alike the distribution.

Decommodification: The extent to which an individual's welfare is reliant upon the market.

Deserving: Those people who through no fault of their own need a welfare benefit. It is thus also implicitly a normative loaded concept given that there can be a different understanding of who is in need through no fault of their own.

Disability: Denotes that a person either by birth or later in life is restricted for either physical or psychological issues in participating on an equal basis with other persons.

Ethnicity: The shared ethnic background of a group of people and a process of self-identity and forms of social stratification. Ethnicity is also a multifaceted concept.

European Social Survey: A survey undertaken in the same way in most European countries making it possible to get information on many value questions. It measures and analyses interaction between Europe's changing institutions and the attitudes, beliefs and behaviour patterns of its diverse populations (http://www.europeansocial-survey.org/).

Evaluation, Evidence: Analysis showing the impact of different types of intervention. Often it is used in order to achieve the most efficient interaction. Evidence can be achieved at different levels.

Family: The notion of a group of people often related to each other by biological bonds, but can be interpreted more broadly as a group of relatives.

Family policy: Various types of policies supporting family life – ranging from benefits in cash to social services.

Fiscal welfare: Welfare distributed through the tax system, for example, by a reduction in the tax to be paid if saving for a pension.

Flexicurity: The notion of a combination of flexibility and security in the labour market. There are many different forms and kinds of flexicurity.

Gender: In welfare analysis gender refers to the often different positions of men and women in societies, and how the impact of state, market and civil society impacts on their position in society, including the labour market. Many welfare states used to follow the male-breadwinner model emphasising that the man was earning the money while women were taking care of the children.

Gini coefficient: Measures the degree of inequality in a distribution, and describes how close or far a country is from full equality or full inequality. It ranges from 0 (full equality) to 1 (full inequality).

Governance: Relates to the use of institutions, structures of authority in order to allocate and coordinate or control activity in a society, and in welfare states it relates to how welfare is steered either in the form of in-kind or in-cash benefits.

Health care: Support to help the individual have or continue to have good health. It can be provided and/or financed publicly as well as privately.

Inequality: A term describing the degree of difference persons have in access to money or certain kinds of goods and services, including also inequality in access to education.

In-kind benefits: Benefits delivered such as housing, food, welfare services or support for people with disabilities. They can be provided directly or through a voucher enabling the user to get the service they are eligible for.

Labour market: The broad connotation of the place where demand and supply of different kinds of labour meet; if there is no balance unemployment occurs.

Legitimacy: Shows the degree of support for welfare state activities, either the welfare state in itself or different parts of the welfare state. There can be different kinds of support to welfare state activities, especially depending on the viewpoint of whether those receiving benefits are deserving or undeserving.

Long-term care: Care taking place over a long time; in welfare states it is therefore mostly related to care for frail elderly individuals.

Market failure: A term to describe that the market is not functioning as it will do in the case of perfect competition.

Marketisation: The process by which welfare states have used the market or market-type mechanisms in the delivery of welfare services.

Means-tested benefits: A benefit where the level and right to receive the benefit is dependent on the person/family's income and/or wealth.

Occupational welfare: Welfare delivered through being in the labour market, it can be paid by the employer either directly or indirectly, but it might also be supported by economic incentives from the state through the tax system.

Old-age care: Care especially focused on and with the purpose of helping elderly people.

Open Method of Coordination (OMC):   A soft-law approach in the European Union with the expectation that an agreed set of goals will be achieved in individual countries by different options.

Path-dependency: The argument that welfare states continue on the path they have developed over history.

Pension: A sum of money an individual can receive when fulfilling a certain number of criteria (the most central being age) in a welfare state given an expectation that the individual no longer is able to work in the labour market.

Poverty: Living in poverty describes a person living below a set limit, which can be absolute (such as 2 dollars per day) or relative (such as 60 per cent of median income in a country).

Prevention: Attempts to reduce the risk that a person will need help or support from the welfare state.

Public goods: Goods where one person's use of the good does not hinder another person in using the good, e.g. air. They are often used collectively such as military, justice, fire brigade, but also individually such as nature, parks, roads, etc. There are borderline cases such as libraries and bridges.

Public welfare: Welfare delivered and/or financed directly by the public sector.

Risk: The probability that a certain situation will occur, e.g. unemployment. In welfare state analysis it often refers to old risk covered by the welfare state (unemployment, sickness, old age, work injury) and new risk, such as breakup of family life, etc.

Sickness benefit: The benefit an individual can receive in case of sickness. This can be by the welfare state, but in principle also by a private insurance or collective agreement (such as full wage income during sickness for a certain time).

Social exclusion: Refers to when a person or groups are not integrated into one or more elements of societal life. This can be the labour market, but also includes social contacts with other people.

Social security: The benefits to compensate an individual for the occurrence of a special social contingency such as sickness, unemployment, etc.

Social stratification: The way a society is stratified along different lines. An individual's position has an impact on his/her ability to act.

Take-up rate: Describes the percentages of a given population having a right to receive a benefit and/or services and that actually receives it.

Taxation: The payment by individuals to the state where there is no right to receive anything back, compared to insurance premiums where when a specific contingency occurs there is a right to compensation.

Unemployment figure: The number of people without a job who are prepared and willing to work in case a vacant job is available.

Unemployment insurance: The coverage with benefit in case a person becomes unemployed.

Universalism: A principle of access to goods and services dependent on being a citizen, or having the right to stay in a country and then after fulfilling certain requirements be eligible for benefits.

Welfare: An encapsulation of elements important for a person's life; in some countries it can imply income-tested benefits.

Welfare mix: The way the state, market and civil society participate in financing and/or delivering welfare benefits and services.

Welfare state: A society trying to ensure its citizens a guaranteed minimum living standard. There is no uniform agreement of what precisely constitutes a welfare state.

Index

index